That's <u>not</u> all Folks!

That's not all Folks!

BY MEL BLANC
And
PHILIP BASHE

WARNER BOOKS

A Warner Communications Company

Warner Books, Inc., 666 Fifth Avenue, New York, NY 10103

W A Warner Communications Company

Printed in the United States of America
First printing August 1988
10 9 8 7 6 5 4 3 2 1

Book design: H. Roberts

Library of Congress Cataloging-in-Publication Data

Blanc, Mel.
  That's not all folks! : my life in the golden age of cartoons
and radio / Mel Blanc and Philip Bashe.
      p. cm.
    1. Blanc, Mel.   2. Motion picture actors and actresses—United
States—Biography.   3. Musicians—United States—Biography.
I. Bashe, Philip.   II. Title.
PN2287.B455A3   1988
791.43'028'0924—dc19
[B]   88-14724
ISBN 0-446-51244-3   CIP

*This book is dedicated to children
from one to one hundred*

Acknowledgments

Thanks to Lucille Ball, Joseph Barbera, Fred Bowen, Frank Bresee, Art and Bill Brink, Richard Clorfene, Dr. Eliot Corday, Dr. Stephen Corday, Eve Crawford, Kirk Douglas, Greg Ford, Friz Freleng, Hal Geer, Bill Hanna, Marilyn Heston, Chuck Jones, Terry Lennon, Rich Little, Michael Maltese, Leonard Maltin, Barry Marx, Marion C. H. Pines, Vincent Price, Don Richardson, Dr. Mark Saginor, Gila Sand, Mike Slosberg, Ron Smith, Dawn Sprock, Dan Vinokur, Jonathan Weiss, and everyone at Hanna-Barbera Productions, Inc., and Warner Bros. cartoons.

Special thanks to Ray Manzella, Kristy Walker, Sarah Lazin, Patty Romanowski, Tom Watson, Walt Mitchell, Charles Stumpf, Mary Lou Wallace, Steve Schneider, Ed Bleier, Kathy Helppie, Steve Green, and to the following friends at Warner Books, Inc.: executive editor James D. Frost, associate editor Charles Conrad, copy editor Steven Boldt, and designer Helen Roberts.

Very special thanks and affection to my wife, Estelle, and my son, Noel.

Contents

Foreword

By Rich Little

Mel Blanc is without question the greatest voice-man of all time. I'm not talking about impersonations, I'm talking about *voice*. His range, his imagination, his energy have put him in a class by himself.

My characters are drawn from real life; his are drawn from his imagination. And in many ways that's tougher to do because you have nothing to compare it to. I think the biggest flaw of today's cartoon-voice actors and actresses is that their natural voices often creep into the characters they perform. This is never true with Mel Blanc. It's hard to believe that Yosemite Sam and Tweety bird are done by the same person.

When I was a kid growing up in Canada, I wanted to be the Mel Blanc of impersonators. He was my inspiration. He was so remarkably versatile. Not content to just voice cartoon characters, he branched into radio and TV with Jack Benny and soon became a household name.

The big question is, Was the cartoon invented for Mel Blanc, or was Mel Blanc invented for the cartoon? Frankly, I think that Mel Blanc invented the cartoon.

Introduction

It sounds unbelievable, I know, but it's true.

The car accident had occurred three weeks earlier, on the night of January 24, 1961. I was on my way to a Hollywood studio for a radio-commercial taping, driving leisurely on the stretch of Sunset Boulevard known as Deadman's Curve. In just the previous year the S-shaped bend had claimed six lives.

Suddenly the harsh glare of headlights blinded me; an Oldsmobile 98 had miscalculated the treacherous turn. It veered across the white line and slammed head-on into my Aston Martin. Both vehicles were demolished, rendered into grisly sculptures of mangled metal and shattered glass, yet somehow the other motorist escaped with only minor injuries.

I was not so fortunate. Virtually every bone in my body was broken, my right leg alone sustaining thirty-nine fractures. Having struck my head against the steering wheel and windshield, I also suffered a severe concussion and lost nine pints of blood during the more than thirty minutes it took a special unit of the California Highway Patrol to free me from the wreckage. I would later be told that a fireman at the scene said of me, "We should have just put him in a sack."

After being attended to all night by a team of eight doctors at the nearby UCLA Medical Center, my chances of survival were put at a scant one thousand to one. With odds like that, it was no wonder why the next day's *Honolulu Herald* carried my obituary, claiming voice-man Mel Blanc, fifty-two, was dead. The paper wasn't that far off. Comatose, and entombed in a heavy full-body cast, it indeed seemed that Porky Pig's signature "That's all, folks!" was about to become my epitaph.

For three weeks I lay there, breathing but silent, though my throat had miraculously been spared from injury. Doctors spoke in hushed tones about the prolonged semicoma possibly leading to brain damage. Meanwhile, my wife, Estelle, and my twenty-two-year-old only son, Noel, kept vigil at my bedside. With anguish etched on their faces, they tried desperately to rouse me out of my unconscious state, calling my name over and over, but to no avail.

That was until the twenty-first day, when Dr. Louis Conway glanced up from my medical chart to see my most popular animated creation, the irrepressible Bugs Bunny, cavorting across the room's black-and-white TV screen. Inspiration struck. Had this been a Warner Bros. cartoon, a light bulb might have blinked on above the neurosurgeon's head. Leaning over the bed, he asked, "How are you feeling today, *Bugs Bunny?*" And from within the thick mass of bandages swathing my head came the reply, "Eh, just fine, Doc. How're you?" The voice was faint but unmistakably Bugs's. Then he inquired, "And Porky Pig, how are you feeling?"

"J- uh-ju— uh-just f-fine, th-th-thanks!" I stuttered. It was as though Bugs and Porky, into whom I had breathed life three decades earlier, were returning the favor. I may have been on the verge of death, but they were very much alive inside me.

At long last, on February 14, I awoke from the coma. Estelle and Noel say it was the best Valentine's Day gift they ever received.

After that, my condition improved rapidly, but a full recovery entailed yet another two months of hospitalization. Far worse than the physical pain was the interminable boredom from being laid up in that damn body cast. To keep myself occupied, one morning I began taking a mental inventory of all the characters whose voices and personalities I had developed for cartoons, radio, and television. Of course there were Bugs and Porky, as well as Sylvester, Tweety, Yosemite Sam, Pepe Le Pew, Foghorn Leghorn, Speedy Gonzales, Woody Woodpecker, Barney Rubble, Professor Le Blanc from "The Jack Benny Program," the Happy Postman from "The George Burns and Gracie Allen Show" . . .

I fell asleep past midnight, having lost count somewhere around four hundred. And that was more than twenty-five years ago.

Not that I recommend it to anyone, but spending so much time flat on your back does give a person ample opportunity for reflection. And while confined at the UCLA Medical Center, I thought a great deal about many things. About my loving family. About my career. About *life*.

Until then, I had taken my talent and my success largely for granted. I didn't truly grasp the impact my characters had on people until learning that during my weeks of unconsciousness, the hospital switchboard was jammed with so many well-wishes from family and friends, extra lines and operators had to be put on just to handle them all. But most touching were the fifteen thousand cards and letters from folks I didn't even know. Children sent carrots wrapped in foil, sticks of gum, and pennies. They fashioned homemade get-well cards containing drawings of their cartoon favorites. "Please, God," many scrawled in crayon, "let Bugs Bunny get well."

Carroll Van Court, a columnist who once labeled me "The Man of a Thousand Voices," published a guest editorial in the *Los Angeles Mirror* asking youngsters to remember me in their prayers. I am certain their warm thoughts hastened my recuperation.

Then there was the kindness shown me by so many of the wonderful entertainers I'd associated with over the years: dozens of telegrams, from George Burns, Red Skelton, Mickey Rooney; and visits from many others, such as Lucille Ball, Orson Welles, Peter Lorre, and my dear friend Jack Benny. In fact, Jack's face was one of the first I recall recognizing upon awakening.

"I'm going to make it, Jack," I whispered.

"You'll have to make it," he said firmly, "because I can't do my TV show without you." Despite the gravity of the moment, his prankish sense of humor was evident as always. "Here, Mel, this is for you." He placed half a candy bar in my left hand. I looked at him quizzically. Half a candy bar?

"Well," explained Benny, pretending to be the penny-pincher he'd played for decades, "I didn't think you were in shape to eat the whole thing, so why waste it?"

The outpouring of love from family, friends, and fans made me feel extremely humble and grateful. I don't think it's an overstatement to say that Melvin Jerome Blanc is one lucky fellow. What is more satisfying than being able to make children of all ages laugh? And to have worked alongside so many talented performers, directors, writers, and animators?

After more than sixty years in show business, this "Man of a Thousand Voices" has a million memories to share with you. And here's a switch: I will do so using my own voice—which, for the record, sounds like Sylvester's, but without the *thspray.*

CHAPTER

1

Voices

*E*ven as a child, I heard voices.
Now, I don't mean to imply
that I was daffy, as in duck. I was simply fascinated by the
way people spoke, particularly immigrants from other coun-
tries. And in the flourishing industrial center of Portland, Oregon, circa 1918, a medley of foreign accents caught my ear.

Straddling the Willamette River, the "City of Roses" was
an ethnic mosaic. My family lived in the southwestern quarter,
which was primarily Jewish. But surrounding us were pockets
of Germans, British, Canadians, Mexicans, and Japanese. Yiddish was the first dialect I mastered, picked up from the elderly
couple that ran the neighborhood grocery. However, no language intrigued me as much as Japanese, with its lilting, almost musical quality. As a ten-year-old, I was tickled by the
way the words seemed to roll right off the tongue.

Around the corner from my family's four-room Jackson
Street flat stood a small produce market whose proprietor was
Japanese. Unwittingly, he became my first and only acting
coach.

**I never had this
much hair again,
that's for sure. San
Francisco, 1911.**

Bounding into his store one day, I pointed to a head of
lettuce. "Excuse me," I called to him, "what's this?"

"Ah, thassa *hedda reddus*," he replied.

"And this?"

"Thassa *hedda cabbash*."

"Hedda reddus, hedda cabbash," I repeated. "Thank you
very much."

Having taken up his time, I felt obligated to buy something. So I did: a hedda reddus.

My parents, my brother Henry, and I had moved to Portland from San Francisco in 1915, when I was six and a half years old. Changing residences was nothing new for my nomadic father, Frederick Blank (yes, spelled with a *k*, not a *c*). At the impressionable age of fifteen he had struck out from his Brooklyn, New York, home for Alaska, his mind swimming with romantic notions of becoming a wealthy gold prospector. As it turned out, he did mine a modest amount of the precious metal near Nome, site of the 1899 Alaskan gold rush. But a pair of gun-toting thieves quickly relieved him of the trouble of spending it.

There he was, flat broke in the desolate north. Anyone with an ounce of sense would have been frightened out of his wits, but then, adolescence is seldom characterized by sound judgment. No, my father wasn't fazed in the least by his predicament. He may not have had much formal education, but Frederick Blank was extremely resourceful, not to mention an artful pool player. Wandering into the nearest town, the fifteen-year-old asked directions to the local pool hall. Several games and two thousand dollars in winnings later, he had more than enough money to journey down to San Francisco. There he managed a shoe shop, sales and repairs done cheaply while-u-wait, and met his future bride.

Eva Katz was a charming young woman with a broad, friendly face and a radiant smile. I assume she flashed it often around my dad, a jovial sort who loved a good joke. Though only of medium height, he always seemed much taller to my brother and me, probably because of his firm jaw, fearless gaze, and robust build. Together he and Eva made a striking couple. Just months after they were introduced, my father called her from Tacoma, Washington, where he had ventured to gamble on a new business, and asked for her hand in marriage.

The former Eva Katz and Frederick Blank. They met in San Francisco
around the turn of the century, shortly after my father returned from
prospecting for gold in Alaska.

That's my older
brother, Henry, on
my mother's right
and me on her left.
Henry grew up to
be lanky and
athletic; I was
chubbier and
preferred playing
violin to basketball.

Eventually my parents returned to San Francisco, opening a ladies'-apparel store called the Factory Sample Shop in the predominantly Spanish Mission District. My father was able to afford a comfortably modest wood-frame house at Bush and Divisadero streets in the residential Western Addition District. It was one of the few areas not destroyed by the catastrophic 1906 earthquake, which had left three hundred thousand San Franciscans homeless, and remains a tourist attraction for its ornate, Victorian-style homes. On Memorial Day, May 30, 1908, the "City by the Bay" gained another resident: Melvin Jerome Blank.

Apparently it took fatherhood to tame my dad's wanderlust, because we moved just once after I was born, to Portland. Our house there was a cream-colored two-story with a beautiful backyard. I can still see its abundant apple, cherry, and pear trees, which I used to sit under.

I have only fond memories of growing up in Oregon. In addition to mimicking voices, I demonstrated an early appreciation for music, studying the violin for eight years. The entire Blank household was similarly inclined, so we frequently conducted evening "jam sessions": me on violin; my father switching among trumpet, cornet, and piano; my mother on vocals; and Henry, who was untrained and had to play by ear, on piano. Together the four of us would perform hit tunes of the day such as "Yes! We Have No Bananas," "I'm Just Wild About Harry" and "Old-fashioned Girl (in a Gingham Gown)." Music was a popular form of home entertainment in the early twentieth century, and few homes, it seemed, were without pianos.

I was extremely close to my parents, who were very loving, generous, and open-minded. Today, I suppose, you would call them progressive. If they found my interest in music frivolous, they kept it secret, always offering encouragement. And they tolerated my penchant for speaking in dialects, even when it got me into trouble at Portland's Commerce and Lincoln high schools.

While still in grammar school, I had begun entertaining classmates and instructors at assemblies, telling jokes and spinning yarns in different voices. The kids would laugh and clap their hands; the teachers would laugh and give me lousy grades. To be truthful, report-card *C*s and *D*s had little to no effect on me, but that applause? What an impression it made on a twelve-year-old! I remember receiving cheers for the first time. As I bowed deeply from the waist, flushed with pride, I thought, *This is definitely for me. I* like *this. This* was peer acceptance and was as important to an insecure youngster then as it is today.

My talents were not appreciated by all, however, in particular a crotchety old teacher by the name of Washburn. When I broke up a classroom discussion by giving an answer in four different voices, she reprimanded me sternly; too sternly, if you ask me. "You'll never amount to anything," she said scornfully. "You're just like your last name: *blank.*" Her stinging insult so shamed me that when I was sixteen, I started spelling my surname with a *c* instead of a *k*. Later, as an adult, I changed it legally. After I became a familiar name on national radio programs and in cartoons, I often wondered if Mrs. Washburn associated *Mel Blanc* with that young student she'd ridiculed so many years before.

Another authority figure less than enamored of my "act" was the Lincoln High principal. I remember him vividly, undoubtedly because I spent so many long afternoons in his office, exiled there by frustrated teachers such as Mrs. Washburn. God, that poor man! I'm sure my good-natured pranks drove him to an early grave, or at the very least, early retirement. Let me recount one such incident for you.

Lincoln High had a cavernous hallway that produced a resounding echo; acoustically optimal, I determined, for trying out this new voice I'd been practicing: a shrill, cackling laugh. "*HELLO!*" I hollered, then stopped to listen. "*HELLO!* Hello . . . hello . . ." A return with dividends! To a fourteen-year-old, this was enthralling stuff. I darted down the hall, perfecting the raucous laugh, when whom did I collide with but the principal.

"What are you doing?" he demanded, rubbing his midsection.

My nervous explanation about utilizing the hallway's nat-

At fifteen, I look almost innocent here. But my schoolteachers in Portland certainly didn't think so; my penchant for mimicking dialects got me into plenty of trouble.

ural echo did not evoke a shred of compassion, the principal's frown deepening by the second. The second I finished, he exploded, "I should kick you out of this school!" but he never did. Fifteen years later I would match the exact same laugh with a redheaded cartoon character destined to make animation history: Woody Woodpecker.

As you might gather, I was no model student, and my scholastic career, inglorious. Except for music class, I loathed school. Whenever the tedium was unbearable, I thought nothing of ducking out a side door and trotting down to the local movie house, on Jefferson Street and Eighteenth Avenue. For a nickel you could take refuge in the darkness, watch a silent cartoon, a one- or two-reel short-subject, and a full-length feature: perhaps *Robin Hood*, with swashbuckling Douglas Fairbanks, or Rudolph Valentino's latest epic, *The Sheik*. Remember that in the early 1920s silent films were not accompanied by even a musical soundtrack, though the nicer theaters provided a pianist, a Wurlitzer organist, or sometimes a full orchestra. On a weekday afternoon, however, words were superfluous, put in the actors' mouths by the other wisecracking truants scattered throughout the house.

To earn some spending money, my brother and I hawked newspapers on the sidewalk. We discovered that business was especially brisk following an important prizefight: heavyweight champ Jack Dempsey versus Frenchman George Carpentier, for instance. With a few coins in my pocket, you could usually find me the next afternoon paying my way into the Orpheum Theatre. A grand old building at Taylor Street and Broadway Avenue, it presented two vaudeville shows daily, just before noon and in the evening. Admission was from twenty-five cents, for a spot way in back, to a dollar, for a choice orchestra seat.

Throughout my boyhood, vaudeville was America's preeminent form of entertainment, though it was to be short-lived. In the East, the largest chain of venues was the Keith-

Albee circuit, comprising about thirty or so "big-time" theaters and dozens of less prestigious houses. West of Chicago, performers played the Orpheum Circuit. These two companies, which later merged in 1927, monopolized big-time vaudeville.

Vaudevillians were itinerant entertainers who trekked from small town to major city to tiny burg, putting on two or more shows a day, seven days a week. Small-time acts could expect to give as many as five performances a day, and for meager wages. But a name showman who, in backstage parlance, was a "riot," a "panic," a "knockout," or better still, a "wow," could command a hefty "doughdy"—that is, weekly salary. When first lady of the American theater Ethel Barrymore appeared on the Orpheum circuit in a one-act play, for example, she reportedly earned three thousand dollars a week, more than the president of the United States.

Vaudeville's essence was quantity, though not necessarily quality; a variety show in the truest sense. In the course of a typical seven-act bill, an audience might be treated to a trapeze act, acrobats, a comedy act, a "girlie" revue, a jazz band, a dramatic sketch or one-act play, a dancing act, a singer with "a swell pair of pipes"—the possibilities were endless. The shows seemed that way, too, sometimes. Animal acts were popular and could border on the bizarre. One that I recall seeing was Swain's Birds: trained songbirds publicized as "feathered thespians."

For me, the highlight of any program was always the comic. It is ironic, but vaudeville provided a rich talent pool for radio and talking motion pictures, the two mediums that ultimately contributed to its demise. Innumerable famous movie or radio comedians had honed their acts to a fine edge on a vaudeville-theater crowd: the four Marx brothers, Groucho, Harpo, Zeppo, and Chico; Bob Hope; Mae West; and Fred St. James, who years later would become better known as Fred Allen, Jack Benny's acerbic nemesis of the airwaves.

Two that I saw at Portland's Orpheum were W. C. Fields, billed as the Eccentric Juggler, and Milton Berle. Back then the man today renowned as Uncle Miltie called himself The

Wayward Youth, acting in two-part skits. Although he was the same age as me, Berle was already a veteran, having gotten his start on the stage when he was just eight years old, in 1916.

By far my favorite was a one-man act called "Fiddle Funology," which I caught as often as I could when it came to town. Its blue-eyed star was in his late twenties and labored under the stage moniker Ben K. Benny. Brandishing a violin, he'd walk out from behind the curtain and greet the audience pleasantly. Then he would ask the orchestra leader in the pit below how the show had been progressing thus far.

"Just fine."

"Well," he'd snap, *"I'll* fix that."

Initially "Fiddle Funology" was a predominately musical act interspersed with self-deprecating gags about the violinist's instrumental prowess, or lack of it. But with each pass through Portland, it seemed as though there was less fiddle and more funology, until eventually the violin was relegated to a mere prop. Little did I know at the time that this comedian from Waukegan, Illinois, would one day become my employer and dear friend: the great Jack Benny.

Of course, for a fourteen-year-old in 1922, movies and vaudeville shows were rare luxuries. So other times when the urge to skip school struck, two like-minded friends named John Wilson and Petey Peterson and I headed down to the docks by the Willamette River. There we hid, sneaking cigarettes until the truant officer had completed his rounds, then we would go swimming. Portland is both celebrated and damned for its mild, damp climate, and on one particular late-spring day, the Willamette's murky water was still bone-chillingly cold.

Petey and I loved diving; John loved wagering. "Betcha can't dive off the bridge," he challenged, pointing to the steel structure connecting the east and west halves of the city. It had to be at least thirty feet high. Too young and impulsive to assess the potential dangers, the three of us dove in repeatedly, sometimes turning somersaults in midair. Then we'd scramble out of the water and hurry back to the bridge, teeth chattering, for another jump.

A busy seaport, Portland's rivers were heavily congested with water traffic. Some of the vessels were still powered by old-fashioned paddle wheels, which churned the water foamy white. To a trio of teenage boys, it looked very inviting.

"Betcha I can dive in closer to one of the boats than you two can!" John was daring me and Petey again.

"No you can't, big mouth!" I countered.

As if on cue, we all leaped in together. John and I splash-landed on either side of the paddle wheeler and swam toward each other, triumphant grins on our faces. Petey, however, was nowhere to be seen, having come down in the whirlpool's swirling midst. Whether it swallowed him or whether he was struck by the enormous wheel, I'll never know. But he died that day, and all during his funeral the pastor's attempts to comfort the assembled mourners were drowned out by Petey Peterson's weeping, disconsolate mother.

Naturally I felt just awful, and my mood was hardly lifted when my father informed me after the service that I was grounded for the imminent summer. My heart sank. I'd been eagerly anticipating vacation from school ever since—well, ever since the previous September. "I want you to think good and hard about what happened, young man," he said gravely. I could only nod my head and swallow hard.

So, stifling July and August afternoons were spent alone in the house. Whenever my brother—four and a half years my senior—was leaving to meet his friends, I'd fix him with a sad-eyed gaze, hoping he'd invite me to play football or to scamper across the tops of empty boxcars down by the railroad tracks. But like any older sibling, he had no intention of letting his kid brother tag along. Henry and I loved each other, but in addition to the gap in our ages, we shared few joint interests. He was a strapping, athletic boy with sinewy arms that could loft a basketball into the net from anywhere on the court. I was shorter, chubbier (cuter, I was often told) and preferred cultural pursuits such as music. Looking back, we were sort of amiable rivals, which I reckon is common in many families.

I might not have survived the summer had my father not brought home a surprise one night: a three-dollar crystal set he bought from a local inventor. Ever since the first commercial station, Pittsburgh's KDKA, broadcasted the 1920 presidential election returns, radio had captured America's fancy like nothing before it. In 1922 alone, sixty million dollars' worth of crystal sets were sold, and President Warren G. Harding was said to be such a radio-telephone buff that he had a powerful long-range receiver installed in a bookcase near his Oval Office desk.

According to the papers, Harding's set could pick up signals all the way from Panama and Hawaii. Most radio amateurs, however, were lucky to tune in frequencies broadcasting from a distance of several miles. I still remember sitting on our front porch with the radio, fiddling with its dials, and all of a sudden shouting excitedly to some pals playing ball in the street, "Hey, come here! I got long distance! Ya wanna hear *long distance?!*" I'd happened upon an Army barracks transmission from Vancouver, Washington, across the Columbia River. Nine whole miles away; in those days that was long distance. As far as I was concerned, the signal might as well have come from the other side of the world.

Crystal sets were portable, but one had to don a pair of headphones to listen. Saintly patience was also needed when trying to dial in a station clearly. You'd bask in the amber glow of the unit's vacuum tube, deftly rotating a "tickler" knob, as it was dubbed, and an auxiliary device called a vernier adjustment. My choice local station was KGW, owned by *The Oregonian,* Portland's first newspaper. I listened regularly to its musical programs and especially to the newscasts that seemed to condense the miles between my hometown and the rest of the country: ". . . Seven men, including Brooke County Sheriff H. H. Duval, were killed in an attack on a nonunion coal mine in Cliftonville, West Virginia. The United Coal

Workers of America strike, meanwhile, heads into its fourth month. . . ."

". . . The Protestant Episcopal Commission will recommend that the word 'obey' be dropped from nuptial rites and that women be regarded as equals. . . ."

". . . Detroit player/manager Ty Cobb went five for five in the Tigers' sixteen-to-seven rout of the last-place Boston Red Sox. The Georgia Peach's batting explosion put his season's average above four hundred. . . ."

It was KGW that gave me my start in radio, soon after Lincoln High and I parted company with mutual sighs of relief in 1927. Apparently word of my abilities as a storyteller, musician, and vocalist reached the station, which was headquartered in the Oregonian Building at Alder Street and Sixth Avenue. Someone in programming phoned and asked me to sing on a Friday evening program called "The Hoot Owls."

"Sure, I'd love to. Which song?"

" 'Juanita,' " I was told, a beautiful traditional Spanish ballad. What splendid luck; I knew its enchanting melody and lyrics by heart: "Soft o'er the fountain, lingering falls the southern moon . . ." However, it turned out the station had a different "Juanita" in mind. The version Mel Blanc warbled over the airwaves, with his family and friends listening raptly to their crystal sets, went like this:

I'd be a wreck when I got the check,
I prayed that she'd get indigestion.
But such luck, it was out of the question.
They say nanny goats can eat soda cans and such,
My girl eats things nanny goats won't touch.
I call her my sweet Wanita:
"Wanna eat, wanna eat," Wanita.

It was an immediate hit with both the audience and the cast, which I was asked to join on a steady basis. The salary? A pittance. But I eagerly accepted, for "The Hoot Owls," a charity show presided over by local businessmen, was a city-wide favorite. Needy citizens could call in, and the Portland police department's Sunshine Division would deliver a free food package to their door.

In addition to serving a worthy cause, "The Hoot Owls" was damn entertaining. None of the cast was a show-business professional, but each could have held his own with some of the comedy writers and performers I would later encounter in Hollywood.

Our little radio troupe was called the Degree Team, and all members were accorded descriptive appellations: My friend Harry Granitt, an insurance salesman, was nearly seven feet tall; hence his sobriquet "The Grand Stringbean." Charles Berg, who ran a downtown department store, was "The Grand Screecher." A local preacher was, naturally, "The Grand Sermon." Because of my faculty for fetching laughs, I became "The Grand Snicker." There were several other regulars, including a prominent judge with a shockingly ribald sense of humor.

We'd hold extemporaneous discussions about current Portland events, and I became quite skillful at ad-libbing, an invaluable asset for an aspiring radio actor. The primitive microphone we used was a far cry from what you'd find in a modern radio station: It had a horn resembling a gramophone speaker, which funneled our voices into the transmitter.

As much as I enjoyed spending Friday nights on the air, the income generated wasn't nearly enough to keep me clothed and fed, so I had to rely on my musical aptitude to make ends meet. I had long ago exchanged my violin for a tuba, having determined I was never going to make the world forget Niccolò Paganini. Too, at sixteen I became obsessed with the pomp and pageantry of a marching band and figured I'd look pretty ridiculous parading down the street with a fiddle tucked under my chin.

I found union-scale work with a couple of nine-man ensembles, Frank Vaughn's Columbians and the Del Milne Orchestra. For the next two years, when I wasn't behind a microphone, I was playing dance halls throughout the Northwest. Rarely did we venture more than seventy-five miles from home; about the farthest I can remember traveling was to Centralia and Chehalis, south of Olympia, Washington.

To commute to and from engagements, the fellows and I took turns carpooling. So as not to wrinkle our black tuxedos, we changed clothes in the backseat "dressing room." Consequently, I always tried hitching rides with saxophonist Fred Greene, whose father owned a roomy sedan. One afternoon Mr. Greene watched us stashing our instruments in the trunk and asked why we weren't wearing our stage outfits. Fred explained the situation, to which his father replied archly, "Well, tell the boys someone left his lipstick and panties in there the other night."

Sometimes we'd perform at divey beer joints; other times, elegant ballrooms. Our primary function was to keep the patrons dancing strenuously to jazz and Big Band favorites such

Director Del Milne and the Portland KGW radio orchestra. I'm on the far right, having traded in my violin for a tuba and having sprouted a mustache.

as Louis Armstrong's version of "Ain't Misbehavin'," Benny Goodman's "A Jazz Holiday," and later in the evening, the more subdued "Nobody's Sweetheart" by Paul Whiteman. At intervals I'd set down my cumbersome instrument and step out front to sing, all the while watching impeccably attired young men make plays for begowned girls with bobbed hair.

Since good tuba players were a precious commodity, I was recruited by yet another outfit, the Bohemians, led by Frank Fogelsong. When he fell ill with hepatitis, I was asked to conduct, over the objections of Wendell Fogelsong, Frank's trombone-blowing younger brother. Wendell believed strongly that *he* should have been next in line for the baton, not this comparative newcomer, and he did little to hide his resentment of me.

It was the Bohemians' custom to open and close with a piece we called our "Salute to Prohibition." Prohibition was the fourteen-year constitutional illegalization of alcohol signed into law in 1919. We'd play a few measures, then the musicians would rise to their feet and shout defiantly, "Whiskey!" A few more measures, then everyone would stand again and holler, "Vodka!"

Everyone, that is, except Wendell, who would take this opportunity to yell obscenities—at me! The patrons on the dance floor couldn't hear him over the general clamor, but I certainly did. This went on until our drummer cooked up a scheme: "The next time we play the salute," he whispered conspiratorially, with Wendell just out of earshot, "everybody stand up but keep quiet."

And so, at a dance the following week, we struck up the composition as usual. But when it came to the part where normally we called out "Whiskey!" the orchestra leapt to its feet, opened its mouths and—

—uttered not a sound, except for Wendell, who crowed, *"F**k!"* at the top of his lungs. After whipping his head left and right to see his bandmates weak with laughter, then slowly turning back around to see the throng of dancers gaping at him incredulously, he gulped painfully and timidly lowered himself into his seat. From that day on, the trombonist was considerably more accommodating.

My next employment opportunity represented a sizable step forward: playing in the NBC Trocaderans radio orchestra on San Francisco's KPO. Because the station was within walking distance of my maternal grandparents' home, it seemed only logical that I reside temporarily with them.

Grandpa Nachum Katz was a kindly, wizened Russian immigrant with snow-white hair and mustache, and a personal history as colorful as that of his son-in-law Frederick Blank. He and my diminutive grandmother, Leah Beyla, were second or third cousins (we're not sure which) who had grown up and labored side by side on a potato farm in their homeland. They fell in love, but poverty prevented them from marrying until the enterprising Nachum devised a fiscal plan: Working unharvested plots of land, he and his bride-to-be gathered potatoes that would otherwise be left to rot, then sold them back to the family in exchange for marriage money.

Upon their arrival in America in the late nineteenth century, the newlyweds settled in Bismarck, North Dakota. They'd heard from other expatriate Russians that the land was fertile for farming. What they weren't told, however, was that the winter temperatures were far too bitter for raising tubers, hovering near zero most of the time. Fortunately, a friend of my grandfather's had discovered more suitable conditions— for both potatoes and people—in Porterville, California. The Katzes took his advice and relocated to the picturesque farming community midway between Fresno and Bakersfield. They lived there for many years before moving to the Bay Area.

My grandparents were not Orthodox Jews but did keep a kosher home. Although naturally I enjoyed their company, to this day I rue having stayed with them. The Trocaderans performed dance and show tunes four nights a week, from ten to eleven on Tuesdays, eleven to midnight on Wednesdays and

Fridays, and ten to midnight on Thursdays. So I generally didn't get home until the wee hours of the morning. I felt like such a selfish s.o.b., disturbing their sleep all the time.

When I received an offer to return to Portland as Orpheum Theatre pit conductor, I grabbed it. Just twenty-two, I was the youngest musical director in the country and had the opportunity to work with many fabulous acts, among them Edgar Bergen and his monocled, sharp-tongued dummy, Charlie McCarthy. At one point the Chicago-born Bergen considered chopping his white-pine partner into firewood and going solo as a comedian. It's a good thing he reconsidered, because together they would achieve national fame, "discovered" in 1936 on singer Rudy Vallee's radio show, generally credited as the first variety program of the airwaves.

Unfortunately, by 1930 there weren't many other high-caliber acts playing the Orpheum anymore. Or any theater, for that matter. Vaudeville was falling out of public favor, having lost most of its top draws—Eddie Cantor, Bob Hope, George Burns and Gracie Allen, Jack Benny—to radio and to legitimate theater. And its most illustrious star of all, Al Jolson, had revolutionized the entertainment world with his starring role in the first motion-picture "talkie," 1927's *The Jazz Singer*.

The unveiling of sound not only led to vaudeville's ruin, it single-handedly delivered film from a similar fate at the hands of radio. Headed for certain bankruptcy, in 1926 the Warner Bros. company gambled on a disc system developed by Bell Telephone Laboratories: Vitaphone. It was little more than an outsize phonograph-record turntable that spun one-reel's worth of synchronous music and selected sound effects. In Vitaphone's first full-length tryout, John Barrymore's *Don Juan*, audiences thrilled to the clashing of swords during the dueling scene.

Interestingly, the Warner brothers merely viewed Vitaphone as a gimmick that would hopefully keep them out of the red a while longer. Satisfied with the reception accorded *Don Juan*, they employed it again on *The Jazz Singer*, the plot of which was drawn from Jolson's real-life story. He was born

Asa Yoelson in Russia and was blessed with such a sonorous singing voice, that his rabbi father resolved immediately that his son would join him at the pulpit as a cantor. When Asa made it known that he wanted to become an actor instead, his father was enraged. The elderly man made no attempt to conceal his bitterness, eventually driving the boy away.

For years Jolson lived the life of a vagabond, singing in saloons and cafes. But by the time of his film debut at age forty-one, he was a vaudeville- and minstrel-circuit legend who had also racked up fourteen years on the American stage. His trademarks were the breaking voice, the dropping to his knees during heart-rending passages, and most of all, the burnt cork he frequently applied to his face.

The Jazz Singer, released on October 6, 1927, featured four musical numbers and snippets of dialogue. Just before launching into "Toot, Toot, Tootsie! (Goo'bye)," he cried exultantly, "Wait a minute, wait a minute. You ain't heard nothin' yet!" Indeed, we hadn't. At the movie house in which I saw the film, people gasped and jaws dropped. Then the theater erupted with wild applause. Vaudeville's death knell had been sounded.

Less than a year later, when Warner's premiered the first full-length talkie, *Lights of New York*, only two hundred twenty U.S. movie theaters were equipped for sound. But public demand was such that by late 1929 the number had soared to more than four thousand. Sensing the end, many vaudeville venues incorporated films into their programs, but it was too late. On May 13, 1932, New York City's famed Palace Theatre at Broadway and 47th Street presented its last two-a-day bill. Almost cruelly, it was a Friday the thirteenth.

The advent of talking pictures affected vaudeville performers and silent-screen actors alike. Dialect coaches were flown in from New York and England, but it was soon apparent that many of the previous era's box-office attractions would not survive the transition. Exotic vamp Pola Negri suddenly found herself unemployable because of her guttural Polish accent and fled back to Europe, while longtime leading man John Gilbert vanished from Hollywood as if he'd never existed.

Of course, one man's misfortune is another man's gain. For me, with a rapidly expanding repertoire of voices, sound-fixated Hollywood held forth great promise.

"Mom, Dad," I announced one evening while the family was relaxing in the parlor after dinner, "I'm thinking of going to Hollywood."

My father put down his newspaper, and my mother, an avid solitaire player, looked up from her game.

"You're going to become an actor?" my father asked, bemused. "Like Gary Cooper?"

To tell the truth, I hadn't decided exactly in which direction to go: film, animated film, or radio. But with all three still in their nascency, I liked my chances.

"There's just not much left for me in Portland," I continued. "I think going to California would really help boost my career."

My father left his chair, walked over to me, and said, "I understand, Mel. This is your chance to do something big, and I'm all for it." I can't say his encouragement came unexpectedly, for my dad was never one to shy away from a challenge himself. But receiving my parents' blessing sure bolstered my confidence, even when he added, "Just remember: If it doesn't work out, or if you don't like it, you can always come back here and work in the store."

Never had my father pressured me to enter the family business, something so many of my peers' parents did. I deeply appreciated that. And although merchandising had never interested me, it was reassuring to know that I always had something to fall back on.

I wound up going to California, all right, although my destination fell about four hundred miles short of the city of dreams. Once again I was back in San Francisco, this time to emcee a Tuesday-night variety program called "The Road Show" on an NBC affiliate, KGO. A network talent scout named Cecil Underwood, who would figure prominently in my career for many years to come, had heard me on the air at KGW and offered me the job. I took it, even though a master-of-cere-mony's duties weren't exactly what I'd had in mind: introducing the various acts and interjecting the odd joke here and there.

But "The Road Show" gave me my largest exposure yet and enough in salary so that I didn't have to impose on my grandparents. Instead, for the 1931–1932 season I rented a hotel room around the corner from the studio. The moderately priced accommodations may not have compared to those at Union Square's opulent St. Francis Hotel, but at least they were clean and cheerily appointed.

Living once again in ethnically mixed San Francisco proved as advantageous career-wise as my NBC hitch itself. The 1840s gold rush had brought scores of foreign adventurers converg-ing on the city, which now claimed districts of English, Chinese, Japanese, Mexican, German, Irish, Italian, and Russian an-cestry. For a voice-man intent on assimilating new dialects, simply walking down the street provided daily education.

When "The Road Show" ended with the coming of sum-mer hiatus, I had mixed emotions. Mostly, though, I was ex-cited about my prospects in Hollywood. I ran back to my hotel and started packing my suitcases for the tedious trip south. It would take about two days in my 1920 Ford Model A con-vertible, which I'd purchased for the then princely sum of $670. For companionship I'd invited along two vaudeville ac-tors from Portland, who were to meet me in front of my hotel early the next morning. They, too, were convinced that fame beckoned.

I barely got any sleep that night, tossing and turning and mulling over my career plans for as soon as I got settled. Before I knew it, the sparkling morning sunshine was nudging me awake, and bleary-eyed or not, it was time to go.

CHAPTER

2

California, Here We Come . . . and Go

*T*oday Route 101 is one of California's major freeways, but in 1932 it was a congested two-lane road that ran beside the Salinas River before snaking westward. Then from Santa Barbara to Ventura it hugged the scenic Pacific coastline.

It was somewhere around San Luis Obispo that the once-lively conversation among my two passengers and me dried up like the scorched earth alongside the roadway. But by the time I finally pulled my Model A into the Hollywood city limits, we were too exhausted to talk anyway.

The local Chamber of Commerce had erected a sign at the corner of Hollywood Boulevard and Vine Street. "Don't Wait for the Good Times," it exhorted, *"Spend Now* and Keep Business Alive." My companions and I, baked a leathery brown from the sun, managed a tired laugh. After having paid out for food and fuel, I had but a few dollars to my name. And the two vaudevillians? Flat broke.

Not that we were any worse off than most people. For two and a half years the country had been mired in the Great

Depression, seeming to sink steadily deeper as time went on. Nearly fifteen million Americans—one quarter of the labor force—were out of work, and many of them were out on the street. Virtually every metropolis had its own ramshackle "cities" of hovels erected next to refuse dumps, where their inhabitants scrounged for food. There was a name for these areas: "Hooverville," a derisive reference to then-president Herbert Hoover.

And in the downtown areas, once-proud people stood in breadlines or outside soup kitchens. Stopped at traffic lights while driving home from work in Portland and later in San Francisco, I would study their grim faces and silently give thanks that I had escaped the Depression's grip; so far. If only my hardworking father had been as fortunate. The formerly prosperous family business, which he'd expanded into four stores—and believed would be there for me to fall back on—eventually went bankrupt.

On the far horizon of a country gone bust, Hollywood loomed as the last boomtown, an oasis in a desert. That motion pictures could provide escape from life's harsh realities was reflected in the growing number of fantastic, lavishly staged film spectacles. Radio, too, helped Americans get through these calamitous times. An early door-to-door survey showed that comedies were preferred over other types of programs by sixty-five percent. Small wonder.

But I think that in addition to fantasy and laughs, the nation needed a Hollywood in order to maintain its trust in the future. The city's fabulously rich were symbols of hope whose material gains could be savored vicariously: by reading gossip-column accounts of extravagant affairs that eclipsed Roman bacchanalias. Some of the era's movie stars and moguls thought nothing of filling their magnificent swimming pools with lotus blossoms, or of importing maple trees and bonsai from Japan for a masquerade ball with an Oriental theme. Then, the next day, they would be discarded without thought, as if the Roaring Twenties had never ended.

Tales of overnight success stories—actresses purportedly

"discovered" while wiping slop off soda-fountain counters—lured swarms of amateurs from all over the country to the city. Most, of course, soon returned to their one-stop towns bruised and battered; like the two actors who accompanied me in my convertible. I never heard from or heard of either one again.

But I did cross paths with another Portland acquaintance, Hymie Breslau, with whom I'd played in the Del Milne Orchestra several years earlier. He was an accomplished violinist and had come to Hollywood seeking work in the radio orchestras. The two of us decided to room together, figuring we could share expenses as well as tips on prospective employment. After some searching, we found a cheap, cramped bungalow at the top of hilly Hyperion Avenue. To get to the front door required hiking up an exterior staircase so steep it could wind a Swiss mountaineer. On days that I returned home after arduously, and unsuccessfully, pounding the pavement for work, dragging myself up those dozens of steps seemed to take forever.

My sights were set on radio, which was ripening as an entertainment medium. Even in the Depression's depth, by 1932 Americans had purchased close to thirty million sets, which they tuned in to over five hundred stations. You could order a five-tube, mahogany-finish Silvertone receiver from Sears, Roebuck for $24.95, four dollars down, with four-dollar monthly installments. Since the first commercial broadcast just twelve years earlier, listening to the radio had become America's favorite nightly pastime.

I can remember my family and I going into the parlor after dinner and switching on one of our best-liked programs. It was much the same as TV viewing is today in many homes, except that, with no visual, everyone had to be quiet. My dad was constantly glaring at Henry and me, placing an index finger to his lips and shushing us.

There were two networks: NBC, the National Broadcasting Company, launched in 1926; and CBS, the Columbia Broadcasting System, started the following year. And plans were underway for a third network, MBS, the Mutual Broadcasting System. It would begin operating in 1934. In effect, even prior to Mutual's arrival on the scene, there were already three national systems. NBC was split into the Blue and Red networks, so named for the colored lines used to designate affiliates on company maps. The former originated from flagship station WEAF in New York, and the latter from WJZ, also in New York. Eventually NBC would be ordered by the Federal Communications Commission to divest itself of the Blue Network, and in 1943 it became ABC, the American Broadcasting Company.

These networks fed national news, dramas, comedies, and quiz shows to local broadcasters, which formerly had been responsible for all their own programming. Now even stations between the East and West coasts' entertainment meccas, New York and Los Angeles, had access to major-league talent. If you lived in Philadelphia, you could hear "The O'Neills" on WCAU, fed by CBS's flagship station WABC, New York; Guy Lombardo and his orchestra on NBC Red's WFIL; and Mary Pickford starring in *Daddy Long Legs* on NBC Blue's KYW. While this was good news for listeners, it put many actors out of work, since the majority of shows were produced in New York. I would have relocated there myself but couldn't afford the cross-country train fare.

I knocked on the doors of every radio station in Los Angeles, including the networks. KFI and KECA were NBC's Red and Blue, owned by Earle C. Anthony, a well-heeled Packard dealer. Coincidentally, his stations' chief ratings rival, CBS's KHJ, belonged to the equally affluent Don Lee, who trafficked in Cadillacs.

It was quickly apparent that I would drive neither luxury car unless my prospects improved rapidly and radically. I landed some bit work at NBC, thanks to Cecil Underwood, who had hired me to emcee "The Road Show" in San Francisco the year before and was now also in L.A. Most of the shows on which I appeared were anonymous comedy-varieties, though on one of them I did get to work with an up-and-coming crooner, Harry Lillis Crosby, better known as Bing. His velvety, rich voice was a joy to listen to even then.

I wasn't much for Hollywood parties but was finally coerced into attending one, where I met Mae West. A veteran vaudeville and stage actress, she'd recently come to Hollywood, too, under contract to Paramount Pictures. I'd heard all sorts of wild stories about her: how one of her self-penned plays, *Sex*, was so salacious (by early 1920s' standards), she was arrested and briefly incarcerated in the New York City prison. But the woman I met was soft-spoken and neither drank nor smoked, not at all like I'd imagined her to be.

"So, you're a radio actor?" she asked in her husky voice. "Yes, ma'am," I replied nervously. "At least, I'm trying to be."

And trying and trying. After hearing "Sorry, we don't need any voices" for the umpteenth time that week, I'd trudge up Sunset Boulevard, deeply discouraged. But then I'd glance at the landmark "Hollywoodland" sign atop Beachwood Canyon Drive and think about Peg Entwhistle.

Peg was a noted New York stage actress who pilgrimaged west with the intention of making a splash in motion pictures. Unfortunately, her legacy was a mere ripple. In despair—and perhaps in hopes of finally making the front page of the *Hollywood Reporter*—she ascended the fifty-foot-high "H" in "Hollywoodland" and leaped to her death. The way I saw it, no amount of rejection was worth killing yourself over. Despite my bleak prospects, I'd say, "If things don't pan out, it's not the end of the world." After repeating it enough times, I eventually convinced myself.

Meanwhile, my roommate wasn't having any easier a time getting work. Back in Portland there was a surplus of freelance musical jobs, but down here you had to belong to the local union. Being an out-of-towner, Hymie couldn't break in right away. Another factor that hampered his progress may have been his looks, because Hymie was—how do I put this?—pretty homely. It's too bad that stood in his way, because he was a lovely fellow.

One Saturday evening, following another futile week of

hunting for employment, we were sitting gloomily around the bungalow, which was festooned as usual with dirty laundry.

"Say, Hymie," I said, rousing him from his doldrums. "What do you say we go see some musicians who *are* working?"

"That's a snazzy idea," he replied. "But where?"

"There's a swing band playing tonight at the Ocean Park Ballroom." The Ocean Park sat right on Santa Monica Beach and held dances at five cents admission. Neither of us was any great shakes at cutting the rug, but we were both "alligators"—popular slang for devotees of swing. Rung in by Fletcher Henderson, Jimmie Lunceford, and the Casa Loma Orchestra, it was the hot new sound. After checking our pants pockets to see if we had two nickels between us, Hymie and I put on suits and ties and drove out there in my Model A.

From a distance away you could hear the strains of the orchestra, and the salt-laden ocean breeze made us temporarily forget our financial woes. The place was already teeming with frantic dancers doing a new step called the lindy hop, so Hymie and I split up and wandered off in search of partners.

Since coming to southern California, I'd dated only sporadically and, frankly, had always been somewhat reserved with the opposite sex. I never had much money, but I must say that I was always immaculate, even if my suits were several years out of date. I sported a pencil-thin mustache—probably the influence of suave leading men such as Clark Gable and Ronald Colman—that gave me a dapper, sophisticated air.

I was standing on the perimeter of the dance floor, scouting around for an available young lady, when my eyes caught sight of a very attractive blonde. Alas, she was fox-trotting with a handsome curly-haired fellow. I thought for an instant about cutting in but noticed she seemed to be having a splendid time in his arms. She had a radiant smile, which she revealed often, tossing back her head and laughing gaily.

What I didn't know was that the source of hilarity was her partner's lack of dancing expertise—and more to the point, that he was her younger brother, receiving some urgently needed lessons. "Ouch, Sonny," I heard her moan, "you're stepping on my toes. Stand a little farther back. Like this," she said, positioning him a safer distance away.

Still watching her out of the corner of my eye, I wound up clasping my hands around another girl, named Vera. We chatted amiably as we slow-danced, and I thought I was giving her my undivided attention, but apparently not. No sooner did the music stop than Vera walked over to the blonde and whispered something in her ear. I stood watching, dumbfounded. What the hell was going on?

It turned out that Vera had come to the Ocean Park Ballroom in the blonde's car, with *her* younger brother as an escort. Rather than being offended by my poorly disguised interest in her friend, Vera immediately grabbed my hand and pulled me over to where the young woman was checking her ankles for bruises. After an awkward moment or two, we introduced ourselves.

"Pleased to meet you," she said brightly. "My name is Estelle Rosenbaum."

"And I'm Mel Blanc. May I have the next dance?"

Not only did we enjoy the next dance together, but the one after that and the one after that. She was a legal secretary, she half-shouted over the blare of the brass section. Originally from Denver. Parents in the restaurant business. I was delighted to learn she shared my interest in radio and sang occasionally with a choral group on station KNX.

"In San Francisco I used to host a program called 'The Road Show,'" I told her, and to my surprise Estelle said that she had listened to it often.

"So you were the emcee, huh? I'm very impressed."

Not half as impressed as I was that she'd even heard of it.

The conversation shifted to what I was doing now. Not much, I had to admit sheepishly.

"Well," she said after a few seconds' thought, "I'm on the Junior League's entertainment committee. We're having a big dance next Saturday; how about being master of ceremonies?

A lot of people come to these events, and it might be a great showcase for you."

This was the best offer I'd had in weeks: the promise of a job, and made by a pretty girl, yet.

"Sounds swell. What's your phone number? I'll call you tomorrow."

"Federal four four nine oh."

Many months later Estelle confessed that she had been crestfallen when I didn't jot down the number. Also, she had assumed I was Italian at first, because of my olive skin and dark-brown eyes. In her diary that night she entered:

"Dear Diary:

"I've met the most wonderful man. He's Italian, I think, with the cutest shoe-button eyes. I offered to help him with his career, but I don't think anything will come of it. When I gave him my phone number, he didn't write it down. Men!"

When it's the right girl, you *remember* her number.

The next day I called to finalize arrangements for the dance and could tell from her voice that she was initially nonplussed to hear from me. We met again the following weekend at the Junior League affair, which was very enjoyable. It never did lead to anything, professionally speaking, but already my relationship with Estelle was blossoming into a full-fledged courtship. For the first time in my life I was in love.

Without even having to discuss the subject, marriage seemed inevitable. But with radio work still scarce, how could I hope to support a wife and a family? In a good week I earned maybe twenty-five bucks.

One evening just before the holidays I staggered up the steps to the bungalow and found in the mailbox an envelope postmarked "Portland."

What on earth could this be? I wondered, tearing it open. Scanning the letter's contents, I started laughing deliriously before letting out an elated whoop. "I don't believe it! This is wonderful!" Hymie, wanting to know what all the commotion was about, came hurrying out of the shower, dripping wet.

Seeing me on my knees, planting kisses on the letter I gripped with both hands, he eyed me warily and wrapped the towel tighter about his waist. "Mel? Are you all right?"

"A job! Hymie, I've been offered a job! Back in Oregon!"

KEX, NBC's Blue Network affiliate, had written to propose my own hour-long show, which I would produce, write, and perform. I practically tripped racing down the steps to my car, then sped to Estelle's to tell her the good news. I was gasping for air when she opened the door.

"You seem ready to burst," she observed, amused. "What is it?"

Holding the letter aloft, I breathlessly blurted out the details: "My own show . . . in Portland . . . produce, write, and act . . . fifteen dollars a week . . . a raise for each new sponsor."

"Isn't that an awful lot of work?" she asked. I was too excited to notice her lack of enthusiasm.

"But it'd be *my* program, and who knows where it could lead? Besides, nothing's happening for me here. I've just got to do it."

Estelle moved to the other side of the living room and gazed wistfully out the window. "Well," she said at length, "I'm certainly going to miss you, Mel."

"No, you won't."

"What do you mean?"

"You won't miss me, because we're going up there together!"

"But Mel, we're not married!"

"I'll solve that." Falling to one knee, I proposed on the spot.

Because we couldn't afford the traditional ceremony and reception, we eloped on January 4, 1933. She was twenty-two, I was twenty-four. "We won't tell a soul," Estelle whispered excitedly as we drove to a justice of the peace in Riverside, about halfway between Los Angeles and Palm Springs. Who would know us there? The justice perfunctorily performed the wedding rites in a solemn monotone, and afterward Estelle and I celebrated over two sixty-five-cent deluxe plates at a nearby restaurant. Not exactly the kind of nuptials a woman dreams about—or a man dreams about, for that matter.

Four days later the job in Portland fell through. As it was spelled out for me, the KEX station manager had decided instead to hire a relation. Needless to say, it was a bitter pill to swallow. Compounding my distress was that since we'd exchanged wedding vows clandestinely, Estelle and I had to return to our previous living arrangements: she with her parents, me with Hymie.

Having a wife, albeit in secret, only steeled my determination to find work in Los Angeles. The very next morning, there I was as usual: sitting in yet another radio-station reception area with my shoes shined and trousers crisply pressed, hoping to get an audience with the talent scout. Probably the most important lesson I learned during these difficult times was to disassociate myself from the rejections, no matter how brusque or insulting. My advice to anyone entering a field, whatever it may be, is to never take rebuffs personally or allow them to erode your confidence. Whenever I strode into a radio station, I always projected the self-assurance of a veteran voice actor, not a struggling novice with a thin waistline and an even thinner wallet. I had faith that eventually my break would come, and shortly after Estelle and I married, it did.

At least once a week I routinely paid a call to NBC Blue's KECA, which broadcast the popular comedy program "The Happy-Go-Lucky Hour." It starred Al Pearce, a San Jose native who'd gotten his start in the business on San Francisco's KFRC. For a time he'd tried selling insurance door-to-door. While the experience didn't net him any sizable commissions, it did at least provide the inspiration for his best-known character: Elmer Blurp, a fainthearted traveling salesman who would do anything to avoid facing up to customers. Blurp's patented line was an imbecilic "Nobody home, ah hope, ah hope, ah hope," intoned without inflection. It never failed to draw big laughs.

"Can't you even get me an audition?" I'd persist, driving

the KECA secretarial staff to distraction. "I just know Mr. Pearce could use me on his show." This went on for months. Finally, one day Pearce's talent agent waved me into his office and with a bored expression said, "Okay, let's see what you can do."

Out came a cornet my father had given me and a well-rehearsed routine designed to showcase my versatility. It was a takeoff on "The Richfield Reporter," a nightly radio newscast that opened with a trumpet fanfare. In my interpretation, however, the flourish was sputtered vulgarly on the cornet, making for the worse damn noise you ever heard. Then the instrument was dropped unceremoniously to the floor. *Clang!* And rather than portray an appropriately sober newscaster, I affected the slurred delivery of a skid-row derelict. Reading fabricated news stories from around the world enabled me to employ several accents. After five minutes I brought it to a close, then looked expectantly at the man behind the desk.

"Pretty good," he said, rubbing his chin thoughtfully. "Yes, sir, pretty good. Let me go get Mr. Pearce; I think he'd like to hear this for himself."

I repeated the bit for the star, who laughed heartily at each gag. When it was over, he turned to his subordinate and ordered, "Book him for next week."

The pay wasn't much—five dollars per show—but I was grateful for the break. Two years later, in 1935, his program would move to New York for transcontinental broadcasts. Al became a bona fide celebrity, and Blurp's "Nobody home, ah hope, ah hope, ah hope," a national catchphrase. He eventually faded from radio in the late 1940s and toiled briefly on television before his death in 1961. A warm, generous man, many years earlier he'd given me a gift black Labrador puppy, and in his honor I'd named the canine Elmer.

Except for my appearances on Pearce's show, however, my career was at a standstill. Finding work became my real full-time job, radio acting merely a sideline. Estelle and I had to continually postpone legitimizing our marriage, which frus-

Portrait of the young man as an artist—a starving artist—in 1933. I was a regular on comedian Al Pearce's NBC program but still found it difficult to line up additional work.

trated me more than my inability to track down steady employment. Finally I couldn't stand living apart from her any longer.

"Estelle," I said to her one night, pacing back and forth in her parents' living room, "this is unbearable. Why shouldn't we tell the truth, that we're married?"

"Because we didn't have a Jewish wedding."

"Then we'll have a Jewish wedding, and right away. My grandfather will know the next correct date." As the operator rang San Francisco for me, I explained to Estelle that it was currently *Sefírah*, a period of mourning in the Jewish religion. During all but one of its forty-nine days, weddings and other festivities were forbidden.

"Hello, *Zéyde?*" I said, using the Yiddish word for grandfather, "this is Melvin. . . . Yes, I'm fine; terrific, in fact. Listen, I've met the most marvelous girl, and we want to get married." I cupped my hand over the receiver and blew Estelle a kiss.

"Yes, of course she's Jewish. *Zéyde*, I need to know the earliest day for having the ceremony. . . . *Lag Baómer?*" It was a holiday on the thirty-third day of *Sefírah*, my grandfather explained, and weddings were permitted.

"Great. I'll expect to see you and Grandma there. Thanks so much."

"Well," I said, turning to Estelle, "it's settled. We're getting married on *Lag Baómer.*"

"I'm thrilled," she replied, laughing, "but Mel, didn't you forget something?"

I clapped a hand to my forehead. "Oh my gosh!" It hadn't occurred to me to ask for the month and day. Redialing my grandfather's number, I joked, "This getting-married business is expensive."

Upon picking up, Grandpa Nachum didn't even wait to hear the voice at the other end of the receiver. "It's in twenty-six days, May fourteenth," he said in heavily accented English. "And *mázel tov*, you should be very happy."

The wedding was held at the Rosenbaum home, with family and friends in attendance. A rabbi conducted the ceremony, the bride wore white, the groom sported a black tuxedo, and though I didn't bother to compute the total expenses of food, flowers, and so on, rest assured that it cost well in excess of the dollar-thirty splurged the first time around. To this day Estelle and I celebrate both wedding anniversaries, in January and in May. But it wasn't until we'd been married for six years that we told her and my parents about our elopement.

Our honeymoon? A drive up the coast to Portland, courtesy of radio station KEX. Just two days after I became a husband—again—the station manager contacted me. Nepotism resulted in a miserable failure, it seems; he'd had to fire the announcer hired in my place four months before. "The job is yours, if you still want it," he said contritely.

I wanted to say, "Sure, so long as you don't have too large a family," but managed to restrain myself.

"Good-bye! Good luck!"

"And write soon. Remember?"

With tears and blinding gray smoke from my new 1932 Ford in their eyes, Estelle's parents bid us farewell. Reluctantly I'd traded in the Model A for a more economical machine, but my good intentions backfired on me. So did the green four-door sedan, which guzzled oil like a lush swigging muscatel. Every few miles I had to pull over and add another quart, while cursing the simpering face of the salesman who sold me the rattletrap.

It was ten o'clock, and I was growing weary from the long drive, so we stopped at a gas station.

"Excuse me!" I called to the attendant, who hustled over.

"Yes, sir?"

"We're looking for a place to stay. An *inexpensive* place to stay. Is there anything nearby?"

He pointed to a darkened apartment directly above the garage and said, "Five dollars for the night."

Estelle and I looked at each other, shrugged, and started unloading our bags. The cozy room may not have been a honeymoon suite at the Beverly Hills Hotel, but at least it was clean. Almost charming, as a matter of fact. And that is where Estelle and I spent our first evening as "newlyweds." I was in such a buoyant mood the next morning, I tipped the garage owner an extra five dollars upon departing.

In San Francisco we stayed with my grandparents, then

proceeded up Route 101, sojourning in a remote town north of Eureka, California.

"Look, Mel." Estelle motioned with her chin to a road sign that read, "Rooms: $1.50."

"Well, the price is certainly right," I said and put my foot to the accelerator. The second we stepped inside the registration office, however, our nostrils flared, assaulted by a heavy, foul-smelling odor. It was probably just disinfectant but was so noxious, my first thought was, *Mustard gas?*

"Would you like a room?" asked the desk clerk.

Before I could answer, Estelle kicked my shin and shot me a look as if to say, "Not in a million years."

"Um . . . w-well," I stammered, "I think maybe we'll come back after we've had some dinner."

"No, you won't," he whimpered. "You won't come back. *They never do.*"

They didn't this time, either.

"Is it really as rainy as people say?" Estelle asked as we neared Portland. Family and friends had warned her that she'd better get used to hoisting an umbrella. "Naw, it's not that bad," I reassured her. "Just look at this gorgeous sky." The sun was shining gloriously, as it had for all ten days of our trip. To afford my wife a breathtaking view of her new hometown, I detoured to Terwilliger Point, a picturesque hilltop in the southwest section. No sooner did Estelle step out of the car than the sky filled with ominous black clouds and rain came pouring down in pitchers. "Welcome to Portland, dear," I said.

We rented a house eight miles outside the city, in a scenic, countrified setting with lush Douglas firs and evergreens. Right away I had to spend so much time at the radio station, Estelle and I didn't get a chance to meet our neighbors. I'm sure they were naturally curious about the new couple down the road. One evening after supper we were relaxing and talking in front of the dining room's lovely picture window. As she was gesturing to make a point, Estelle inadvertently struck her funny bone on a table edge.

Springing from her chair, she shimmied about in agony. Not that I wasn't sympathetic, but it was a riotous sight, made all the more riotous when I turned and noticed that the elderly couple next door were observing my wife's antics through *their* lovely picture window. From the startled expressions on their faces, God only knows what they thought we were doing. When her pain subsided and Estelle demanded to know what was so funny, I simply pointed. Horrified, she dove to the floor like an infantryman hitting the dirt to dodge a bullet.

"Welcome to the neighborhood, dear," I said.

In order to get to know the Blancs, all our neighbors needed to do was to set their radio dial at 1190 megacycles. KEX was where Estelle and I resided sixteen hours a day, Mondays through Saturdays, assembling my program, "Cobwebs and Nuts." Don't ask me what the title meant. Although she wasn't a paid employee, my wife was integral to the show. Not only did she assist me in thinking up material, she eventually assumed several on-the-air roles. I had pleaded with the station to hire an actress for the program's comedy sketches but was told there wasn't the budget for it. Management's helpful suggestion? "Stop writing women into the script." For a time I played the female characters myself, until Estelle offered her services. I was delighted, as I'm sure were KEX's miserly owners to find noncompensated talent.

I don't know of too many couples that could withstand spending so much time cooped up together, but Estelle and I always got along famously. "Cobwebs and Nuts" broadcast live at eleven P.M. Therefore, mornings and early afternoons were for penning material, which I presented to my one-woman audience for approval. If Estelle didn't think something was funny, believe me, she never minced words in telling me so. And many times she suggested subtle changes in punch lines or contributed dialogue. Then she deciphered my scrawly handwriting and typed the scripts.

Once each show had taken shape, we relaxed, sometimes

by driving down to the Hollywood Theater for a late-afternoon movie. Because the venue was owned by a sponsor, admission was free, which on a fifteen-dollar-a-week salary did not go unappreciated. After dinner, around ten o'clock, it was on to the studio to get ready for the broadcast. By that time the building was deserted except for us and an engineer who functioned dually as announcer. Shortly before eleven, scripts were stacked in order, sound effects were all lined up—and my nerves, frayed. Then the engineer lifted a finger to his lips, introduced the program, cued me, and "Cobwebs and Nuts" was underway, fifteen hours after preparations had begun.

The format was unconstrained, juggling skits, commentary, and recorded music. In that sense I was one of the original disc jockeys, only unlike most DJs, I thought nothing of grabbing the microphone and crooning along over the air. It was like singing in the shower, but with thousands of strangers eavesdropping. KEX listeners were treated to such duets as Mel Blanc and Bing Crosby, Mel Blanc and Rudy Vallee, and Mel Blanc and Louis Armstrong howling "I Gotta Right to Sing the Blues."

One of our repeated gags centered around the time checks given on the hour and half-hour. Instead of sounding a conventional tone or chime, I rattled a huge metal barrel full of tin cans, bells, and rusty nails, generating a terrible racket. Then I gave the time in painfully accurate degrees: "It is presently nineteen and two-fifths minutes past ten o'clock." Anything for a laugh.

About the only similarity between "Cobwebs and Nuts" and the big-budgeted, national-network shows hosted by Jack Benny and Fred Allen was its odd assortment of recurrent characters. There were Mr. and Mrs. Travellog, for example, a vacationing couple who tumbled into every conceivable traveler's pitfall. They'd wear the wrong shoes while hiking and wind up with burning blisters, get arrested for picking berries in no-trespassing zones, find their tent overrun by insects, and so on. We also wrote around regular themes including Westerns and murder mysteries, for which Estelle emitted such bloodcurdling screams that the engineer had to whisk off his headphones and cup his hands to his ears.

Many of Estelle's characters were big hits with the auddience, including the coquettish Toots Waverly. People even began referring to her as "Toots" off the air and sent fan mail addressed to Mrs. Waverly. Her best-loved creation of all, though, was snooty, upper-crust Mrs. McFloggpoople IV. In our most famous sketch involving Mrs. McF., her husband (me) has been gone for three years in search of a pack of cigarettes. When he finally returns, he whistles and says, "Boy, that line sure was long. . . ."

The night it was performed, Estelle and the engineer anticipated the gag line and laughed so uproariously that few listeners could make it out. We received dozens of letters and phone calls demanding to know what Mr. McF. had said. From then on, loyal fans began materializing at the station just before airtime, setting up folding chairs right there in the studio. Before long, we had spectators nightly, adding to the show's anarchic, anything-can-happen appeal.

To maintain audience interest six hours a week, I had to come up with countless voices and must have multiplied my repertoire every month. More and more I relied on the improvisational skills I'd first cultivated on "The Hoot Owls." Estelle became a pretty good ad-libber too, but one impromptu remark of hers topped them all.

It happened on a night when she was nursing a hangover. My wife has never been one to drink, but the evening before she'd sipped from a bottle of peach brandy. Out of curiosity (she claims). She continued sipping until it was nearly drained and woke up the next afternoon feeling demon alcohol's wrath. Came show time, and her head was still throbbing. All night she rushed through her lines, figuring, I suppose, that the quicker she said them, the quicker she could get home and crawl into bed. Trying to slow her down a bit, I said kiddingly, "Hey, Toots, where's the fire?"

And my wife, in her throatiest Mae West, replied, "In your

eyes, big boy, in your eyes!" The studio audience just about toppled out of their folding chairs.

"Cobwebs and Nuts" 's following grew so much, the show was moved to sister station KGW, with its greater wattage and prestige. We became local celebrities of sorts, occasionally getting stopped on the street to sign autographs. While it was very flattering, of course, public notoriety wasn't putting food on the table. Frugal living? A laughable understatement.

The entire cast of "Cobwebs and Nuts": Mel and Estelle Blanc. We'd been married for two years (not to mention married twice) when this photo was snapped in 1935.

Because Estelle was the more budget-minded Blanc, she managed our limited funds. Of the sixty dollars earned monthly, eight went toward rent, and thirty was earmarked for food: one dollar a day. Luckily a nearby restaurant called Crouch's charged only twenty-five cents for dinner; thirty-five cents for the deluxe plate. But rarely did we have any money left over for such luxuries as gas in the car.

With the shift to KGW, "Cobwebs and Nuts" now aired at six o'clock, making for a slightly less frantic lifestyle. Following a show one evening, I suggested to Estelle that we break our increasingly dreary routine and drive to Vancouver, Washington. "I know a place there that makes the best caramel corn you've ever tasted, for a nickel." She nodded in agreement.

We got to the shop just before it closed, I ordered a bag, dug my hand into my coat pocket, drew out some change, and began counting. "One, two, three, four . . . Four cents? Darn it, I know I had five pennies." My wife and I looked at each other helplessly, for her purse was empty. Rushing back to the car, we nearly tore apart the upholstery searching for the missing coin, but it was nowhere to be found. The drive home that evening was one of the most silent on record.

Eventually, just to cover sundry household emergencies, I had to sell the eight measly shares of Bank of America stock I'd purchased for our future. And although I was already working seventy-hour weeks, I started moonlighting as host of KGW's "Sunday Morning Breakfast Club" and of a KEX amateur talent show.

Oregon winters can be extremely harsh, and one merciless blizzard so paralyzed the city that all the talent-show contestants canceled. So, not knowing what else to do, I assumed the identities of hillbilly yodeler, guitarist, female singer, and violin soloist. The listenership was never the wiser. No, I don't remember who won, and no, I didn't collect the winning prize, either.

It makes for an amusing story, but it especially points up why I loved radio so much: It is a medium of illusion, even more so than film, television, and cartoons. During radio's golden era, expert voice actors could transport listeners to wondrous places or immerse them so deeply in a drama, the line between reality and fantasy became imperceptible.

No one exploited radio's illusory power better than Orson Welles, with whom I later worked. His infamous October 30,

1938, "The Mercury Theatre on the Air" adaptation of H. G. Wells's *War of the Worlds* sent thousands of panic-stricken listeners into the streets, certain that Martians in flying cylinders were vaporizing New York City and New Jersey. What with preexisting jitters over the escalating European conflict, plus convincing acting and inventively applied sound effects from Welles's radio troupe, Americans from Maine to Washington conjured terrifying scenes of an extraterrestrial invasion. A Pittsburgh woman was ready to swallow poison rather than perish from Martian death rays. The film version made some years later wasn't nearly as chilling, for what soundstage prop could equal the images generated by an audience's fancy?

I think it's a shame there aren't more radio comedies and dramas today. Children have been deprived of exercising their imaginations, which are so fertile at that age. This is just a theory of mine, but one reason why modern youngsters don't read as much as did previous generations might be that their enjoyment is hampered. They haven't been encouraged to shape their own fanciful images from the words on a printed page. Instead, they are force-fed someone else's interpretations of a story or a song by way of television, rock-music videos, and the like. Not only is it stifling, it's tragic, to think of the pleasure and self-discovery they are missing out on.

"Cobwebs and Nuts" certainly encouraged me to use my imagination: practically stark raving mad after eight or nine hours of writing, I'd envision myself on a sun-swept tropical beach; anywhere but in the dank, dark KGW studio. My dissatisfaction soared after I was awarded a paltry five-dollar raise, far below management's original promise to boost my salary commensurate with the number of show sponsors. By 1935 "Cobwebs" had eleven. Five dollars? My paycheck should have increased by *fifty*-five.

For the first time in my life I became so disheartened that I seriously considered quitting. Harry Granitt, my old cohort from the "Hoot Owls" show, knew Estelle and I were barely scraping by and made me a tempting offer: sell insurance for fifty dollars weekly. "I'll discuss it with the missus," I said to him, "and get back to you."

That evening at dinner I told Estelle about the opportunity dangling before me.

"Fifty dollars a week? That's a lot of money," she said thoughtfully. "But don't take it, Mel."

"Don't take it?"

"I know you. You wouldn't be happy selling insurance. You're a voice-man, and you belong on the air."

I walked over to her and hugged her tightly. Without my wife's unwavering faith and support I might very well have opted for a quick monetary fix—and a dull career. But Estelle was insightful and selfless enough to understand that I'd only be trading in the future for the present.

She also knew when I had reached the end of my rope. After two years of incessant pressure for me to turn out original material, the show's title had taken on new meaning: Cobwebs were forming between my ears, and I was slowly going nuts. One night Estelle looked over at me, racking my brain to fill reams of paper with dialogue, and said, "Do you want to have a nervous breakdown, or do you want to go back to Los Angeles?"

My pencil point snapped.

"What did you say?"

"Do you want to go back to Los Angeles? Mel, if we're going to be broke, at least let's be broke someplace where it's warm."

I didn't have to give her proposal a second thought.

"You're right," I said, forcing a smile. "Besides, we can't do much worse down there, can we?"

It was a rhetorical question, just in case.

Before returning to California, we had to do something about improving our mode of transportation. Several months back, the troublesome green Ford had been customized by a reckless driver who ran a red light and into our bumper. He forked over twenty-five dollars for his negligence, but the money quickly disappeared: Food and rent took precedence over auto cosmetic surgery. We both knew, however, that it would be a miracle if the car limped even as far as Eugene, Oregon. "Let's trade it in for a new model," Estelle suggested.

"Are you kidding? Who in his right mind would give us anything for this piece of junk?"

"Trust me."

There was a newly opened Ford dealership in Portland, and my wife marched up to and accosted the dealer. "We'd like to trade in our old car for a new one," she said coolly.

"What condition is it in?"

She gestured out the showroom window to our jalopy, which at Estelle's prompting I'd parked across the street so that the damaged side wasn't visible. "What'll you give us for it?"

"About three hundred forty-five dollars," the salesman replied. It was a struggle for me not to burst out laughing.

"What does that new model over there sell for?" I put in, pointing to a gleaming 1935 tan coupe with radio and rumble seat.

"Six hundred forty."

"Would you excuse us a moment?" My financial coach and I huddled.

"We'll make you an offer," Estelle said at last to the salesman. "Take our old car as down payment, and we'll pay you the two-ninety-five balance within four months."

To my amazement, the salesman cried, "Deal!" *Steal* was more like it.

"I haven't sold a single car since I started this job," he explained while filling out the necessary paperwork. "Believe me, I'd have done anything to make a sale." We believed.

Since we didn't have enough money for lodgings on the long drive to Los Angeles, the coupe served additionally as a motel on wheels. Estelle slept in the front seat; I took the rumble seat. As cramped as it was, we snoozed peacefully, contented smiles on our faces. Estelle was coming home, and I was about to take my second stab at making it in Hollywood.

CHAPTER

3

Porky Pig to the R-R-Rescue

Estelle's parents were delighted to have their daughter and son-in-law back in Los Angeles and insisted we stay with them until I got on my feet financially. So we moved into their large four-bedroom, two-bathroom flat at the corner of Sixth Street and St. Andrew's Place. Estelle and me, her mother and father, her brother, Sonny, and a cousin, Rose.

It wasn't at all as intolerable as it probably sounds. For one thing, because there were two married couples among us, no one had to share a bedroom; at least, no one that wasn't legally wed. And for another, Mr. and Mrs. Rosenbaum were two of the kindest, most fun-loving people I ever met. Don't think I didn't appreciate their good-heartedness; I knew that for most husbands, living with their in-laws usually constituted grounds for divorce within a matter of weeks.

Actually the Rosenbaums and I hit it off from the very start, and I quickly discovered where their daughter inherited her keen sense of humor. The first time I met Estelle's mother and father, she was half an hour late getting home from a horseback-riding session. As my wife later told me, she was concerned about not being there when I arrived. *What if my parents and Mel don't get along?* she worried.

When she burst in through the front door, she heard me entertaining her parents in the parlor, telling stories in my different voices. Mr. Rosenbaum's hearty laughter erased any anxiety she was still feeling. It was a good thing Estelle's mother laughed easily, too, or else I very easily could have gotten on her bad side. A fabulous cook, that night at dinner Mrs. Rosenbaum made a mushroom and barley soup that was so delicious, I wolfed down two bowlfuls.

"Would you like some more, Mel?" she asked.

Hoping to impress her with my fluent Yiddish, I replied, "No thank you. *Geférlakh.*" Loosely translated, it means, "That's pretty bad" or "That's dangerous." What I'd meant to say was *"Geéndikt"*: "I'm finished."

She sensed my slip of the tongue and began laughing. I couldn't help but laugh along, wondering what the hell I'd said that was so funny.

Like their daughter, Mr. and Mrs. Rosenbaum never tried to dissuade me from pursuing my dreams in Hollywood. They were once involved in show business themselves, employed by the old Fox film studios commissary. The restaurant was divided into two areas: a very plain section in which electricians, key grips, and other crew members ate, and an elegantly appointed section for cast, directors, and producers, replete with white-lace tablecloths and white-linen napkins. Estelle and her brother often accompanied their folks to work. But the day when young Sonny came racing up to his father and shouted, "Daddy, come quick and look! A naked lady!" Mr. Rosenbaum realized a movie-studio lot was probably not a proper environment for growing children.

They quit to open a small grocery store; Estelle's father ran the butcher department, while her mother tended to the fruits and vegetables. Like most Depression-era families, they struggled, but the Rosenbaums made a comfortable life for their children.

Estelle insisted on joining the work force, and I insisted just as vehemently she stay at home. I realize that seems pretty chauvinist in these days of women's liberation, but bear in mind that in the 1930s, a wife's not having to work was a source of male pride. After several heated discussions on the subject, Estelle turned down an offer to become a theatrical agent, which I'm sure she would have been very good at. Perhaps today I'd react differently; then again, maybe not. I suppose I'm just old-fashioned that way.

The funny thing was, my wife was fielding more job propositions than I was. In radio's early days competition was especially fierce because a multivoice artist such as me was a rarity. Studios were used to hiring one person for one part only. Fortunately I had the benefit of not one but five personal agents: Estelle and her family. I'd instructed Mrs. Rosenbaum that if a call came in for *any* radio work, grab it, no questions asked. So when a local station phoned to ask if I could imitate a German dialect, "like Lew Lehr," she replied cheerfully, "Of course he can." No questions asked.

When she relayed to me the good news that evening, however, *I* had a question: namely, "Who's Lew Lehr?" A Fox newsreel in which he starred was playing at the nearby Wiltern Theatre on Wilshire Boulevard, so Estelle and I hurried down and bought two tickets. Lehr was a Philadelphian who'd played the vaudeville circuit with his wife, actress Nancy Belle, before entering radio and motion pictures. He is best remembered for his phrase "Monkeys iz der craziest peoples," proclaimed in a German accent as dense as the head on a stein of beer. Interestingly, it became such a familiar expression that it was later used in several Warner Bros. cartoons, in various permutations: "Ducks iz der craziest peoples," and so on.

I did the voice the next day—just a few lines—and the producer expressed extreme satisfaction. But as much as I appreciated the work, imitating someone else rubbed me the wrong way. As I got up in front of the microphone, I even asked, "If you wanted Lew Lehr's voice, why didn't you get Lew Lehr himself?" The reason, of course, was money. A relative unknown was cheaper. It seemed dishonorable to me then, like stealing, and except for those occasions when an impersonation was needed for satirical purposes, I never did it again.

After several more weeks of feeling the breeze from doors slammed in my face, I nabbed a regular spot on KFWB's Gaffers and Stattler Stove Company–sponsored "Johnny Murray Talks It Over." Once again I auditioned using my five-minute World News Report, working in French and Swedish accents this time. Murray, a singer and radio personality of some renown, was as amused as Al Pearce had been two years earlier.

"I've got to find a spot on the show for you!" he bellowed, adding almost as an afterthought that I'd be paid thirty-five dollars weekly—more than double what I had earned in Portland.

Estelle and I celebrated by splurging on dinner at King's Tropical Inn on West Washington Boulevard. "No deluxe plate, either," I said to her. "Let's have some real food." I ordered my favorite, a generous-size steak, which I was beginning to think I'd never taste again. Ah, heaven.

I was still hungry to get on a national program, so crucial to furthering a radio career. You know the saying that it's easier to find a job when you've already got one? How true. Shortly after picking up the Murray show, I received a call from Nate Tufts, producer and talent scout for CBS's widely popular "The Baker's Broadcast," sponsored by Fleischmann's Yeast.

"You're calling *me?*" I asked suspiciously. Tufts, a blunt, bearish sort of fellow, had never endeared himself to me. I'd approached him at least a half dozen times about auditioning, and he always seemed to take perverse pleasure in refusing me.

"Yeah, I'm calling you," he answered. "Listen, Blanc, we're giving you guys who think you're so funny a chance to prove it." His voice dripped with sarcasm.

Go ahead and insult me, you s.o.b., I thought. *I'll show you.*

The tryout was for the show's star, Joe Penner. Though he is not well remembered today, he was a 1930s sensation, beginning with his guest spots on Rudy Vallee's radio program. Born Josef Pinter in a village outside Budapest, Hungary, he was a peculiar-looking man who chain-smoked cigars and favored derby hats to cover his slicked-back hair. He'd floundered in vaudeville for years until coining a phrase that rescued him from certain obscurity: "Wanna buy a duck?"

I know, it doesn't read especially uproarious, and even Penner himself was hard put to explain why audiences found it so funny. What put it across was his comically nasal delivery and his penchant for interjecting the line unexpectedly. In the middle of a scripted gag he'd blurt, "Wanna buy a duck?" or "Wanna buy a rhinoceros?" and crowds just ate it up, as if there were some profound meaning behind it. Two other stock Penner-isms were "You *nah-h-sty* man!" and "Don't ever *do-ooo* that!"—both stretched like taffy. But "Wanna buy . . ." remained his most memorable, so much so that the duck was eventually given a name, Goo-Goo, and a voice: one of mine.

When I auditioned, Penner sat in the listening booth. The moment I finished, the door flew open, and he hustled into the studio. He pumped my hand and spouted superlatives as if he'd just discovered a cure for polio. "Why the heck didn't you come to me before? I could have used you in so many sketches!" I learned a valuable lesson: Whenever possible, bypass the middleman and go directly to the star.

In addition to the ubiquitous Goo-Goo, I supplied various voices. Nothing illustrious. But being on the show suddenly whisked me out of the pack and placed me among the voice-actor community elite. As more calls like Tufts's came my way, I sensed momentum building.

Unfortunately, Joe's career was headed in the opposite direction, a downward spiral. He was an extremely ethical man whom I admired greatly. After he'd been named radio comedian of the year he quit "The Baker's Broadcast," voicing dissatisfaction with the show's quality and format. He returned a year later in a situation comedy, "The Joe Penner

Show," which never took off. By decade's end it was back to the stage for Penner, who for all intents was washed up.

He died in 1941 at just thirty-six years of age. The night before, he'd dined in Philadelphia with Ozzie and Harriet Nelson, "The Baker's Broadcast" 's bandleader and vocalist. He was in a low-grossing road-company production of *Yokel Boy* at the Locust St. Theatre, and according to the Nelsons it was painfully obvious that Penner was down on his luck. The newspapers barely made mention of his passing, from an apparent heart attack in his sleep.

This is what I believe happened to Penner: Back in 1935 he received a "fan" letter that essentially said, "Your duck routine stinks, and I'm never going to listen to you again." Now, most actors form thick skins against such criticisms and would simply have tossed the epistle in the nearest wastebasket without a second thought. But Joe was extremely sensitive and let it gnaw at him. Imagine, one lousy letter! I'm convinced that was the real reason he dropped out of "The Baker's Broadcast" a short time later.

I was deeply saddened to hear about his death. By 1941 my career would be flying high, while the man responsible for my first national exposure died in obscurity. It was a sobering thought.

Any headiness I may have felt about my rising star was tempered by the awareness that one cancellation could hurl me back where I started. With more entertainment choices than ever before, audiences had grown increasingly fickle. Just as vaudeville quickly toppled from public favor, who knew if radio wasn't destined to be displaced too?

That in mind, I wanted to branch into other areas. Film was out of the question because I didn't feel comfortable in front of cameras. But *animated* films, that made sense. Following in the footsteps of motion pictures, cartoons had also gone full-sound. From what I'd seen, however, the majority of voice characterizations didn't come close to matching the animation's level of ingenuity. I was positive I could do better.

And from what I'd heard through the grapevine, it seemed that cartoon studios paid well.

The first animated film I recall seeing was a silent short, *Felix Saves the Day*, starring Felix the Cat, when I was about fourteen. But cartoons' origins go back at least a decade further. Gertie the Dinosaur, brainchild of newspaper cartoonist Windsor McCay, is generally accepted as the original cartoon character. By today's standards the animation was primitive: austere black-line drawings come to life. Nevertheless, audiences were astounded, and Gertie stole their hearts, though she did little else besides devour anything remotely edible in her path.

In animation's early days, simply showing pictures that moved was fantastic enough. Therefore, storylines were secondary to milking this new technology the public clamored to see. Characters were made to wiggle, to walk upside down, and to contort themselves into impossible positions. Realism was not at all an aim; fantasy was. Like radio, cartoons fired my young imagination.

The animation process used today was conceived around 1914; characters and backgrounds are inked on the front and then painted on the back of clear celluloid, or cels. Until then, they had been drawn sequentially on sheets of translucent rice paper, which were then filmed frame by frame.

By the time I forayed into the field, there existed dozens of cartoon characters appearing in full-sound productions. Eight major studios dominated the industry: Max Fleischer Studios, then famous for Popeye the Sailor, Betty Boop, Koko the Clown, and other box-office bigwigs; Terrytoons (Farmer Al Falfa); Walter Lantz Productions (Oswald the Lucky Rabbit); Ub Iwerks's Celebrity Productions (Flip the Frog and Willie Whopper); Charles Mintz's productions for Columbia Pictures Corporation/Screen Gems (Krazy Kat and Scrappy); MGM (the Happy Harmonies series); Walt Disney Productions; and Leon Schlessinger Productions, distributed by Warner Bros.

The latter two studios interested me the most; Disney, because he was to cartoons what producer D. W. Griffith was to motion pictures. Without question he was the most innovative and influential animated-filmmaker of the late 1920s and 1930s.

Often overlooked is the fact that Disney was a brilliant cartoonist, even though his formal art training was confined to a night course at Chicago's Academy of Fine Arts when he was sixteen and a brief tenure at a Kansas City, Missouri, art school. Considering that drawing animals was to become his forte, he probably received his finest education by growing up on Midwestern farms. When bored by his studies at Kansas City's Benton school, he sketched pictures of animals in his schoolbooks' margins, then flipped the pages with his thumb so that the illustrations appeared to move. I always get a kick out of that story because it reminds me of how I accidentally discovered Woody Woodpecker's voice in a high-school hallway. Obviously, adolescent boredom has its practical applications.

In 1923 twenty-two-year-old Disney arrived in Hollywood with forty dollars in his pocket. He also clutched the rough designs for an experimental film, *Alice in Cartoonland*, to feature a live-action girl romping among animated backgrounds and animals. Thanks to a five-hundred-dollar loan from his uncle, he and his brother Roy set up a tiny garage studio at 2719 Hyperion Avenue. If the address sounds familiar, it's because it was just down the hill from where I later lived with Hymie Breslau. We could see the Disney studio from our front door.

Three months went by, and a discouraged Disney was ready to go back home, when distributor Margaret J. Winkler was impressed enough by his sketches to bankroll an *Alice in Cartoonland* series. Next, Disney and associates Ub Iwerks, Rudolf Ising, and Hugh Harmon designed a merry character they christened Oswald the Lucky Rabbit. Truthfully speaking, Oswald didn't look much like a rabbit at all. But he certainly brought luck, even if not for Walt, who in 1928 fell victim to unscrupulous studio politics. I will spare you the convoluted details; suffice to say that the profit-generating bunny wound up the property of distributor Winkler's husband, Charles Mintz.

Undaunted, Disney set about developing the hare's heir. As I've heard it, his inspiration was a real live mouse that had taken up residence in his office wastebasket when Disney was working for a farm journal. He grew so attached to the rodent that he named it Mortimer, then Mickey, then Mickey Mouse. Mickey Money would have been more fitting, although two silent shorts introducing him, *Plane Crazy* and *Gallopin' Gaucho*, were so poor they were temporarily shelved.

The third was the first "talking" cartoon, *Steamboat Willie*. There was no dialogue per se, but for the first time animal sounds, laughter, and exclamations were heard. Mickey Mouse was at once the Al Jolson of animated films.

With sound tracks cartoons took on exciting complexities and possibilities. Disney was heralded as the field's undisputed giant: Of the first ten Academy Awards handed out to cartoon makers, he collected nine.

The last Disney cartoon to contain any of Walt's artwork was his most ambitious to date: 1937's *Snow White and the Seven Dwarfs*, the first full-length animated picture. It entailed *two million* drawings and sketches, a quarter million of which were photographed; cost Disney $1.6 million in production alone; and took three years to complete. Despite his irreproachable track record, most Hollywood moguls thought Walt was daft and began referring to the cartoon as "Disney's Folly." But just as when he lost custody of the soon-to-be-forgotten Oswald, Disney enjoyed the last laugh: Within months of release *Snow White* took in eight million dollars, at the time making it Hollywood's highest-grossing film ever.

I don't think anyone who worked for Disney once doubted his genius, but because he was such an obsessive perfectionist, many found him difficult to work for. My personal experience with him was problem-free, although, admittedly, it was minimal. In fact, my lone contribution to a Walt Disney picture was a single, solitary hiccup. Allow me to explain.

For some time I'd been calling on the Disney studio, trying to ingratiate myself to his young receptionist. At first she was cool to me, another pain-in-the-neck actor pestering her for an appointment, but eventually she warmed up, and we became friendly.

"Gee, I sure wish Mr. Disney would give me a listen," I sighed one day, hoping to evoke some compassion. "I'd love to work for him."

"What sort of voices do you do, anyway?" she asked.

"Well . . ." I thought for a moment. "I do a great drunk." Which I proceeded to demonstrate in all its hiccuping glory.

"That's really funny," she said, laughing. Then noticing my beseeching expression, she rolled her eyes. "Okay, okay. I'll see if I can get Mr. Disney." Sure enough, when she returned to her desk, her boss was behind her. Having seen his photo in newspapers and magazines, I recognized him instantly. He had a slender build, dark, combed-back hair, and a small, neat mustache. Walt enjoyed my characterization so much, he cast me as Gideon the cat in *Pinnochio*, Walt Disney Productions' second full-length feature. Costs for this one mounted to $2.5 million, due primarily to Disney's exacting ways: Six months into the project he scrapped every cel when they failed to meet his approval. I don't imagine his artists were too pleased.

My *Pinnochio* dialogue was recorded in sixteen days, at fifty bucks per. After I collected my eight hundred dollars, I waited like everyone else for the film to open. When it finally did, in 1940, to my great surprise Gideon was mute. Between the time I'd been taped and the picture was released, Disney, concerned that children might think the cat was a lush, edited out every utterance; except for one hiccup. At eight hundred dollars, it undoubtedly remains the most expensive glottal spasm in the annals of motion pictures.

*   *   *

While I wanted to work for Walt Disney because he was the best, I wanted to work for Warner Bros. because it was far from it. The voices for its otherwise inventive Looney Tunes and Merrie Melodies characters were then among the worst in the business. I soon found out why: Stand-ins from the studio's films were conscripted off the lot to supply cartoon dialogue at no extra pay. And for many actors, the greater the piece of change, the greater the dramatic range.

In every other aspect of its productions, though, Warner's seemed poised to challenge Disney. No surprise, that, as many of its creative guiding lights had previously worked for Walt. When the studio opened in 1929, its core was comprised of directors Hugh Harman and Rudolf Ising, one half of the original Disney axis. They were later joined by other Disney alumni: directors Jack King, Tom Palmer, Isadore Freleng, and Ub Iwerks, who subcontracted his work to the house for a brief time.

Harman and Ising were extremely talented. But they were so determined to vie with their former boss that the early Warner Bros. cartoon characters never acquired distinctive personalities and were little more than pale Disney facsimiles. Not that Warner Bros. was the only studio guilty of flattery by way of imitation; every other production company seemed to claim Mickey Mouse's illegitimate offspring. The situation got so out of hand, in 1931 Disney filed a temporary court injunction against the Van Beuren Corporation, which in two of its cartoons had cast a pair of male and female mice virtually indistinguishable from the famed Disney originals.

Just as it had underestimated the importance of sound, Warner Bros. initially saw cartoons merely as an enticement for movie-theater owners: Buy one of our feature films, and we'll throw in a six-minute short free, was the proposition. Its first was the 1930 black-and-white *Sinking in the Bathtub*, which starred a sweet-faced, mush-mouthed black boy named Bosko. He was the studio's mainstay until Harman and Ising left Warner's three years later after repeatedly butting heads with management over budgets. When they took Bosko with them, few tears were shed.

His replacement was Buddy: little more than Bosko with white pigmentation. Bright-eyed Buddy starred in roughly two dozen productions over two years before being sentenced back to the inkwell for criminal blandness. Foxy, essentially Mickey Mouse in fox's clothing, and Beans, a high-spirited cat, were two other seminal Warner Bros. creations that are little remembered.

I came to Warner Bros. in 1936, by which time most of the founding brain trust was replaced by young directors, animators, and writers with fresh ideas. Actually, let me rephrase that: I finally gained entrée to the studio that year. But I'd been trying for eighteen months.

Without fail, I would pay biweekly visits to Leon Schlessinger Productions, located around the corner from Warner's stately southern-mansion headquarters. Schlessinger was a savvy businessman who'd helped the four Warner brothers finance *The Jazz Singer*. Now they distributed his Looney Tunes and Merrie Melodies animated films. Every time I bounded up the steps and through the door of his Bronson Avenue building, the same scene was repeated:

"Excuse me," I'd say to the casting director, a churlish fellow whose last name was Spencer, "I'd like to audition for you."

"Sorry," he'd reply haughtily, "we have all the voices we need." He never even had the courtesy to look up from his desk at me. This went on from summer 1935 to winter 1936. When I first came calling, I had few credits to my name, so perhaps his indifference was understandable. Yet even when I'd protest, "But I'm a regular on Joe Penner's radio show," or Johnny Murray's (which was broadcast over Warner-owned KFWB), his condescending response was always the same.

One late-December afternoon I walked up to his desk as usual, readying myself for yet another rejection. A different person sat there, engrossed in paperwork.

"Excuse me, but what happened to the guy who usually sits here?"

"He dropped dead last week."

"Jeez, that's too bad. Say, pal, how about giving me an audition?"

"Sure," replied the new face, whose name was Treg Brown. "Let's hear what you've got."

I nearly passed out. Having been turned down every other week for a year and a half, I'd come to expect it. But I regained my composure enough to do a creditable rendition of—what else?—my World News Report, which Brown thought enough of to corral the directors for a second opinion. A lively Christmas office party was in progress, so the entire cartoon division was present, albeit in various stages of mood alteration.

He brought back the four directors: Isadore Freleng, whom everyone called Friz, Frank Tashlin, Bob Clampett and Fred "Tex" Avery. The diminutive Freleng was a holdover from the old regime and a Walt Disney refugee. At the time, he was involved primarily with the Merrie Melodies in-color short-subjects. Tashlin had only recently arrived at Schlessinger Productions, directing several of the black-and-white Looney Tunes. A comedy writer and cartoonist, he later went on to a distinguished film-directing career beginning in the 1940s. Clampett was an even newer addition to the staff; a handsome fellow with dark, wavy hair and a lantern jaw. Then there was the portly Avery, who'd gotten his start as an animator for producer Walter Lantz. At Warner's he gained distinction as one of the most wildly inventive directors of all time.

Of the quartet, Avery seemed most taken with my routine. "Hey, Mel," he said, "I've got this new cartoon character in the works, and you might be just the person for its voice."

"What kind of character is it?"

"Hold on a minute and I'll show you." He ran into his office and returned with a drawing of a bull.

"We need a drunken bull," he explained as I studied the sketch. "Think you can do it?"

Asking Mel Blanc if he can sound like a drunk is like

asking Marcel Marceau "Can you mime?"—though I'm a social drinker at most. A few years later, when I was a regular
on singer/actress Judy Canova's radio show, I sometimes
frightened her by pretending to have hit the bottle just before
airtime. "Oh, my God, Mel's drunk!" she'd shriek, panicked.
"What are we gonna do?" It must have been pretty convincing.

"Sure," I told Avery confidently, "I think I know just what
you're looking for."

**Presto, change-o: From mild-mannered Mel to drunken bull. This
characterization was my very first for Warner Bros., in 1937's *Picador Porky*.**

Screwing up my face, squinting through one eye and af-
fecting a lazy southern drawl punctuated by hiccups, I slurred,
"Well, a drunken bull (*hic!*) would sound a li'l (*hic!*) loaded,
like he wuz lookin' (*hic!*) fer the sour mash." I discharged one
final, head-shaking "Hic!" and the directors—plus lanky ani-

mator Chuck Jones, who'd joined the group—broke out in applause.

"That's terrific!" Avery exclaimed. "Tell me, can you come in for a recording session next Tuesday?" It goes without saying that I didn't have a damn thing scheduled for that Tuesday or any Tuesday thereafter. But not wanting to appear too overanxious, I thought for a moment before replying nonchalantly, "Yes, I think I can make it."

The bull character was to be used in an upcoming production titled *Picador Porky*, starring a Friz Freleng creation, Porky Pig. Porky had bowed in a 1935 cartoon, *I Haven't Got a Hat*, supporting Beans the Cat. After another secondary role in the Avery-directed *Gold Diggers of '49*, he ascended to top billing, beginning with 1936's *Boom, Boom*. By now he had thirteen shorts to his credit and was incontestably Looney Tunes' biggest star.

Like many of the animated animals I was to voice, Porky went through several physical transformations shortly after

Porky Pig had already appeared in sixteen theatrical shorts when I replaced actor Joe Dougherty, who stuttered in real life. *Illustration © 1987 Warner Bros. Inc.*

conception. In *I Haven't Got a Hat* he's an adorable piglet. But several cartoons later, he's been bloated into an enormous adult, a bedeviled ham who can barely stand upright. Eventually it was decided that audiences best responded to Porky as an innocent little creature, so the artists tapered his pronounced girth.

Porky's voice was tinkered with accordingly. The pig's stutter was Friz's idea, one for which he initially tolerated a good deal of criticism. But he wanted to distinguish Porky from the many homogenous animated-film characters, and in hindsight the distinctive speech impediment did just that. Originally the role went to Joe Dougherty, a debonair actor whose film credits included *The Jazz Singer*. Talk about typecasting: Dougherty stuttered. For real.

It must have seemed ideal at first—need a stammering cartoon pig, hire a stammering actor. But problems unfolded. Recording was still done on expensive optical film, and Dougherty's inability to come in on cue wasted a lot of it, irritating budget-minded Leon Schlessinger. The producer liked my drunken bull so much, he called me into his office, closing the door behind us with an air of secrecy.

"I've got a problem here, Mel," he said gruffly, flicking ashes from his cigarette. Leon was short and stocky, with dark hair that was draped over his balding pate in a last-ditch but ultimately futile effort at camouflage. He went on to explain about the difficulties Dougherty presented. "Joe's a nice enough fellow, and he does his best, but . . . I was wondering if you'd try Porky's voice."

"You want me to be the voice of a pig? That's some job for a nice Jewish boy." I was joking. Schlessinger was in no mood for laughing.

"Well?"

Not really knowing what a cartoon pig should sound like, I asked if I could have a few days to research the role. Leon looked at me in disbelief. "You're kidding, right?" Not this time.

"You know, Leon, method acting." Method acting was a

theory propounded by the celebrated Moscow Art Theatre director Konstantin Stanislavsky, who contended a performer should become his character. For many actors his Method could be God's law. Grudgingly, Schlessinger agreed.

That afternoon I drove out to a pig farm near Saugus, north of San Fernando. As I explained to the owner why I needed to observe his prize swine, his expression grew increasingly bewildered. But he told me to take all the time I needed. "Just don't fall in the mud," he cautioned.

Once satisfied that I could translate a stout-bodied omnivore's grunt into a comical cartoon voice, I headed back to the office, to demonstrate for my boss the fruits of my intensive probe.

"Now, Leon, if a pig could talk, he'd talk with a grunt, right?" I began emulating a series of grunts, progressively raising them in pitch so that they sounded, indeed, like stutters. But adding to Freleng's original concept, I used the impediment as a means for inserting a running gag: having Porky attempt to spit out a particular word, then several alternatives (which he can't enunciate either), before he finally settles on an entirely different word to express the original thought.

"So, Porky would say good-bye like this: 'Bye-b—, uh-bye-b—, so lo—, uh-so lon—, auf Wiede—, auf Wiede—

" 'Toodle-loo!' "

I finished by ad-libbing, "Th— uh-th— uh-th—that's all, folks!"

Schlessinger jumped up from behind his heavy desk and stabbed a finger in the air. "You're it!" he shouted.

"Y-y-ya mean I'm P-Porky Pi— uh-Porky Pi— uh-P-Porky—ya mean I'm him?"

"Yes, Mel." He was laughing. "You're him." We shook hands, and I headed for the door.

"Just one more thing, Mel." Schlessinger's voice turned me around.

"Yes, Leon?"

"Go home and take a bath, will you?"

* * *

When handed my first Warner's paycheck, I had to blink my eyes. Two hundred dollars! I'd never seen three digits on a check before; at least, not one made out to me. I immediately phoned my parents in Portland to tell them the good news. "Two hundred dollars? A *week?*" My father couldn't conceive of drawing such a salary. With suspicion he asked, "What else do you have to do?" assuming that for that amount I probably had to sweep the studio floors as well.

"Nothing else, Dad, just voices."

"You work hard for them," he said to me seriously, "you hear me?"

"I will, Dad, I promise." The pride in his voice was unmistakable, and it put me on top of the world.

Picador Porky, released in March 1937, was my first cartoon for the company. Animated by Chuck Jones and Sid Sutherland, the plot is as follows:

Porky and two pals come across a sign publicizing a bullfight and a thousand-dollar grand prize. Together they hatch a scheme: The pig will masquerade as a matador, and his friends as a bull that will purposely fall upon *el matador gordo*'s sword, so that afterward the trio can split the winnings.

However, Porky's cohorts get so drunk prior to the bullfight, they're unable to rouse themselves. (The drunken bovine, of course, was the character for which Tex Avery initially recruited me.) Poor Porky, not exactly a master of *doblando* and *muletazo* moves, is confronted by a real, ferocious, snorting bull, played by veteran character actor Billy Bletcher. I would work many times over the years with Bletcher, who stood just over five feet but possessed a deep, resonant, villainous voice.

The impostor bull finally shakes off its intoxication, drags itself into the ring, and collapses at Porky's feet. But in a fit of conscience our hero awards the prize money to the real bull. Good-hearted Porky never was a very credible scam artist. While this character trait made him beloved by audiences, ironically, it ultimately led to his downfall.

Still, in his late-1930s prime, Porky was Warner's top attraction, so identified with the studio that all its cartoons ended with his bursting through a big bass drum and uttering the classic "Th— uh-th— uh-th— That's all, folks!" The gentle pig starred in many wonderful productions, including one of Friz Freleng's most innovative and inspired: *You Ought to Be in Pictures* (1940).

It opens with a black-and-white filmed sequence of the Schlessinger Productions rank-and-file straggling in to work. Cut to an artist's glancing at the clock and bellowing, "Lunchtime!" In fast-motion the workers bolt out of the building as if it were on fire. Come to think of it, that scene wasn't far from the truth.

Porky and a relatively new Warner's creation, Daffy Duck, strike up a conversation from their respective easels. Little does the gullible pig know, but the wily duck is gunning for his position. "You call this a job?" Daffy sneers in disgust. "Working in cartoons? Poop!" You can do much better for yourself in feature films, he tells Porky, "as Betty Davis's leading man. Three grand a week."

Combining live-action footage and animation, Daffy is shown prodding his victim down the hall to Leon Schlessinger's office. Go ahead and knock, he orders. Porky does, meekly. "Naw, like this!" Daffy says impatiently, and hammers the door so hard it nearly comes unhinged.

Once inside, Porky finds himself face-to-face with Schlessinger himself, in the flesh. "Hello, Mr. Schle—, Mr. Schle—, uh-hello, Leon," he splutters, claiming that he wants out of his contract. Much to his dismay, Schlessinger agrees all too readily, shaking Porky's hand and wishing him the best of luck. But as soon as the pig leaves his office, the studio boss turns to the camera and says with a conspiratorial wink, "He'll be back." I have to say, Leon turned in a very commendable performance, though it was nothing compared to his melodramatic poverty-pleading whenever I hit him up for a raise. *That* piece of acting deserved an Academy Award.

Porky's excursion into the real world is plagued by one mishap after another. He tries talking his way into the Warner

Bros. lot, but gets tossed out by a security guard played by one of our writers, Michael Maltese. (Incidentally, all voices, including Maltese's and Schlessinger's, were mine, dubbed in later.) After finally sneaking past, the pig enters a soundstage where an elaborate dance routine is being filmed, only to let go with a violent sneeze that blows over stacks of film canisters. This time it's the stagehands who bodily eject him.

Desperate to retrieve his old job, and to escape the Warner Bros. lot in one piece, Porky leaps into his animated automobile and zooms off, but he gets caught in the middle of a horse stampede. For this Friz Freleng used footage from one of the studio's Westerns. Next the poor pig is shown weaving frantically through a maze of traffic on his way back to Bronson and Fernwood. The panicked expression on his face is hilarious, and the technical wizardry outstanding. Other studios experimented with merging film and animation, but most film historians regard *You Ought to Be in Pictures* as the best of its kind.

Meanwhile, in Porky's absence, Daffy has perched himself on Schlessinger's desk, bending the producer's ear about granting him top billing. "Why, I'm a better actor than him," he brags. "Porky never did anything; *I* did all the work." Schlessinger, however, isn't nearly as convinced of Daffy's talent as is the narcissistic duck.

Just then Porky returns breathlessly. But before throwing himself at Leon Schlessinger's mercy, he has a debt to repay: The normally pacifist pig pummels Daffy until there are enough feathers on the floor to stuff a pillow. Then he timidly enters his boss's office, where Leon tells Porky that he didn't tear up his contract after all. "Now get back to work."

The final scene depicts Porky and Daffy back safely on their easels, the duck bandaged from head to webbed toe. Never one to admit defeat, this time he tries piquing the pig's interest by insisting Porky could earn twelve thousand dollars a week playing opposite Greta Garbo. In response he receives a faceful of paint. *Splat!* The end. Viewed today, *You Ought to Be in Pictures* is every bit as funny as when it was made and remains one of my favorite Porky Pig adventures.

By then, however, Porky's headlining days were nearing an end. With the emergence of Daffy, Bugs Bunny, and other Warner Bros. characters, he was relegated to either playing Daffy's foil or to ensemble work. In 1940 fifteen Porky Pig cartoons were produced; in 1950, just three; and in 1960, none. The studio even repossessed his "That's all, folks!" tag line, which as far as I'm concerned was like ripping the stars off a general's uniform.

Porky Pig made his theatrical-short farewell in *Corn on the Cop* in 1965. By that time many considered him a mere hasbeen. Discarded bacon. But I'll always have a soft spot in my heart for Porky. I owe him a lot.

For instance, if it weren't for Porky, Estelle and I couldn't have afforded our own apartment, which we rented in the summer of 1938. It was half of a two-flat house at 625 Alta Vista Boulevard, near Melrose Avenue. I was reluctant at first because although it was roomy enough, the yard was so over-grown it looked like the Everglades. Inside wasn't much better: warped floors and a heavy blanket of dust. I was ready to head for the door, but my wife said, "I see potential in it, Mel. I think we should take it." I'd learned long ago to trust Estelle's instincts, and as usual she was right. A little paint, some elbow grease, and the assistance of a gardener, and we transformed it into a lovely home.

We needed to be on our own because the Blanc family was about to expand, much like Estelle's stomach. Her doctor had told her in the spring that she was pregnant. Due date: first week in October.

"That's my kid," I joked to friends, "just in time for the start of the radio season!"

But the first week of the month came and went: no baby. The second week: no baby. On the morning of October 17, Estelle nudged me awake.

"I'm not feeling too well," she said. Due at a radio-program rehearsal, I immediately reached for the phone to cancel.

"No, you go on and do the show," my wife insisted. "The pain will go away."

Estelle knew full well she wasn't merely suffering from an upset stomach and that her water had broken. But she wanted to surprise me. As soon as I kissed her good-bye and drove off to the studio, she got dressed, hailed a cab, and checked herself into Cedars of Lebanon Hospital. Late that afternoon I returned home to find the note she'd left me. Jittery with excitement, I rushed to the hospital, where I was apprised that Estelle was already in labor.

While pacing the floor, I was spotted by a radio crew setting up its equipment.

"Hey, aren't you Mel Blanc?" a technician asked me.

"Yes, I am. Why, what's going on?"

"We're doing a broadcast about expectant fathers."

"Well, I'm here waiting for my first child to be born. My wife's in labor right now."

Figuring it would help to calm my nerves, I consented to an interview, and it's a good thing I did. In my race to Cedars of Lebanon, I'd forgotten to inform the Rosenbaums that their daughter was about to give birth. As it happened, Estelle's parents were tuned in to that station. Once they recognized the shaky voice of the expectant dad, they threw on their coats and came down to walk the floors alongside me.

When the program's producer offered me ten dollars for going on the air, I told him to make the check out to my child instead. "I'll call in the name as soon as I know if it's a boy or a girl," I instructed him.

However, that would take another twenty-four hours. Estelle's pregnancy may have been easy, but her labor was another matter. The baby had turned, and rather than rush a breech birth, a cesarean section had to be performed. Nowadays, of course, the procedure is more routine, but back then not much was known about the effects of having a baby re-

I love this family portrait, taken when our son Noel was three years old.

moved surgically. Needless to say, both my wife and I were upset by the news.

Finally, a day and a half after Estelle entered the hospital, October 19, our son was born, weighing seven pounds, fourteen ounces. We named the dark-haired, brown-eyed child Noel, after my much loved Grandpa Nachum, who had passed away the previous year. Noel? Nachum? An explanation is in order:

When my grandfather arrived in America from Russia, the immigration officials recording names and other pertinent background data misunderstood his heavily accented English. Instead of "Nachum," they wrote down "Nolan," a broth of an Irish name. A cousin of mine had already named a son Nolan in our grandfather's honor, so Estelle and I searched for a variation. We came up with Noel, associating it with the famous English actor and dramatist Noel Coward. Imagine our surprise when we later learned that *Noël* is French for *Christmas*, and *blanc* is French for *white*, as in *white Christmas*. It was a hell of a name for a Jewish boy.

CHAPTER

4

Those Wonderful Warner Bros. Characters

Warner Bros.'s cartoon comedy troupe may have been wild, but wily Bugs Bunny, loony Daffy Duck, and the others were tame compared to some of the flesh-and-blood characters who created them. We had so much young, enthusiastic talent, the studio atmosphere practically crackled with energy. It was a pleasure to come to work, even if it was in a place nicknamed Termite Terrace.

Early on, Leon Schlessinger sensed that something special was brewing in his production house, though he didn't quite know what. He decided to shift most of the cartoon unit into its own quarters on the Warner Bros. lot. Some quarters: a ramshackle cottage on Fernwood Avenue, near Van Ness Avenue. But despite its dilapidated condition, Termite Terrace became the laboratory where animated-film history was made.

Because of their conflicting objectives, clashes between the business's creative and commercial ends were inevitable. Warner Bros. was no exception, for Leon Schlessinger was as cost-conscious as any other producer. But while he may not have been the most popular boss, to his credit he knew not to tamper with success. Thus Termite Terrace's denizens had free artistic rein, so long as budgets were adhered to and the finished product generated profits.

Compared to some of his colleagues, Schlessinger was a maven of the arts. Eddie Selzer, who succeeded him as producer when Warner Bros. bought the company in 1944, had no cartoon experience whatsoever. A few weeks with Eddie and the boys were ready to beg Leon to come out of retirement. And vice president Jack L. Warner himself, roundly despised by his employees, knew even less about animated films than either Schlessinger or Selzer. When once informed that Walt Disney had beaten us out of an Oscar, Jack L. is alleged to have said, "What the hell, at least we've still got Mickey Mouse."

How a cartoon is produced may surprise some readers, for the process is entirely opposite of what many assume it to be. This is how we did it at Warner Bros. for four decades:

First the writer, or story man, cooked up a basic plot, which was shown to an artist whose job was to illustrate the writer's ideas. Each rough drawing of a scene was cut up and thumbtacked in sequence on a large wall. This visual script is called a storyboard.

Here is where even rabid cartoon buffs get confused. Rather than add audio to video, it was the other way around. Only in the earliest days of talking animated films was sound synchronized to film, an agonizingly exacting procedure. At Warner's, I consulted with the director and the story man in a sort of brainstorming session: ad-libbing lines, deleting or changing others I felt were out of character. To illustrate how intertwined my identity became with those of the cast members, I'd say something like, "Bugs Bunny wouldn't do that, he'd do *this.*" And who could argue?

These creative meetings thrived on collective inspiration. The visual rendering of a character enabled me to settle on an appropriate voice, which in turn helped the animators to refine physical characteristics. Together, writers, artists, and voice-men imbued a mere sketched animal with a distinct personality.

Naturally each director had his own style, and at Warner Bros. I had the privilege of working with some of the industry's finest: Freleng, Tashlin, Clampett, Avery, Chuck Jones, and Bob McKimson, among others. For me, McKimson was easiest to work with because he always knew what he wanted and how to communicate it. The only one I had any trouble with was Clampett. He was an egotist who took credit for everything, yet in the studio he could be irritatingly indecisive.

Which director was the best? Hell, how do I answer? Certainly each had his area of expertise: Jones was the best animator of the lot, Avery probably the cleverest gag man, Freleng unsurpassed for sheer imagination, and Tashlin a technical innovator, introducing to cartoons motion-picture devices such as off-kilter camera angles, montage effects, and quick cuts. All were tremendous talents, but I'll go out on a limb here and put Freleng, Jones, and Avery just slightly ahead of McKimson and Tashlin, with Clampett just slightly behind them. If this were a horse race, it would be a photo finish.

Originally the directors selected from a collective of writers and artists, but eventually they assembled their own teams. For example, as a rule Freleng collaborated with story men Tedd Pierce and Warren Foster, animators Virgil Ross, Arthur Davis, Gerry Chiniquy, Ken Champin, and Manuel Perez, layout man Hawley Pratt, and background artists Paul Julian and Irv Wyner; Chuck Jones, with writers Rich Hogan and Michael Maltese, animators Ken Harris, Ben Washam, Lloyd Vaughan, Phil Monroe, Abe Levitow, and Richard Thompson, layout men Robert Gribbroek and Maurice Noble, and background artist Philip De Guard. Bob McKimson shared writers Pierce and Foster with Freleng, but his cartoons were usually animated by his brother Charles, Phil De Lara, Herman Cohen, Rod Scribner, and Emery Hawkins, laid out by Robert Givens or Cornet Wood, and the backgrounds were drawn by Richard H. Thomas.

But it's important to note that these weren't teams in the

I am fortunate to have worked with some of the finest directors in animation history, including Friz Freleng (center) and Chuck Jones (right). *Photo by LPI*

conventional sense, competing against one another. On the contrary, members of McKimson's staff felt free to pitch ideas to one of Chuck Jones's men, and vice versa. Such communal spirit was vital to Warner Bros.'s success, with no person ever fully responsible for the finished product.

Once everyone had agreed on the script, we taped the dialogue. When I was first hired by the studio, this was done in sequence from beginning to end, a time-consuming method that took a day and a half. For a six-minute cartoon? It struck me as inefficient and presented problems when I had to record multiple voices for a single cartoon. Not to blow my own horn, but I have to take credit for changing the manner in which cartoons are recorded.

Back in early 1937 we were putting down the sound track for *Porky's Duck Hunt,* which marked the coming out for my second Warner's lead character, Daffy Duck. Switching voices back and forth from pig to duck to pig resulted in several flubbed takes. Why not, I reasoned, record each character's lines separately, then have the tape editor reassemble the dialogue in sequence? All it would take was a razor blade, splicing tape, and a steady hand. The directors agreed reluctantly. First we put down all of Porky's lines, then all of Daffy's. Total time? A mere hour and a half.

By the late 1940s I had such a considerable inventory of voices that many Warner Bros. theatrical shorts feature only me. The most characters I ever played in a single production, I believe, was fourteen. For these one-man recording sessions I stood alone at the microphone, with just an engineer and the director looking on from the control room. All I needed was a pitcher of water, a wastebasket, and my script, which I either held or propped on a music stand.

Earlier in my career I worked more in ensembles with some marvelous voice actors, each of us at his or her own microphone. Arthur Q. Bryan played Elmer Fudd, as did Daws Butler, among other characters. Additional studio presences included Billy Bletcher, Stan Freberg, Hal Smith, Kent Rog-

**Director Bob McKimson and me at a 1948 taping session. I frequently
played all the characters in a single cartoon, recording each voice
separately. Later, a tape engineer edited them together.**

ers, Dick Beals, Vance D. "Pinto" Colvig, Robert C. Bruce, and Cliff Nazarro. Even several of the writers and directors contributed characterizations: Tedd Pierce, Cal Howard, and Tex Avery.

Because high-pitched female voices taxed my vocal cords, I tended to work more with actresses such as June Foray: Granny from the Tweety and Sylvester cartoons, as well as other supporting Warner Bros. players. A lovely gal, she is probably best known as the voice behind Rocket J. Squirrel from the long-running television cartoon series "The Bullwinkle Show."

Several other actresses lent their talents to the Warner's characters: Julie Bennett (Miss Prissy the hen, and also Granny) and Bernice Hansen (Sniffles and miscellaneous voices). In the 1930s and 1940s most female roles went to Sara Berner, who in addition was a fellow cast member on radio's "The Jack Benny Program" and "Nitwit Court." Following in her footsteps during the mid-1940s was Bea Benaderet, also from the Benny show as well as countless others. Between animated films and radio, we spent so much time together in studios that I used to refer jokingly to her as the "other woman" in my life.

Whether I recorded by myself or as part of a group, once the taping was completed, the director timed the action frame by frame. Next, the layout man physically staged the scenes, combining action and backgrounds. Some merely tidied up the director's poses, while others drew from scratch. Only when the layout man was finished did the four or five artists go to work penciling the approximately sixteen thousand drawings and sixty backgrounds it took to make a single Warner Bros. cartoon.

To help capture the characters' facial expressions and to match lip movement to the sound track, the animators kept a tape recorder and a mirror on each of their desks. Repeating the prerecorded dialogue aloud, they used their own reflections as models. And physical movements were often acted out for accuracy. It wasn't unusual for me to poke my head into one

of the guys' offices and see Lloyd Vaughan looking very much
like he was about to take an ax to Ken Harris's helmeted head.
A stranger visiting the studio might well have wondered why
the walls were covered with peeling paint and not rubber
padding. Fortunately I generally completed my parts without
a hitch ("First-take Blanc," they called me) and was able to
get the hell out of Termite Terrace just in case their insanity
was contagious.

There were months of work between recording the voices
and the inking and the painting. The finished panels were
traced onto celluloid in India ink and brushed with opaque
paint. These cels were then placed over the appropriate background and shot individually, using a stop-motion camera.

Now came time for music and sound effects, two de-
partments headed, respectively, by musical director Carl W.
Stalling and film editor Treg Brown. Stalling, an urbane sort
with a prematurely receding hairline and a faint mustache,
was a former Disney associate from Kansas City who joined
Leon Schlessinger Productions in 1936. When it came to com-
plementing cartoon action with a musical score, he was peerless.

Stalling's music was predominately his own original work,
but he would often insert several bars from a popular tune to
advance the plot. Because of his background as a onetime
silent-film accompanist, he had an uncanny recall of titles.
Therefore, when the Roadrunner and pursuer Wile E. Coyote
are shown zigzagging around a highway cloverleaf in *Fast and
Furry-ous* (1949), Stalling has the Warner Bros. orchestra strike
up "I'm Looking Over a Four Leaf Clover." A cat gone fishing
in *A Fractured Leghorn* (1950) is backed by the soothing "By
a Waterfall," from a 1933 Warner Bros. film starring Dick
Powell and Ruby Keeler, *Footlight Parade*. The frequent inclusion of Warner's-owned material was no coincidence, the
company's logic being that movie-house audiences might then
go out and buy its sheet music.

One song Warner Bros. purchased the rights to was a
lively novelty number called "The Merry-Go-Round Broke

Down." It would become widely known as the Warner Bros. cartoons theme from the late 1930s until the mid-to-late 1940s, at which point just a snippet of the theme blared behind the "That's All Folks!" graphic. When Stalling retired in 1958, the directorship went to longtime arranger Milt Franklyn, also a musical mastermind with an encyclopedic knowledge of popular songs.

Treg Brown, of course, was the man responsible for my getting into Warner Bros. in the first place. Not only did we look like cousins—at least that's what others said—we had a lot in common. He, too, was a musician, having played guitar and sung with famed jazz cornetist Red Nichols and his Five Pennies, a group that at varying times had included Benny Goodman, Jimmy Dorsey, and Artie Shaw. Of all my Warner's coworkers, Brown was my favorite. What a character! But then, I suppose you have to be in that line of work.

Anyone who marvels at how I've earned a living should consider Brown's occupation: shooting off a .45-caliber pistol to achieve the sound of a door's slamming shut, smacking an anvil to accompany footage of a cartoon character getting bonked on the head, or simulating a cataclysmic crash by dropping two armfuls of metal objects from the top of a ladder onto a concrete floor.

The real challenge for any animated-film sound-effects man wasn't to simulate realism but to defy it. Much Warner's cartoon hilarity stemmed from Brown's outlandish imagination. Why always apply the fitting sound effect, went his thinking, when something completely incongruous would be so much funnier? For example: In 1938's *The Daffy Doc*, Daffy Duck assists in a risky operation. When a colleague asks him to be so quiet "I can hear a pin drop," the duck lets go of one. Instead of *ping*, Brown whipped up the biggest tumult possible. So in addition to dialogue and sight gags, cartoons contained yet another comic element.

Isn't that six-minute cartoon finished *yet?* you're probably wondering. Patience. Imagine how those of us who made animated films felt. The final step was to record the edited animation and dubbed sound track onto a master reel, in sync. *Voilà!* Or as French skunk Pepe Le Pew would say, *Viola!* Fifteen months after production started, having passed through the hands of 125 people, the 540-foot reel of film was now ready for viewing in movie theaters across America.

During Warner Bros.'s peak production year, 1939, this process was repeated forty-four times: twenty-seven Merrie Melodies and seventeen Looney Tunes. Back then a typical theatrical short took nine months to complete. As the studio's adventurousness expanded, so did the production time. After World War II, output stabilized at approximately thirty productions per year.

The directors, artists, writers, and actors gave life to a stable of funny-looking animals. In turn, those much-loved Warner's cartoon characters gave us success.

Certainly the one most closely associated with me is Bugs Bunny. I employ the rabbit's name as my citizen's-band-radio handle, and his bewhiskered visage adorns my ties, tiepins, shirts, sweatshirts, cuff links, even one of my watches. As you know, Bugs literally helped save my life after my near-fatal 1961 car accident. But he's gotten me out of other scrapes as well. Some years ago I was driving on Interstate 10 near Tucson when a policeman pulled me over. The car, a brand new Rolls-Royce, handled so smoothly that I hadn't even realized I was speeding.

The officer peered down at my license, then at my face. "Are you *the* Mel Blanc?" he asked warily.

About the best proof I could offer was to reply affirmatively in Bug's voice.

His face broke out in a grin.

"Well, I guess I'm going to have to let you off with a warning," he said. "My kids would never forgive me if I gave a ticket to Bugs Bunny!"

Thanks again, old buddy.

In the wake of Bugs's universal success, few recall how

close Warner Bros.'s preeminent cartoon star came to having his rabbit hole permanently erased. He had been around in different guises for several years, appearing without much fanfare in the 1938 Looney Tune *Porky's Hare Hunt,* two 1939 Merrie Melodies, *Presto Change-O* and *Hare-Um Scare-Um,* and a 1940 Merrie Melody, *Elmer's Candid Camera.*

Few fans of the current Bugs would recognize him from his early career: oval-shaped head, jelly-bean nose, and wide, innocent eyes. Frank Tashlin always contended that the original rabbit conspicuously resembled Max Hare from Walt Dis-

This is what the original Bugs Bunny looked like. "Happy Rabbit" was his name. In 1940 I suggested we rechristen him after his animator, Ben "Bugs" Hardaway. Hence: Bugs Bunny.
Original Warner Bros. artwork © 1988 Steve Schneider

ney's Oscar-winning 1935 animated short *The Tortoise and the Hare*. In addition to being a mere shadow of his future self, Bugs wasn't even called Bugs, but "Happy Rabbit."

"*Happy Rabbit?*" I exclaimed, nearly gagging while reading the script for *Porky's Hare Hunt*. "That's terrible," I said to Leon Schlessinger. "I hate it."

"What would you suggest then, Mel?"

"Why not call him Bugs, after Ben Hardaway?" Hardaway had drawn him, so it seemed only fair. For reasons never explained, he'd been nicknamed Bugs as a child, and it stuck. Not that Hardaway in any way looked like a rabbit. He had a prizefighter's mug: square, with a cast-iron jaw.

"Bugs *Rabbit?*" said Schlessinger, recoiling as if he'd just been asked to sign an extra payroll that week.

I suggested we make it alliterative: Bugs Bunny. "Like Porky Pig," I said, popping my *P*s, then doing the same for *Bugs Bunny*. The producer nodded in agreement, and like that, Happy Rabbit was rechristened. If we'd given him a voice yet, I just know he would have thanked me.

Settling on a definitive characterization was a lot more difficult than selecting the name, if for no other reason that that Hardaway kept changing the rabbit's features on me. In *Hare-Um Scare-Um* he was an orthodontist's dream, with badly protruding front teeth. The only way for me to incorporate this physical trait into his delivery was to speak with a pronounced lisp, but that made the voice hard to understand.

Clarity is perhaps the most crucial element for any cartoon or radio characterization. Devising unique voices always came easily to me, but if one wasn't absolutely intelligible, it was useless. Frankly I always believed Donald Duck's popularity—great as it is—was hindered by the fact that he always sounded as if he were drowning in a cup of water. I don't mean to knock Clarence Nash, a good friend and a splendid voice-man, but some of Donald's lines were difficult to decipher.

By the time of *A Wild Hare* (1940), which is considered Bugs Bunny's debut, he'd obviously had some work done: His posture had improved, he'd shed some weight, and his over-bite wasn't as pronounced. The most significant change, how-ever, was in his facial expression. No longer just goofy, he was a sly-looking rascal. "A tough little stinker, ain't he?" Harda-way remarked while admiring his portrait of the new Bugs.

A *tough little stinker*... In my mind I heard a Brooklyn accent; not to insult the integrity of those living there. But to anyone living west of the Hudson River at that time, Brook-lynites were associated with con artists and crooks. Without a doubt the stereotype was derived from the many motion-picture gangsters who always seemed to speak in Flatbush Avenue-ese. Consequently the new, improved Bugs Bunny wouldn't say *jerk*, he'd say *joik*. And the boisterous laugh I'd originally given him no longer fit. It was redeposited in my memory bank, to be withdrawn several years later for another Ben Hardaway creation: Woody Woodpecker. Likewise, a hep cat such as Bugs wouldn't say, "What's cookin'?"—which orig-inally was to be his singular phrase—he'd employ something more contemporary.

"What's up, Doc?" became the most famous ad-lib of my career. It was incomplete, however, without the sound of the rabbit nibbling on a carrot, which presented problems. First of all, I don't especially like carrots, at least not raw. And second, I found it impossible to chew, swallow, and be ready to say my next line. We tried substituting other vegetables, including apples and celery, but with unsatisfactory results. The solution was to stop recording so that I could spit out the carrot into a wastebasket and then proceed with the script. In the course of a recording session I usually went through enough carrots to fill several.

Bugs Bunny did for carrots what Popeye the Sailor did for spinach. How many lip-locked, head-swiveling children were coerced into eating their carrots by mothers cooing, "... but Bugs Bunny eats *his* carrots." If only they had known.

Despite his many incarnations, one aspect of the rabbit remained constant: his audacity, apparent even in *Porky's Hare*

BUGS BUNNY
in
★★ **Yankee**
Doodle
Bugs ★★

a Looney Tune
CARTOON
color by
TECHNICOLOR

© WARNER BROS. CARTOONS INC.

A WARNER BROS. CARTOON

"A tough little stinker" is how Ben Hardaway described the new, improved Bugs to me. What type of voice to give him? A harsh Brooklyn accent, of course! *Illustration © Warner Bros. Inc.*

Hunt. "Here I am, Fat Boy!" he mercilessly taunts the hapless hunter. In another scene the rabbit declares, "Of course you realize, this means war," a phrase that would be repeated in dozens of Bugs Bunny episodes and that would practically come to define the pugnacious character. It was soon obvious to everyone involved, however, that he deserved a more imposing adversary than a mild-mannered pig.

Enter Elmer Fudd, destined to spend the next three decades continually being outsmarted by his prey. The only similarity Elmer shared with Bugs was that he, too, had evolved from an earlier character: Egghead. In keeping with his name, this Tex Avery oddity had an elliptical dome and a voice borrowed from my onetime mentor Joe Penner. In another tribute to Penner, Egghead wore a derby, which when doffed took his entire head with it.

From 1937 to 1939 Egghead starred in nine cartoons, none of which provoked much public reaction. After *Believe It or Else* he was modified into Elmer, and voice-man Cliff Nazarro was replaced by genial, heavyset Arthur Q. Bryan. Many radio actors were never able to adapt to the cartoon medium. For reasons that baffled me, they froze in the studio, exasperating fellow actors and directors alike. Not Arthur Q., a regular on a multitude of radio programs, including "Al Pearce and His Gang" and "The Great Gildersleeve."

We collaborated on many, but spent most of our time together standing shoulder to shoulder in the Warner Bros. studio. In addition to more than thirty Bugs-and-Elmer cartoons, Bryan and I also recorded dialogue for other character combinations: Sylvester and Elmer; Daffy and Elmer; Bugs, Daffy, Porky, and Elmer. And so on.

The tone of Elmer and Bugs's combative relationship was set with their very first confrontation, in *A Wild Hare*—the title of which was just one of many hair-raisingly excruciating puns (*Hare Tonic*, 1945; *Bushy Hare*, 1950; *Oily Hare*, 1952). Clutching his trusty shotgun, the dim-witted hunter tiptoes lightly through the woods and warns the audience: "Be vewy, vewy quiet, I'm hunting wabbits." Suddenly he spies Bugs leaning casually against a tree, dashes over, and levels his double-barrel at the rabbit's chest. But Elmer is befuddled when instead of cowering in fear, his target slaps a white-gloved mitt on the weapon and nonchalantly asks, "Eh, what's up, Doc?"

Though Bugs always gains the upper hand, he is ultimately a pacifist, disarming the gun-toting Elmer with his wiles and appealing to underdog-rooting audiences. Director Bob Clampett always contended it was no coincidence that the rabbit first achieved his tremendous popularity during the war years. To a public outraged over Pearl Harbor and Nazi atrocities, headstrong, brain-dead Elmer symbolized the bru-

tish Axis Powers. Cocky, fearless Bugs, naturally, was the quin-
tessential Yank.

It's an interesting theory, but I can't say I agree that Bugs's
success was so directly tied to the events of World War II.
(Although I will concede that chrome-dome Elmer did look
like a distant relation of Italy's Fascist premier, Benito Mussolini.) Personally I think it's much less complicated: Everybody loves a winner, and Bugs Bunny always wins.

To further prove my point, who were the leading men of
the early 1940s? Clark Gable, Humphrey Bogart and Jimmy
Cagney. Bugs possessed Gable's impertinence, Bogart's cool-
headedness, and Cagney's New York–bred toughness. We cheer
him on because he has the moxie to say and to do what he

**Elmer Fudd, looking
befuddled as usual.
The dim-witted hunter
and wily Bugs Bunny
first costarred in
1940's *A Wild Hare*.**
Illustration © *1987
Warner Bros. Inc.*

wants. If only *we* were so dauntless. To top it off, he gets away with it! Bugs Bunny appeals to the rebel in all of us.

Strangely, for two so embroiled in perpetual conflict, the rabbit and the hunter do an awful lot of smooching. That, and Bugs's proclivity for cross-dressing—in *Rabbit Fire* (1951), *Rabbit Seasoning* (1952), and *What's Opera, Doc?* (1957), to cite several examples—have raised some concern among viewers. On numerous occasions fans have asked me, Are Bugs and Elmer . . . well, you know . . . are they? . . .

No, they're not sweethearts. During a production meeting for *Elmer's Pet Rabbit* (1941), someone suggested we have Bugs startle his new owner by planting a smacker on Elmer's lips. The gag worked, the gag stayed. That's all there is to it.

When Arthur Q. Bryan passed away in 1959 at age sixty, Daws Butler and then Hal Smith supplied Elmer's voice, but apparently not to the studio's satisfaction. Friz Freleng cornered me one day and asked me to take it on. I stubbornly shook my head no.

"You know how I feel about imitating someone else," I said to him, but Friz was so insistent I finally relented.

"So you'll do it, Mel?"

"I don't know if I can," I said, "but I'll *certainwy twy* . . ."

Elmer appeared in more cartoons than nearly any other Warner's star, but in the end he suffered from the same drawback as Porky Pig: not a challenging enough foe for Bugs Bunny. Poor elocution wasn't Fudd's only impediment; he was also too damn dumb. Since the rabbit had become the studio's main attraction, Friz Freleng devised a new character for him to tangle with: ornery Yosemite Sam.

The pint-size, pea-brained, hirsute cowboy with the big, big voice bowed as Bugs's latest victim in 1945's *Hare Trigger*. Freleng not only conceived the character; whether he knew it or not, he also served as Sam's inspiration. Like Yosemite, Friz was very short. When he stood next to Chuck Jones, who was six-feet-plus, they resembled the comic-strip duo Mutt and Jeff—which is what Jack L. Warner took to calling his

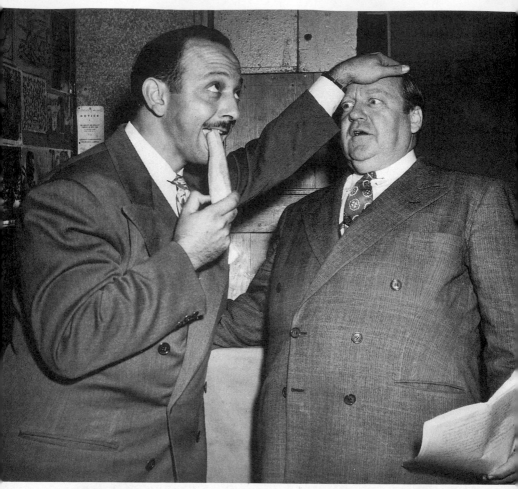

Affable Arthur Q. Bryan (right) and I spent countless hours together in the studio, me as Bugs Bunny, he as Elmer Fudd. After his death in 1959 I took over the role.

two top directors. Additionally, both Sam and Freleng possessed powder-keg tempers.

When Friz first showed me the rough sketches, I had to laugh, for Sam was ridiculous looking: not much more than an oversize cowboy hat roosting atop eyes that peered out from under bushy eyebrows; a bulbous nose; and a droopy, flaming-red mustache that would take hedge shears to trim. I originally bestowed the truncated desperado with a mild Western drawl, but neither the director nor I were pleased with it. Practicing the voice while tooling down Santa Monica Boulevard one day, I was cut off by another driver and yelled at him with all the volume I could muster. It occurred to me, *That's what Sam should sound like!* Volume was just the ticket.

Yosemite's vociferousness makes his the toughest voice for me to perform. Imagine screaming at the top of your lungs for an hour and a half, and you have an idea of what it's like. Fortunately I rarely get sore throats, even though I'd been a pack-a-day cigarette smoker from the time I was eight. Some friends and I got started by smoking pieces of wicker that we'd snapped off my father's favorite chair. One evening he went to sit down with the newspaper and fell clear through! From wicker we graduated to leaves, then to corncob, before trying tobacco. I kept up the habit until several years ago, when I developed such severe emphysema that I needed oxygen just to breathe. So I quit, like *that,* and can't say I miss cigarettes at all. Today I no longer need the oxygen, and I feel terrific.

As for my rather remarkable throat: I had it x-rayed once, and the doctor marveled at what he saw. Shaking his head, he told me I had the same musculature as the great Italian tenor Enrico Caruso. So, even when I do lose my voice, it usually returns to full strength within an hour or so.

My only home remedy for soreness is to mix one teaspoon each of salt and baking soda in a glass of extremely hot tap water and gargle with it. It tastes every bit as lousy as it sounds, but it works. Interestingly, rather than deteriorating with age, my larynx has actually gotten stronger, probably from the wide range of pitches it's had to produce over the years. Even now I can effect Yosemite's robust roar for up to an hour without a trace of hoarseness.

Whereas audiences felt sorry for witless Elmer Fudd, Yosemite evoked no sympathy at all. Impulsive and obstinate, he was his own worst enemy. Just when you think he'll finally concede defeat, he issues the rabbit yet another ultimatum,

Ornery hombre Yosemite Sam is the hardest character for me to voice. Conceived as a more challenging adversary for Bugs Bunny, he bowed in Hare Trigger *(1945).*
Illustration © 1987 Warner Bros. Inc.

as in *Bunker Hill Bunny* (1950): "Ya better say yer prayers, ya flea-bitten varmint! Ah'm a-gonna blow ya to smithereenies!" But the outlaw is a one-man gang that can't shoot straight, and despite his bluster, his plans always go awry. One of my favorite Sam scenes is from the Friz Freleng–directed *High Diving Hare* (1949):

Yosemite learns that the high-diving act he's paid to see has canceled and accosts emcee Bugs with his six-guns a-drawn. "Ah paid six bits to see a high-divin' act," he fumes, practically gusting back the rabbit's ears, "and ah'm a-gonna *see* a high-divin' act!" He forces Bugs up the ladder to the diving platform but is repeatedly tricked so that again and again he plummets to the water-filled tank below.

The action intensifies: Yosemite scrambles up the ladder, but plunges right back down. Yosemite scrambles up the ladder, but plunges right back down *again*. The only sign that Sam realizes the bunny is getting the better of him is his resigned growl, "Ah *hates* rabbits."

Yosemite Sam proved compatible with other characters

as well, including Speedy Gonzales the Mexican mouse and Bugs Bunny's leading rival, Daffy Duck.

Daffy preceded Bugs by three years, envisioned by Tex Avery as a sort of web-footed, animated Marx Brother. Indeed, in his early roles Daffy did little more than strive to uphold his first name. One of his early lines, from *Porky's Duck Hunt* (1937), could have served as a calling card: "I'm just a crazy, darned fool duck," he says to Porky Pig, a tormented hunter on the verge of a breakdown. With that, the screwball duck laughs maniacally, *"Hoo-hoo!,"* and backflips into the horizon. The *hoo-hoo*s, incidentally, were lifted from a popular vaudeville and film comedian of the day, Hugh Herbert, but were softened as Daffy's persona lost its wacky edge.

After two cartoons opposite Porky and one opposite the forgettable Egghead, he was given a shot at stardom in the black-and-white Looney Tune *The Daffy Doc* (1938), directed by Bob Clampett. Daffy's role as an inexpert medical man liberally references Groucho Marx's nutty Dr. Hugo Z. Hackenbush from the Marx Brothers comedy *A Day at the Races*.

The action opens at the Stitch-in-Time Hospital, where a sign out front proclaims, "As We Sew, So Shall Ye Reap." Daffy is "Dr. Duck," about to assist "Dr. Quack" in performing a delicate operation, but his incompetence causes his superior more headaches than a malpractice suit. Already the animated fowl's features were altered noticeably from *Porky's Duck Hunt:* To further emphasize his battiness, he was drawn with mad, gleaming eyes and a long bill. The latter characteristic figured prominently in creating Daffy's voice.

It seemed to me that such an extended mandible would hinder his speech, particularly on words containing an *s* sound. Thus "despicable" became "de*sth*picable." And here's a little-known fact: An engineer sped up the voice slightly on a variable-speed oscillator. Lines were recorded at eighteen percent below normal speed, then were played back conventionally, raising the pitch but retaining the clarity. The same machine

Early in his career Daffy Duck strove mightily to live up to his first name. He had a maniacal laugh —"Hoo-hoo!"—which I borrowed from comedian Hugh Herbert. *Illustration © 1987 Warner Bros. Inc.*

was also utilized for Porky Pig and three subsequent characters, Henery Hawk, Speedy Gonzales, and Tweety, the latter of whom was recorded at twenty percent below.

Daffy and Porky appeared together for nearly fifteen years, the affable pig reduced to acting as the egocentric duck's protégé. In *Deduce You Say* (1956) he plays Watson to Daffy's Sherlock (Derlock) Holmes. "Holmes was moodily engaged in his favorite pastime," Porky narrates, "deducting." Daffy is deducting, all right, from his income-tax returns: ". . . I can deduct six pounds, eight shillings for a magnifying glass and gumshoes . . ." London is being terrorized by a criminal known as "the Shropshire Slasher," whom crafty Daffy plots to capture. But much to his chagrin, the unflappable Watson calmly convinces the thug to give himself up.

In *Drip-Along Daffy* (1951) the duck portrays a sheriff committed to upholding the peace, and Porky, his stubble-chinned sidekick. They mosey into the lawless Western town of Snake Bite Center, where rampant gun battles are monitored by traffic signals, even *horses* pull pistols on one another, and the inhabitants live in fear of bandit Nasty Canasta. Once again it's Porky to the rescue, outdrawing the outlaw in a duel. The grateful townspeople install him as sheriff, while Daffy gets his wish to clean up this one-horse town: working for the sanitation department. "Lucky for him it *is* a one-horse town," the newly appointed sheriff observes.

Under the brilliant direction of Chuck Jones, Daffy evolved into Warner's number-two drawing card. Did success spoil the little black duck? Absolutely. He went from naughty to downright vengeful. Whereas Porky Pig gracefully accepted Bugs Bunny's ascension to top banana, Daffy's resentment festered until it became an obsession. Jones parlayed this theme into a series of riotously funny cartoons starring Bugs, Daffy, and sometimes Elmer Fudd. The first was *Rabbit Fire* (1951), leading off a trilogy that included *Rabbit Seasoning* (1952), and *Duck! Rabbit! Duck!* (1953). The plots follow a similar line, with Daffy trying to lasso Elmer into allying with him against the rabbit.

In *Rabbit Fire* there's Daffy in prosthetic bunny feet imprinting tracks leading right up to Bugs's rabbit hole. "Survival of the fittest," he snickers, "and besides, it's fun. *Hoo-hoo!*" Hunter Elmer follows the path until he and Bugs Bunny are locked in a familiar pose: Fudd training his gun on the rabbit, itching to pull the trigger.

Typically, Bugs coolly convinces the hunter that it's duck season, not rabbit season. When Daffy overhears this, he stalks out of hiding and insists belligerently, "It's rabbit season!"

"Duck season!" Bugs counters, sparking a debate:

Daffy: "Rabbit season!"
Bugs: "Duck season!"
Daffy: "Rabbit season!"
Bugs: "Rabbit season!"
Daffy: "I say it's *duck* season, and fire!"

Elmer shrugs and does what he's told, the shotgun blast singeing the duck's feathers and spinning his bill around and around. Other novel mandible configurations follow, as does

Daffy's resentment of Bugs's popularity festered until it became an all-consuming obsession. His most famous line, directed at the rabbit: "You're desth*pic*able!" *Illustration © 1987 Warner Bros. Inc.*

the debut of Daffy's most famous line. Defeated, he struts over to his archrival, presses his glowering face into Bugs's, and mutters, "You're desth*pic*able!" It was to become as identified with Daffy as "What's up, Doc?" is with Bugs.

Even though he always winds up clutching the short straw, Daffy finally presented Bugs with a worthy opponent: an equally cheeky alter ego. The difference between them is that while fate smiles on the rabbit, it thumbs its nose at the duck. Chuck Jones always said that victorious Bugs is an aspiration—what we'd all like to be. Victimized Daffy, on the other hand, is more the reality of what we truly are, whether we want to admit it or not.

After years of continually absorbing humiliation at Bugs Bunny's hands, Daffy's bitterness develops into an acute persecution complex. Studio politics, he's convinced, are behind his inability to outsmart the rabbit. In Jones's wonderfully inventive *Duck Amuck* (1953), the duck's most paranoid fantasies come true.

Daffy leaps into the first frame dressed as a musketeer but looks over his shoulder to see that the background has vanished. No castles. No knights with whom to do battle. Just white. His demand that the artist furnish some scenery is answered with a farmhouse.

"Okay, have it your way," he growls contemptuously, tramping off the set and returning in a pair of overalls. Daffy is just several bars into "Old MacDonald Had a Farm" when he realizes the artist has switched scenes on him again, supplanting the farmhouse with a frigid arctic icescape. The merciless animator keeps changing backgrounds with greater frequency, until Daffy is fit to be straitjacketed.

"In all the years," he gripes, "I've . . ." While he's pouring out his bitter tirade, the artist is busy erasing his body. From behind the empty panel comes Daffy's exasperated voice: "All right, wise guy, where am I?"

The torment continues: Daffy is recast as a cowboy but can't speak. When sound is finally added, he opens his bill in protest and is horrified when out comes a rooster's shrill crow. A squawking jungle bird. A mewing kitten.

"This is the very, very last straw!" he screams hysterically. "Who is responsible for this?! I demand that you show yourself! Who are you?!"

The camera pulls back to reveal the animator is none other than Bugs Bunny, who says coyly to the audience, "Ain't I a stinker?"

Desth*pic*able, if you ask me.

Sylvester, Tweety, and Other Terrible Twosomes

*T*he success of Bugs and his sundry antagonists encouraged the directors to try combining other characters. When the chemistry worked, it would salvage relatively minor careers, as in the case of Sylvester and Tweety. The canary had inconspicuously bowed in 1942's *A Tale of Two Kitties* and appeared in two subsequent cartoons, while the cat had starred in but one short, an Academy Award nominee called *Life With Feathers* (1945). Friz Freleng decided to pair them in 1947's *Tweety Pie*, which won Warner Bros. the first of its five Oscars for cartoons.

Sylvester has always been a favorite of mine. He's a great deal like Daffy: a perpetual fall guy with a near-identical voice. Daffy's is pitched up slightly, while Sylvester's is recorded at regular speed and sounds the closest to my natural way of speaking. He's always been the easiest character for me to play.

It had never occurred to me before to base one voice characterization on another, but when I was first shown the

model sheet of Sylvester, with his floppy jowls and generally
disheveled appearance, I said to Friz Freleng, "A big, sloppy
cat should have a big, *shthloppy* voice." He should spray even
more than Daffy, I continued, which the director probably
found difficult to imagine. While recording Sylvester cartoons,
my scripts would get so covered with saliva I'd repeatedly have
to wipe them clean. I used to suggest to actress June Foray,
who played Tweety's vigilant owner Granny, that she wear a
raincoat to the sessions.

The writers, directors, and I always tried to endow each
character with a distinctive expression. Keeping in mind
Sylvester's spluttering delivery, I wanted a phrase with two or
more *s*'s in it. Since I had already borrowed his voice for Daffy,
I had no compunctions about nicking a line from another of
my creations: traveling salesman Roscoe E. Wortle from radio's "The Judy Canova Show." The line, of course, was "thsuf-
ferin' thsuccotash."

Tweety, the baby-faced, baby-voiced yellow canary, was
already well-known for the phrase "I tawt I taw a puddy
tat!"—an ad-lib of mine. It became so popular that in 1950
Warner Bros. story man Warren Foster used it as the title of
a song he composed, which I recorded for Capital Records.
The single sold in excess of two million copies and was also
a novelty hit in England.

Tweety and Sylvester shared top billing in thirty-nine animated films between 1947 and 1964, and the secret of their
success is no mystery. The canary was so adorable, audiences
felt as protective of him as did Granny. I've even sat in movie
theaters where young viewers became so involved in the action, they actually shouted warnings to Tweety whenever sly
old Sylvester came skulking around his birdcage.

Innocence versus evil? On the surface, perhaps, but it's
not so cut-and-dry. Each character embodies a little bit of
both. Sylvester may spend every waking moment plotting to
swallow the canary, but what would you expect of a famished
feline? He's merely doing what nature intended. By the same

Two minor characters, Sylvester the cat and Tweety bird, were paired in 1947's *Tweety Pie*. The cartoon won an Oscar, as did their *Birds Anonymous* ten years later. *Illustration © Warner Bros. Inc.*

token, Tweety isn't nearly as ingenuous as he seems. An example:

In *Tweety's S.O.S.* (1951) bespectacled Granny takes her precious pet along on a cruise, refusing to let him out of her nearsighted sight. Sylvester, scavenging for food by the dock, glimpses Tweety through a porthole. "Hello, breakfast," he purrs, already beginning to salivate, and he stows on board.

But Sylvester is a far-from-hardy sailor, and the ship's rocking brings on seasickness. In between chasing the chubby-cheeked bird about the deck, he has to make frequent pit stops at the water cooler. Tweety takes immediate advantage of his adversary's affliction, holding up a picture of a ship and moving it back and forth until the cat is once again green-faced and gulping for air. He heads for the cooler, which Tweety has filled with nitroglycerin. "Dat's a nice puddy tat," he says as Sylvester guzzles the highly explosive liquid, "dwink it all down!"

In the final scene Sylvester is back to pursuing Tweety. Suddenly he's confronted by frail old Granny, who packs a Henry Aaron wallop when it comes to swinging a broom, umbrella, or other similarly long-handled implement of destruction at the pesky cat. *Ka-boom!* Sylvester ignites and goes rocketing into space.

The cat-canary combination won another Oscar in 1957, for *Birds Anonymous* (1957), also directed by Friz Freleng. Its premise is that Sylvester joins an Alcoholics Anonymous–type fellowship of formerly bird-addicted pussycats. At his first meeting he hears others' testimonials of how they kicked their feathery habits and gets caught up in the fervor. "Fellow members," Sylvester pledges, "from now on my motto is, Birds is strictly for the birds."

Not for long, as he encounters temptation at every turn. Back home, the reformed cat switches on the TV, only to see a commercial for roast turkey; "a succulent morsel that will melt in your mouth," according to the announcer. Poor Sylvester's eyes glaze over. His mouth waters. His stomach doesn't growl, it roars. He steals a peek at the canary, swinging in its cage, impervious, then slaps himself. If cats took cold showers, he'd be under one right now.

To get his mind off Tweety, Sylvester turns on the radio. Which song is playing? "Bye Bye Blackbird," of course. Coming up next, promises the disc jockey, "When the Red, Red Robin Comes Bob, Bob, Bobbin' Along." *Gulp.* Following several more nights of torturous withdrawal, the cat can resist no longer. With a sinister laugh he is about to devour the bird when his Birds Anonymous counselor appears at the window. He halts Sylvester's fall from the wagon by pouring a box of alum down his throat and snatching Tweety away.

Like an addict scrounging for a fix, Sylvester is so desperate he falls kicking and screaming to the floor. "I can't stand it! I gotta have a bird! After all, I'm a pussycat!"

"Oh, come, come, now, there's no need for this demonstration," the other cat condescends, going on at length about how cats and birds can live together in harmony. All of a sudden his resolve goes the way of Sylvester's, and the two wind up wrestling over Tweety, who philosophizes: "Once a bad ol' puddy tat, always a bad ol' puddy tat!"

Birds Anonymous stands as my all-time favorite cartoon, and I'm proud to have the Oscar for it in my home. How I came to acquire the seven-pound, gold-plated statuette is a story in itself. Frankly, I was always disappointed that the Academy of Motion Picture Arts and Sciences never recognized individual contributions but made awards only to producers.

Warner Bros. producer Eddie Selzer owned all five Oscars, for *Tweety Pie* (1947), *For Scent-imental Reasons* (1949), *Speedy Gonzales* (1955), *Birds Anonymous* (1957), and *Knighty Knight Bugs* (1958). In the late 1950s he became very ill and sent for me. "I'm not going to be around much longer, Mel," he whispered from his bed.

"Don't talk that way, Eddie. You'll be up and about in no time," I said. But my optimism failed to rouse his spirits.

"I want you to have one of the Oscars. Which would you like?"

Somewhat uncomfortably I told him my preference.

"It's yours, then," he said.

As it happened, Selzer recovered, and I forgot all about his touching gesture. When he did pass away a year or two later, I received a phone call from his wife. She hadn't forgotten and insisted that I take the *Birds Anonymous* award. "Eddie wanted you to have it, Mel."

I will never forget Eddie's generosity.

Watch *Birds Anonymous* or any other Tweety and Sylvester cartoon and you'll notice that although the canary always receives top billing, he never actually says or does much. Most of the plots center around the exhaustive lengths Sylvester goes to try devouring him. In the end the cat never did get to dine on Tweety, but he did develop into Warner Bros.'s most versatile performer, teamed up with Elmer Fudd, Porky Pig, a couple of canines named Spike and Chester, Speedy Gonzales, the Roadrunner, and Hippety Hopper, a kangaroo. Sylvester was also the studio's only star to sire a son: Junior. Not only was Junior the spitting image of his pop, he expectorated like him too.

Didn't I write several pages back that Sylvester was easiest for me to voice? A qualifier: among characters that spoke whole sentences, true. But the easiest of all had to be the Roadrunner, whose only sound was a plain "Mbeep-mbeep!"

Because the Roadrunner's scripts, such as they were, didn't change the least bit from cartoon to cartoon, I had to tape "Mbeep-mbeep!" but once, for the second Roadrunner–Wile E. Coyote short, *Beep Beep* (1952). In the duo's debut, 1949's *Fast and Furry-ous*, sound-effects man Treg Brown used an electronic horn called a claxon. But in the nearly three years between cartoons it had been misplaced. When production for *Beep Beep* was under way, he nabbed me in a Termite Terrace hallway to ask if I could mimic the sound vocally. I could, I did, and I never had to do it again. Call the Roadrunner one of my less challenging parts.

The Roadrunner's would-be attacker, scraggly Wile E., didn't speak either, except in an early cartoon opposite Bugs Bunny, *Operation: Rabbit* (1952). The coyote is a self-professed genius, even handing out business cards to that effect, so a mannered English accent seemed well suited. But director Chuck Jones's concept for the Roadrunner-Coyote series would become increasingly restrictive, and Wile E.'s voice was taken away, just one of many mortifications he had to bear.

In addition to lacking dialogue, the cartoons are all set in a Southwestern U.S. desert and are driven by the same plot: the coyote's futile attempts to catch the Roadrunner, who, according to a Western cookbook he reads in *To Beep or Not to Beep* (1963), is "possibly the most delicious of all Western game birds." Not that the coyote will ever find this out personally.

Most even open the same exact way: with an aerial view of the lightning-quick Roadrunner easily outdistancing his pursuer. Suddenly the action stops. Both species are identified

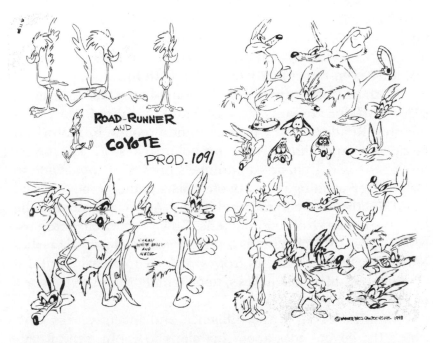

This early model sheet illustrates different poses and expressions for the Roadrunner and the coyote, specifying "white belly and neck" for Wile E. *Original Warner Bros. artwork © 1988 Steve Schneider*

on screen in pseudo-Latin: first the Roadrunner (Burnius Roadibus, Incredibus Accelleratii), then the coyote (Famishus-Famishus, Carnivorous Vulgaris). These changed from cartoon to cartoon.

Yet with all its inherent limitations, this series ranks among Jones's and Warner's best. Wile E. is a comical-looking beast: haggard and spindly, with permanently bloodshot eyes, and clutching knife and fork, which prove about as useful as the Acme products he consumes endlessly. As persistent as Elmer, Daffy, Yosemite, and Sylvester were in their pursuit of Bugs, Bugs, Bugs, and Tweety, respectively, none was as tenacious as the beleaguered coyote, who is engaged in the ultimate futile exercise. He *never* will catch the Roadrunner, and what's more, he knows it. When he began his quest, we presume, it was to satiate his appetite. Not anymore. At this point he hungers solely for the thrill of the chase. If the coyote ever did defy kismet and catch the Roadrunner, one senses that he wouldn't even remember what to do with him.

Each cartoon turned on the bang-bang blackout technique introduced years before by Frank Tashlin: Coyote tries undoing Roadrunner by placing hand grenade in motorized model airplane. But only the propeller takes off, leaving its fuselage— and grenade—in animal's paw. *Ka-boom!* Fade to black. Over winding road, coyote hoists piano, to be dropped when Roadrunner comes streaking by. At precise moment he lets go of rope: Nothing happens. Lowers himself onto suspended piano, which plunges toward canyon below and crashes musically. Wile E. emerges from wreckage to reveal mouthful of white-and-black piano keys, upon which he taps out "Taps." Fade to black.

Funniest of all is the diligence and inventiveness with which the coyote goes about his plans to capture the Roadrunner, always importing a surplus of products from the fictitious Acme company: Acme Giant Rubber Bands, Acme Jet Motors, Acme Rocket-Powered Roller Skates. From these he painstakingly designs and builds hundreds of Rube Goldberg–type contraptions—which all backfire. Yet in the next sequence there he is trying them again, actually expecting them to work.

And when his blind faith proves misdirected (translation: He's about to go *smash* or *crash*), he turns to the camera and fixes the audience with a woeful gaze, ears and nose drooping pathetically. A predator, technically speaking, Wile E. is a tragic figure with whom viewers empathize; because every

You know it, I know it, and what's more, Wile E. Coyote knows it: He never will catch the Roadrunner, no matter how many Acme products he employs. *Illustration © Warner Bros. Inc.*

now and then, who doesn't feel the world is conspiring against them? The next time you find yourself snagged in a rush-hour traffic jam, take a look around you at the other drivers. You'll see a lot of Wile E. Coyotes behind the wheels.

My favorite visual gag involving the coyote, from *Gee Whiz-z-z-z* (1956), more or less sums up his existence: In its final scene, another of Wile E.'s schemes has gone awry, sending him hurtling to the ground below. He holds up a sign reading "How about ending this cartoon before I hit?"—but his appeal is ignored. *Crash!*

Another of my characters, Foghorn Leghorn, was the silent coyote's exact opposite, never giving his beak a rest. The rooster is such a gasbag that he even interrupts himself, delivering a steady stream of asides to the audience. Given his name, there was nothing to do but to match it with a broad bellow from the diaphragm. It's the second-most-difficult voice for me. Because both Foghorn and Yosemite Sam require so much volume, I've mixed the two up on occasion.

When director Bob McKimson, the writers, and I first tossed about ideas for the new character, someone suggested we give him a southern accent. Thus is raised the controversy over which came first, the chicken or Senator Claghorn.

Beauregard Claghorn was the name of a Deep South politician on Allen's Alley, a popular segment from CBS radio's "The Fred Allen Show." Played by talented actor Kenny Delmar, he sounded identical to Foghorn Leghorn. Now, Delmar claimed he based the voice not on my character's, but on that of a Texas rancher he'd once hitched a ride from. Bob McKimson claimed Foghorn's voice was derived not from Senator Claghorn's, but from someone on another old-time radio program, "Blue Monday Jamboree." And *I* claim I first heard the accent at a vaudeville show at San Francisco's Pantages Theatre when I was twenty. As I recall it, in one of the skits an actor played a clownish half-deaf southern sheriff. Further complicating the issue, Foghorn Leghorn debuted in 1946, the same year that Senator Claghorn became a national sensation.

So who's right, Delmar, McKimson, or Blanc? Damned if I know.

Regardless of who preceded whom, the animated rooster was an instant audience favorite, even though in his first cartoon, *Walky Tawky Hawky,* he was merely a supporting player to Henery Hawk. Henery was a precocious little chicken hawk with big ambitions to catch chickens. He'd been featured in 1942's *The Squawkin' Hawk* but had to wait another four years for a second opportunity. One production opposite Foghorn, however, and the billings were quickly reversed.

From an animation standpoint the Leghorn is one of Warner's funniest characters. The artists saddled him with a lumpy body, an immense beak, a bright red comb to crown his lunk-

Foghorn Leghorn (top) and Henery Hawk (bottom). Controversy arose over the origins of the bellowing rooster's voice. I first heard something like it at a 1928 vaudeville show. *Illustrations © 1987 Warner Bros. Inc.*

ish head, and similarly colored tail feathers that should have
had a handle attached for dusting. Because Foghorn's ego is
as bloated as his physique, he feels it his duty to take the
young chicken hawk under his wing, so to speak. "Pay attention now, boy," he constantly reprimands his reluctant pupil.

Both fowls seem perpetually irritated with each other:
Foghorn, because the little hawk is always mistaking him for
a chicken; and Henery, because the overfed rooster is so full
of hot air.

"You're built too low," Foghorn informs the hawk. "The
fast ones go over your head. You got a hole in your glove; ah
keep pitchin' 'em, and you keep missin' em. You gotta keep
your eye on the ball." Whenever the rooster thinks he's stumbled on a pun, his face brightens and he jabs a finger in the
air. "Eye; ball. Eyeball! Ah almost had a gag, son." Henery is
never amused, though.

One of this series' regular subplots involved Foghorn's
run-ins with a cantankerous barnyard dog whom Henery also
mistakes for a chicken. "Now pay attention, boy," the Leghorn
coaches him. "You lookin' for chickens? You see that little
house over there? Says D-O-G? That spells *chicken*. Now go
get 'im, boy!"

Unfortunately for Henery, although he matched Foghorn
Leghorn wit for wit, he had little charm and was dismissed
following 1955's *All Fowled Up*. The rooster had already shown
he could carry the weight by himself and with other character
combinations, including the barnyard dog and a slithery wea-
sel. Two favorites of mine were Miss Prissy, a spinster hen
whose romantic interest in Foghorn is unrequited; and her
son, Junior, a bookwormish child prodigy who earns the Leghorn's everlasting contempt because he'd rather read than
pitch a baseball.

All twenty-six Foghorn Leghorn shorts were directed by
Bob McKimson, who replaced Bob Clampett in 1946. The
animated-film industry was always incestuous, with personnel
shifting allegiances from studio to studio. In addition to Clam-

pett, directors Frank Tashlin and Tex Avery had departed by the mid-1940s.

However, Warner Bros. boasted unusual loyalty from its cartoon unit, McKimson, Chuck Jones, and Friz Freleng all remaining with the studio into the 1960s. Among them they directed over six hundred theatrical shorts and received twenty-two of Warner cartoons' twenty-six Oscar nominations.

Nearly a decade into my animated-film career I had yet to test myself on a romantic lead. Chuck Jones must have read my mind when in 1945 he introduced the studio's newest hopeful, a French *bon vivant* named Pepe Le Pew. I was delighted because Gallic accents had been among the first I'd perfected as a child. Pepe's voice was warm and seductive, inspired by Charles Boyer, the French matinee idol whose bedroom murmur made women swoon.

Pepe had the same effect on people, but not due to any Continental charm. He was a skunk. As amorous as he was aromatic, Le Pew provided story man Michael Maltese with ample opportunities for gags, and audiences found him adorable. Or was that odor-able? He won an Oscar after just three screen appearances, for 1949's *For Scent-imental Reasons*.

The action takes place in a Parisian beauty shop, where always vain Pepe is in atomizer heaven, dousing himself with perfume. Suddenly he spots a female skunk; at least, he thinks she's a skunk. In truth she's a cat who accidentally backed into a counter, spilling a stripe of white hair dye onto her back.

"La femme skunk fatale!" Pepe exclaims. In a flash he is ravishing her while she struggles to slip out of his embrace. "Ah, my leetle darling," he whispers, about to cover her with kisses, "it eez love at first sight, eez eet not?" Apparently eet eez not, for the cat bolts from his embrace. Pepe is so intoxicated by *amour*, he doesn't realize he is kissing his own paw; what's more, the skunk is so unashamedly full of himself, he doesn't particularly care.

Unlike Foghorn Leghorn or the Roadrunner, Pepe is not a physical character. His laughs are derived more from the manner in which he mangles the English language. "Where does eet that you are secreting yourself, you?" he implores of his intended Juliet in *Scent-imental Romeo* (1951). "Where eez eet, your hiding place?" William Shakespeare would spin in his grave if he heard Pepe's paraphrase of perhaps his most famous line: "Au revoir, pigeon. Sweeting is such part sorrow."

Ironically, all of his romantic blathering is just that: blathering. Like Wile E. Coyote, he's excited by the thrill of the chase. In *For Scent-imental Reasons,* when the cat abruptly changes her mind and makes advances on *him,* Pepe is clearly unnerved. "Control yourself, madame! You cannot be een earnest. A joke, yes?" The roles reversed, Pepe races off with the

Pepe Le Pew (left), French bon vivant and skunk. His characterization was inspired by matinee idol Charles Boyer. Some female viewers were so smitten by Pepe's Continental charm, they sent *me* amorous fan mail. *Illustration © Warner Bros. Inc.*

My final Warner's star, Speedy Gonzales (left), the fastest mouse in all of Mexico. His voice was later used for TV pitchman the Frito Bandito. *Illustration © Warner Bros. Inc.*

cat on his scented trail. "You know," he sighs, "it eez possible to be too attractive."

He may have been right. Believe it or not, some women were so smitten by Pepe Le Pew's accent, they sent *me* amorous fan mail.

Far more triumphant with the opposite sex was my final Warner Bros. leading character, Speedy Gonzales the Mexican mouse. In his second cartoon a handful of rodents are discussing his romantic exploits.

"Speedy Gonzales friend of my seester," says one, prompting another to add, "Speedy Gonzales friend of *everybody's* seester!" Presumably his designation as the "fastest mouse" in all of Mexico did not apply to his lovemaking prowess.

A nameless Speedy prototype bowed in an undistinguished 1953 Bob McKimson–directed short, *Cat Tails for
Two.* It's no wonder he failed to catch on with audiences at
first, because he was repellent: a scrawny little thing with oily
hair and glistening buckteeth. But when he returned to the
screen under Friz Freleng's direction in 1955's Oscar-winning
Speedy Gonzales, the mouse was impish looking, with an oversize sombrero covering the top of his head.

Speedy Gonzales's plot is typical. It opens with several
mice staring forlornly at the Ajax Cheese Company factory,
guarded zealously by none other than Sylvester the cat.

"There ees only one mouse who can get the cheese," one
of them declares, "and that ees Speedy Gonzales!" Speedy,
sympathetic to his friends' cheddarless plight, offers his services. As his pals view from a grandstand (an empty egg car-
ton), Speedy drives Sylvester berserk, all the while chattering
in ersatz Spanish, "Yeeha! Andalay! Arriba!" He ricochets past
the cat, under the cat, around the cat, even through the cat,
returning each time with armloads of cheese. By cartoon's
end, his comrades have enough to harden the arteries of every
mouse in Mexico, while "Señor Pussycat" bangs his head against
a telephone pole in frustration.

Compared to Bugs Bunny and Daffy Duck, Speedy was
fairly one-dimensional, but he became Warner's most prolific
star during its final years. In 1966 and 1967, out of twenty-
five productions, eighteen featured the mouse. Moreover,
Speedy's cartoons received more Oscar nominations (four)
than any other character in the studio's history.

Though Speedy was finished by 1968, his voice was sub-
leased to the Frito Bandito, animated TV pitchman for Frito-
Lay corn chips. Admittedly, when first brought to the screen,
the Bandito was not the most savory character: unshaven,
gold-toothed, and he leered a lot. But I was hardly prepared
for the controversy he would spark. Frito-Lay's advertising
agency recommended the Spanish-accented shill be sanitized,
which was done. Yet in 1969 the Mexican-American Anti-
Defamation Committee complained that the Bandito perpe-

trated a "racist message" that Mexicans are "sneaky thieves," and television stations around the country began boycotting the spots.

Frankly, though the charges were never directed at me personally, I was deeply hurt. Certainly it was never intended that the Bandito reflect negatively on Mexican Americans. He was simply a humorous character. Just as amorous Pepe Le Pew in no way insinuated that all Frenchmen were Lotharios. Did Foghorn Leghorn purport to represent everyone living south of the Mason-Dixon line? Of course not. Basing a character on a particular ethnic group is a standard comedic device, from the unmistakably Jewish "The Goldbergs," which was a 1930s and 1940s radio sensation; to "Life With Luigi," another popular show whose main characters were three Italian immigrants; to the Scandinavian Hansens of early TV's "Mama."

Incidentally, the majority of viewers did see the humor of the Bandito, including many Mexican Americans: A Frito-Lay survey showed that nearly ninety percent claimed to *like* the character. Only eight percent said they did not. Had it been another time and not the late 1960s, marked by extreme sensitivity to racial stereotypes, undoubtedly the only people upset by the Frito Bandito would have been rival corn-chip manufacturers.

Not all of my characters were stars the magnitude of Bugs Bunny, Tweety, Sylvester, and Speedy Gonzales. Because Jack L. Warner eventually decided it was more economical, financially and time-wise, for me to portray entire cartoon casts, I added many other voices to my repertoire. Some of them are quite memorable, even if the characters were merely bit players.

One of the most popular was the Tasmanian Devil, who appeared in a handful of shorts beginning with 1954's *Devil May Hare*, opposite Bugs. He was a fearsome whirling dervish who buzz-sawed through trees, rocks, and anything else that obstructed his path. Bob McKimson came up with him, Eddie

For reasons that defy
explanation, the
slobbering, growling
Tasmanian Devil was
a favorite character
of Warner Bros. veep
Jack L. Warner.
Illustration © 1987
Warner Bros. Inc.

Selzer hated and canceled him, and Jack L. Warner reinstated him. This was the same Jack Warner who was so in the dark about his cartoon unit that he thought Mickey Mouse was in his employ; yet he was smitten by the Tasmanian Devil.

McKimson described the character to me, and I have to admit that at first I was stumped. *What the hell would a Tasmanian Devil sound like?* Because of his ravenous appetite, it seemed that he should growl slobbering, indecipherable gibberish. I demonstrated it for the director and said, "I defy you or anybody else to tell me he doesn't sound like a Tasmanian Devil."

Probably the most unusual of all my voices belongs to Marvin Martian. You might remember him playing opposite interplanetary rival Daffy Duck in Chuck Jones's *Duck Dodgers in the 24 1/2 Century* (1953). He's a preposterous-looking little alien described best by Bugs Bunny as "that character wearing the spittoon." Actually I think it's a scrub brush atop Marvin's steel helmet the rabbit was referring to. The Martian also appears to be wearing running shoes; obviously the animators weren't striving for accuracy in their depiction of extraterrestrial life forms.

Marvin's nasal voice is delivered as if he's suffering from sound-barrier-breaking motion sickness. He's comical but also deeply philosophical, editorializing eloquently about the escalating tensions on earth in 1952's *Hasty Hare:*

"There is a growing tendency to think of man as a rational being," he muses aloud, "which is ab-*surd*. There is simply no evidence of any intelligence on the earth . . ." Proof that the studio's writers didn't only crack gags, sometimes they subtly inserted messages—and yet left you laughing.

Still other Warner Bros. characters of mine included:

Hubie and Bertie—two mice with harsh Brooklyn accents that can peel paint; they starred in four cartoons between 1943 and 1952, as well as three with another marginal troupe member, Claude Cat. One of their collaborations, *Mouse Wreckers* (1949), was an Oscar nominee.

The Goofy Gophers—this team starred in eight shorts from 1948 to 1965 and spoke with stiff upper lips; *vedy* British, precious and understated. After nearly going over a raging waterfall on a log, they observe calmly to each other:

"My, but we were in a very precarious predicament, weren't we?"

"Yes, very precarious. Oh, yes, indeed."

Stan Freberg, who for a time was Hubie, of Hubie and Bertie, played opposite me in these cartoons as well.

Charlie Dog—this mangy but lovable mutt first appeared with Porky Pig in *Little Orphan Airedale* (1947) and spoke like a deeper-voiced Bugs Bunny: "Oh, bruddah!"

Wolf and Sheepdog—Ralph Wolf was essentially Wile E. Coyote in disguise; equally devious and luckless. He exerts much effort trying to slip past Sam Sheepdog, but the shaggy-haired flock protector foils Ralph at every turn without breaking into a sweat. The pair was featured in seven cartoons from 1953 to 1963, and they merely grumble, "Hello, Sam," "Hello, Ralph," to each other as they punch in to work on the "set."

Sometimes the most distinctive voice I could give a character was my own. So when you hear Sam Sheepdog and Claude Cat, you're really listening to Mel Blanc playing Mel Blanc. In addition to the abovementioned characters, I portrayed approximately seven hundred incidental, unnamed animals and humans. That was at Warner Bros. alone, so when people call me Man of a Thousand Voices, they're not exaggerating.

No matter who—or what—I play, during the recording I *become* the character and even take on its physical characteristics. Engineers, directors, and fellow actors had told me so for years, but I didn't fully believe them until one day Treg Brown brought a camera to the studio and had me run through my most famous voices. Sure enough, when he showed me the developed photos, I was astonished.

When performing Bugs Bunny, I jut out my front teeth, just like the rabbit.

When performing Pepe Le Pew, I affect a suave look, arching one eyebrow a *leetle beet.*

When I perform slobbering Sylvester, I puff out my cheeks and try my damnedest not to bite my tongue.

Perhaps you're wondering what home life is like with a man of a thousand voices. Oddly enough, I never rehearse at home. Naturally there are some times when sudden inspiration strikes, and I have to amplify the sounds I hear in my head. But generally, aside from the studio, the only place I practice is in the car. I'll be stuck in traffic on Franklin Avenue, notice a kitten frolicking in somebody's front yard, and imagine what it would sound like if given human qualities and a voice. That was something I'd done ever since I was a youngster watching my first Felix the Cat cartoon. Long before Felix

Like any method actor, when I play a character, I *become* that character. I even look like that character. See for yourself. First, Bugs . . .

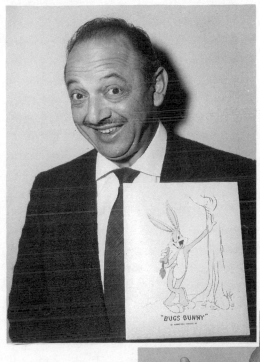

. . . Porky Pig . . .

was presented with a voice, I'd already given him one of my own.

Some people assume mistakenly that I devised characterizations and later assigned them to appropriate characters. Rarely was that ever the case. Normally I wouldn't even begin experimenting until I'd met with the directors, artists, and writers and studied the rough sketches. Many times the voice simply seemed to materialize. Some required months, even years, to perfect, but most were developed quite quickly. And once I was satisfied with a voice, it remained permanently embedded in my memory. I never have to rehearse. Just hand me my script.

What does it take to be a voice-man? Certainly the voice box's elasticity and versatility are important. But just as vital are the ears and the brain: the ears, to be able to consistently reproduce the same timbres, tones, textures; and the brain, because a voice actor has to be keenly sensitive when it comes to shaping each character's persona. My job has always been to take emotions, interpret them through a French skunk, a bigmouthed rooster, and so on, translate them back to human terms, and still coax a chuckle out of the audience.

I'm often asked why it is that the Warner Bros. cartoons are so timeless, still amusing adults who may first have seen them a half-century ago, while at the same time thrilling youngsters who've never seen a theatrical short in their lives. Bugs Bunny was recently voted the best-loved cartoon figure of all time. Figuring in fourth place was the Roadrunner, just behind Jim Henson's Muppets and my own Barney Rubble from TV's "The Flintstones."

Indeed, why them? Why Warner Bros.?

As is true of most success stories, several factors contributed to the cartoons' everlasting appeal: obviously the writing, the animation, and the characters themselves. However, I think it's chiefly the playfulness and irreverence with which we approached our work. Hell, compared to the staff at Walt Disney's production house, we were downright anarchists. Just

. . . Daffy Duck . . .

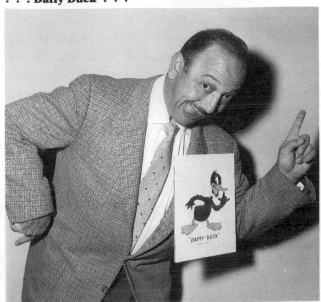

. . . Yosemite Sam . . .

compare the characters most associated with each studio: Disney's ingenuous Mickey Mouse and our shrewd Bugs Bunny.

One reason why Warner's overtook Disney in theatrical shorts was that after the phenomenal success of *Snow White* and *Pinnochio*, Walt turned his attention more to full-length animated features. But in the end, it boiled down to the fact that Bugs, Daffy, Yosemite, and the rest were a lot more fun than Disney's beautifully drawn goody-goodies. Too, our characters were truer reflections of the human condition; they could be sweet and magnanimous, or they could be nasty and vengeful. They had foibles just like real people.

Probably because some of them were based on real people. For Porky Pig, Friz Freleng tapped his memories of two chubby brothers from his Kansas City, Missouri, neighborhood; one nicknamed Porky, the other, Pig. Sylvester the cat was animated with jowly executive producer Johnny Burton (Eddie Selzer's successor) in mind.

Though we were always conscious that the cartoons were intended primarily to amuse youngsters, we ultimately entertained ourselves. If something appealed to one of the story men's sense of humor, it went in the script, so long as it was within the boundaries of good taste. How else can you explain whimsy such as several knights of the Round Table who bear titles such as Sir Loin of Beef and Sir Osis of Liver, for *Knighty Knight Bugs* (1958)? I'm sure that those puns went over the heads of children in the audience, and probably eluded some adults, too. But writer Warren Foster and the rest of us laughed ourselves silly.

Watch the cartoons carefully and you'll notice countless in-jokes. A billboard in *Hare Do* (1948) shouts, "Try Friz, the wonder soap." In *Gonzales's Tamale* (1957) a "Hotel Mel" dominates the background. And according to an opera-house sign in *Rabbit of Seville* (1950), the singers that night include Messrs. Eduardo Selzeri, Michele Maltese, and Carlo Jones. We even poked fun at other studio creations, as in *Tabasco Road* (1957):

Two tipsy Mexican mice aren't sure if a ready-to-pounce feline is for real or merely a drunken delusion. "I theenk I saw

. . . Foghorn Leghorn . . .

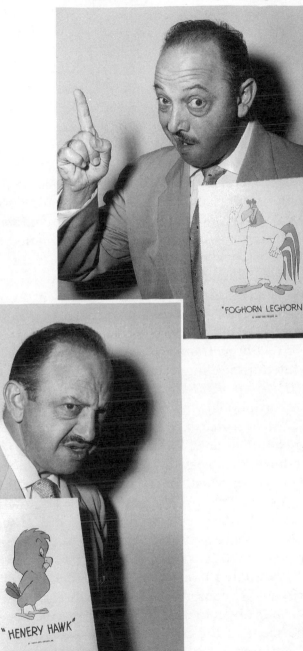

. . . and Henery Hawk.

a pussy *gato*," one says in a slurred paraphrase of Tweety's famous line.

"You did, you did saw una pussy cat!" his companion replies.

Yet another reason for the cartoons' longevity was the versatility of nearly each character. Different combinations— Bugs and Elmer; Bugs and Daffy; Bugs, Elmer, and Daffy— produced different sets of sparks. One grand-scale production, *The Scarlet Pumpernickel* (1950), stars Daffy, Porky, Sylvester, Elmer, Henery, and various incidental characters in a feudal-England setting, thus raising another point: Not only could we experiment like mad scientists with character chemistry, we could drop the members of our animated acting troupe into almost any scenario.

So our directors and writers were free to plunder:

History: Bugs and Yosemite in ancient Rome, where the sign in front of the Coliseum proclaims, "Detroit Lions in Season Opener"; referring not to the football team, of course, but to real lions (*Roman Legion Hare*, 1955).

Literature: Elmer Fudd starring as Pilgrim John Alden in *The Hardship of Miles Standish* (1940), taken from Henry Wadsworth Longfellow's nineteenth-century poem *The Courtship of Miles Standish*. When a marauding Indian's arrow busts a log-cabin window, Elmer hustles out, yelling, "Hey, one of you fellows has to pay for that *gwass*," like a modern-day next-door neighbor chastising a junior Joe DiMaggio.

Cinema: *The Last Hungry Cat* (1961), in which Friz Freleng cleverly satirizes master of macabre Alfred Hitchcock, who is cast here as a narrating bear and is impersonated by yours truly. In this cartoon Sylvester believes erroneously that he has murdered Tweety. My mock Hitchcock jabs away mercilessly at his conscience until finally the cat breaks down. Just as he's about to turn himself over to the police, he returns to the scene of the crime, where Tweety is very much alive and as tummy-tempting as ever.

The narrator delivers the story's moral in appropriately solemn, belabored tones—" . . . in the words of the Bard, conscience makes cowards of us all"—to which Sylvester sneers, "Aw, shuddap!" and conks Alfred on the skull with a brick.

Opera: *What's Opera, Doc?* (1957), a condensed version of Richard Wagner's epic tetralogy *Der Ring des Nibelungen*, featuring Bugs Bunny in drag as the Valkyrie maiden Brünnhilde and Elmer Fudd as the heroic warrior Siegfried. As in genuine opera, all lines are sung, to hilarious effect: for instance, Elmer's grandiloquent "Kill the wa-bbit, kill the wa-bbit, kill the *wa*-bbit!" set to the melody of *Ride of the Valkyries*, the orchestra whipping up a storm behind him. But unlike the German composer's fifteen-hour original, this one falls fourteen hours fifty-four minutes short.

Besides the inventive plots and character development, the Warner Bros. cartoon stars simply *looked* funny. When Foghorn Leghorn strides on screen, there's snickering among the audience before he even opens his giant beak. They looked like no one else, which helped define their personalities, and vice versa. It's no wonder that just as our studio started out imitating Walt Disney's animation, from the 1940s on many competitors began introducing characters that were thinly disguised Warner's impersonators.

But none could match our peerless sight gags: In *Feather Dusted* (1955) Foghorn Leghorn swallows a cannonball, which rumbles down his windpipe like a bowling ball down an alley. Then, *crash!* It lands in his stomach to the accompanying sound effect of a perfect strike, causing the rooster to wobble back and forth like a tipped pin.

Or how about a scene in *High Diving Hare* (1949), where Bugs Bunny catapults Yosemite Sam from a high-diving board? "Uh-oh," says Bugs, feigning concern, "forgot to fill the tank with water." He empties a pailful after Yosemite, who frantically waves the cascading water on past, kneels in fervent midair prayer, and manages miraculously to shove the water ahead of him and into the tank—which the squat cowboy then misses by several crucial feet, smashing through the floorboards.

Another sequence featuring Bugs and Yosemite, from the Oscar-winning *Knighty Knight Bugs*, is often cited as a prime example of Warner Bros. animation. Armor-suited Sam stands on the far side of a castle moat. "Open that bridge, ya varmint," he calls, "open it, ah say!" The rabbit complies, letting the drawbridge collapse on top of Yosemite, who's crushed into an armor-plated accordion with feet. From under the bridge comes a muffled, furious, "Close it! Close it! Close it up again!"

Sadly, it was Warner Bros.'s imaginative full animation that eventually led to its demise. In the 1950s increasingly cost-conscious studios began seeking alternatives to the expensive process of drawing, inking, and painting each frame. They found it: limited animation, which reduced drastically the number of necessary cels and hence, time. And time equaled money. Budgets could be slashed from fifty thousand dollars to ten thousand. Warner's never wavered from its commitment to quality animation, but many other houses opted for limited. While they certainly can't be blamed for wanting to economize, unfortunately this was often done at an aesthetic expense.

In addition to production cutbacks, movie theaters were leasing fewer animated films. For one thing, children could watch them on television now, and for another, why book a six-minute short several times a day when you could sneak in an extra showing of the feature film, thus taking in more money at the box office and the concession stand? A contributing factor may have been the nature of today's movies, which are predominantly violent and/or sexually explicit. I wonder if there isn't too much of a contrast between them and the cartoons' comparatively light fun. It's hard to imagine Tweety bird followed by Rambo, if you know what I mean.

For nearly two decades Warner Bros.'s cartoon unit averaged thirty theatrical shorts yearly, but by 1960 output had dwindled to twenty. By 1963 it was down to sixteen. With animated films a dying art form, the studio hierarchy gave notice that Termite Terrace would be left to the termites. A golden era was over.

Friz Freleng started his own production company with Warner executive David H. DePatie. Just as they were settling down to work, Warner Bros. belatedly reversed its decision and, ironically, was forced to lease cartoons from one of its former directors. Since DePatie-Freleng worked on the same lot, in some respects it wasn't much different from the old days. Except that most of the veteran writers and artists were gone, and budgets were slim: about $16,500 per short. Obviously, quality suffered. To further confuse matters, in 1967 Jack L. Warner resumed in-house production, so that now there were two groups making Warner Bros. cartoons.

It didn't last long, however, and two years later production was halted for good. Considering the shoddiness of many of the cartoons, perhaps it was just as well. Why tarnish a legacy? How sad that after thirty-nine years of featuring some of the most memorable characters in animation history, Warner Bros.'s 1969 swan song, *Injun Trouble*, starred Cool Cat. I know: Cool who? The undistinguished short's only link to the past was its director, Bob McKimson. It was the studio's 1,003rd cartoon, of which I'd voiced 848. For the next eighteen years, that was to be all, folks.

CHAPTER

6

Making Air Waves

*T*he best raise I ever got was the one I didn't get.

Don't bother rereading it. I'll explain.

The arrival of our son Noel stretched the Blanc household budget to the breaking point. Since I supplied the voices for Warner Bros.'s two major animated stars, Porky Pig and Daffy Duck, my business manager (Estelle) felt a raise was in order.

While I had never been very assertive when it came to money, Estelle was just the opposite. Eventually I simply left most financial matters in her hands, telling my employers, "Work it out with my wife." They'd always respond with awkward laughter, not knowing whether or not I was serious. I wasn't kidding at all.

At my better half's urging, I marched into Leon Schlessinger's office to demand a salary increase. It wasn't going to be easy because the producer was notoriously tightfisted with money.

Dragging on his ever-present cigarette, Leon listened politely to the appeal Estelle and I had rehearsed all morning.

Then, leaning back in his chair and using his hands as a headrest, he had the gall to say, "What do you want more money for, Mel? You'll only have to pay more taxes." Even *I* wasn't naive enough to be duped by such a ridiculous ploy, and I continued pointing out my value to the studio. But it wasn't enough to sway my boss, who kept repeating, "Insufficient profits."

"Well, if you won't give me a raise," I countered, "how about at least giving me a screen credit?"

Schlessinger bolted upright.

"Credit? Who ever heard of a voice-man getting a screen credit?"

Precisely my point.

"All right," he said hesitantly, "you'll get your screen credit."

And I did: "Voice Characterizations by Mel Blanc," listed just below the directors, writers, and animators.

Once talent agents discovered Mel Blanc was the man behind Porky, Daffy, and the nascent Bugs Bunny, I received a bounty of offers from other studios, as well as from radio shows. Opportunities were so plentiful, I even had to turn some down. At one point in the mid-1940s, in addition to voicing Warner Bros. animated films, I was on eighteen transcontinental programs a week and bringing home two thousand dollars a week.

It made me the envy of my peers, especially certain veterans who saw me as a relative newcomer. I'm sure that some probably referred to me ever after as Mel Blankety-Blanc. What can I say other than, if I hadn't been the first to insist upon screen credit, someone else would have. That every other cartoon contributor should be recognized but not actors was unconscionably unfair.

It was a good thing I was still a young man, because in retrospect I don't know how I summoned the energy to assume so much work. For example, on a typical Sunday night during the 1944–45 season, I performed on "The Jack Benny Program," "The Great Gildersleeve," "Baby Snooks," and "Blondie." Each half-hour show required one or more weekly rehearsals. The following night, it was "Major Hoople," "The George Burns and Gracie Allen Show," and "Point Sublime," with the rest of my seven-day week shaping up as follows: the Chesterfield "Supper Club" and "Fibber McGee and Molly" on Tuesdays; "Camel Comedy Caravan," "The Eddie Cantor Show," and "Icebox Follies" on Wednesdays; "The Abbott and Costello Show" on Thursdays; "Amos 'n' Andy" on Fridays; and "The Judy Canova Show" on Saturdays. That's not including the many bit parts I was tapped to play on yet other shows.

With the exception of "Point Sublime," broadcast over the Mutual–Don Lee network, all the abovementioned programs aired on either CBS or NBC. Thank God, too, because their studios were just a couple of blocks from each other. CBS's impressive Columbia Square complex was on Sunset Boulevard, between El Centro Avenue and Gower Street, while NBC's sprawling Hollywood Radio City was at the corner of Sunset and Vine. Not that I ever walked it, but I had occasion to sprint back and forth between the two many times.

There was one Saturday night when, after finishing a sketch on "The Judy Canova Show," I dropped my script and ran out of the NBC building like Olympic medalist Jesse Owens, up the boulevard, into Columbia Square, down a hallway, around a corner, into a studio, and up to the microphone, just in time for my cue. All to deliver one line, a baby's bawling—"*Wah! Wah! Wah!*"—while trying not to pant. I don't even remember what program it was.

Between all the shows and rehearsals, sometimes the pace became so dizzying I'd forget which brand of tobacco I was smoking. That may not sound terribly important, but with many series sponsored by savagely competitive cigarette manufacturers, believe me, it was. Lucky Strike sponsored Jack Benny's show; Chesterfield, Bing Crosby's; and Camel, Abbott and Costello's, as well as "Blondie." To play it safe, I used to keep a pack of each on my Packard's dashboard.

Absurd, isn't it? Especially since this was radio; who could tell which brand you were smoking? But the companies were so insistent that actors comply, they even hired inspectors, who carried out their duties with gestapolike zeal.

"Excuse me, Mr. Blanc, but what are you smoking there?" an inspector at "The Jack Benny Program" asked me one time.

"Uh, Pall Mall," I replied absentmindedly, engrossed in studying my script.

"Dammit, Mel," he snapped, "this is a Lucky Strike show, and you sure as hell had better have that Lucky green in your pocket the next time I come around." It becomes even more preposterous when you consider that both brands were manufactured by the American Tobacco Company.

Another time, at a Burns and Allen rehearsal, out of the corner of my eye I caught the Chesterfield inspector heading in my direction. I glanced down and much to my dismay, discovered some other make wedged in my shirt pocket. *Where the hell are my Chesterfields? Right! In my pants pocket!* Just as his fingers were poised to snatch the offending product from my pocket, I deftly switched packs and, raising my eyebrows, smirked in his face. The man grunted and stalked away, seeking another victim. Incidentally, I couldn't *stand* the taste of Chesterfields.

That should give you an idea how powerful shows' sponsors were: too damn powerful, if you ask me. Company representatives regularly sat in the glass-enclosed listening area called the sponsor's booth. They weren't merely spectators but went so far as to make recommendations regarding script content, cast members, and so on. True, they were footing the bill, but a cigarette maker's dictating to seasoned actors and writers made about as much sense as us telling them how much tar and nicotine to put in their product.

Sometimes it seemed as if those products were more integral to the shows than the performers themselves. Many program titles contained the toothpaste's or insurance company's name, but not the celebrity's. For instance, Jack Benny's show was initially called "The Jell-O Program." Personally, I always thought folks tuned in to hear Jack and the cast, not jingles touting a six-flavored gelatin dessert. Likewise, at one

time Bob Hope's program was entitled the "Pepsodent Show,"
Al Jolson's, "The Lifebuoy Program," et cetera, et cetera.

Sponsor influence became so flagrant, commercials were
even woven into scripts, a practice started in the early 1930s
on "The Fire Chief," starring Ed Wynn. At first many radio
personalities resisted, but after a while it became a challenge
to see how seamlessly one could incorporate them into the
storyline. Jack Benny was a master at this, opening his program with the cheerful greeting "Jell-O again." Sometimes
he'd even plug a nonsponsor, knowing that an on-the-air mention might net him anything from free shaving cream to free
liquor. On one occasion he asked his faithful valet Rochester
to fetch his General Electric blanket. "But boss," the butler
replied, puzzled, "you don't have a General Electric blanket."

Said Benny smugly, "I have *now*." Sure enough, the next
day the company sent over electric blankets for the entire crew
and cast. If only Jack had thought to plug Cadillac.

There were several other voice actors in Hollywood with
equally hectic schedules, and over time we became as close
as the CBS and NBC studios in which we worked together.
This little circle included Bea Benaderet, Joe Kearns, Mary
Jane Higby, Sheldon Leonard, Verna Felton, Hans Conried,
and Gale Gordon. To list all of the shows they appeared on
would be a chapter in itself. Suffice to say, each boasted a
substantial, impressive résumé.

I was probably closest to Bea, if for no other reason than
that we performed side by side so often in cartoons and on
radio and television. It was via the latter medium that she
truly made her mark, first as next-door neighbor Blanche Mor-
ton on "The George Burns and Gracie Allen Show" in the
1950s, then as Kate Bradley, star of "Petticoat Junction," from
1963 until her death from lung cancer five years later.

Bea wasn't exceptionally pretty, but someone so warm,
generous, and funny couldn't help but be attractive. Both she
and her husband, Eugene Twombly, were "Jack Benny Program" cast members: she as telephone operator Gertrude

Gearshift, he as a sound-effects technician. Tragically, four days after Bea passed away, Eugene died of a heart attack. To lose them both was very sad and painful.

About the only person in our informal clique that I didn't get along with was Gale Gordon, the 1930s radio voice of Flash Gordon, among many others. He also played Lucille Ball's crusty, tormented foil on TV's "The Lucy Show" and "Here's Lucy." If ever there was an example of typecasting, Gordon as Theodore J. Mooney and Harrison Otis Carter (essentially a reprise of the same role) was it.

I ran into him a few days after Noel was born and announced proudly, "Gale, guess what—I'm a father!"

His eyes narrowed, his mouth puckered—the same sour-puss expression for which he'd later be paid exorbitantly—and he sneered, "Big deal!" Not only didn't I receive his good wishes, Gordon went into a tirade about never wanting children because they "pester you to death." I thought to myself, *You schmuck.* Ironically, he and his wife eventually adopted. But from that day on, I steered clear of him.

It wasn't always easy, since most radio actors clustered around one or two microphone stands, scripts in hand. Because I often voiced as many as a half dozen characters on an individual show, my script resembled a child's coloring book; to distinguish one part from another, I'd underline each in a different color with a mechanical pencil I always carried with me.

Most programs were performed in front of studio audiences ranging in size from several dozen to several hundred. After spending so much time cooped up at Termite Terrace, interacting with a handful of actors at best, it was terrific fun for me to watch the audience's reactions. The director and one or more engineers, meanwhile, observed the show-in-progress from behind a glass partition; and in the client's booth there always lurked the ominous presence of someone from Rinso Soap, Sanka, General Electric, Kraft—whoever the sponsor might be.

Perhaps the true star of any old-time radio program was

the sound-effects man, stationed in the studio along with an assistant, amplified turntables for spinning prerecorded effects, and loads of odd props for creating sounds on the spot. Effects were even more vital to radio than to cartoons. For example, without sound technician Jack Dick's rhythmically beating coconut-shell halves in a dirt-filled box—*clippety-clop, clippety-clop*—the Cisco Kid and his sidekick Pan Pancho wouldn't have been able to make their quick getaways on horseback.

In fact, the best-remembered gag from the classic "Fibber McGee and Molly" revolved around a lone sound effect. McGee, played by Jim Jordan, kept a closet filled to overflowing with every piece of junk imaginable. Whenever the door was opened, the towering pile came tumbling down like the walls of Jericho. *Crash!* Frank Pittman presided over the "closet," heaving barbells, tin pie plates—you name it—down a flight of steps. Other times, McGee went to the door, placed his hand on the knob, listeners held their collective breath in anticipation, and—

Nothing. Dead silence. Either way, audiences were red-faced with laughter. For heightened comic effect, following the last *clank* and *clatter*, Pittman sometimes jingled a tiny bell. *Ting-a-ling*. It was the same device Warner Bros.'s Treg Brown employed: eliciting laughs by applying inappropriate noises. But generally speaking, the sound-effects man's job was to simulate realism and to stir the listenership's imagination.

To do that, he had to rely on ingenuity. For a tranquil Sunday-morning scene around the breakfast table, he might recreate the sizzle of frying bacon by crinkling cellophane next to the microphone. And simulating footsteps evolved into a veritable art form.

On "The Jack Benny Program," Eugene Twombly effected distinctive walks for each character so that listeners could imagine scenes even without the benefit of dialogue. Jack's walk, naturally, was heavier than that of his wife, Mary Livingstone, and so on. Before permitting Twombly on the air,

Benny spent hours with him, pacing back and forth so that the sound man could faithfully reproduce his steps' rhythm. Most of the time Eugene slipped on a pair of shoes with wood soles and heels and walked in place on a wood board. To heighten the realism, he later experimented with concrete slabs and gravel-filled boxes.

During showtime, the sound-effects man resembled the Hindu god Shiva, appearing to have four arms in constant, frantic motion: creating thunder by violently shaking a piece of sheet metal, while simultaneously cuing up the next effects platter. The pace was so quick that mistakes were inevitable. On a comedy program this could add to the hilarity, but such mishaps could ruin the mood of a serious drama. One famous example is from a show on which a prop pistol jammed just as the gunman was about to fire. Thinking quickly, he ad-libbed that he'd have to stab his victim instead. "Take this!" he shouted, to the accompanying *bang!* of a gunshot.

One mechanical error resulted in a new role for me. It happened during a Jack Benny rehearsal outside a Palm Springs radio theater. The venue's air-conditioning had broken down, so we had no choice but to practice our lines alfresco, where it was a balmy one hundred ten degrees. All the men in the cast, including guest star Al Jolson, were stripped to the waist, our bodies drenched with sweat.

At the show's conclusion Jack was to drive away in his 1924 Maxwell, a rattletrap whose engine coughed and sput-tered as if stricken with acute bronchitis. I happened to notice a look of panic on the sound technician's face and followed his stare along the length of the turntable cord: The machine wasn't plugged in. Precisely at the moment of ignition I stepped up to the mike and mimicked the sound vocally: "P-tui, p-tui, b-lit, b-lit, *p-tui.*" That last *p-tui* was so final, garage attendants should have drawn a white sheet over the expired automobile. In between laughs Benny exclaimed, "Mel, you've gotta do that on the show!" From that day on I was Maxwell.

If producing a radio program seems very much like pro-ducing an animated film, it was, except for one crucial difference: Radio shows were broadcast live. If you flubbed a line, you couldn't gesture for the engineer to stop recording; somehow you had to claw your way out of the hole you'd dug. Some actors found the pressure inhibiting, others, inspiring, especially when part of an ensemble that was *on*. Then it was as if the entire cast were conductors of electricity, all being powered by the same current.

The element of spontaneity made it as exhilarating for the audience as for the players. You never knew when a quick wit such as Fred Allen or Fanny Brice would convert a miscue into an uproarious gag.

During my decades in radio I was called on to portray so many characters, readers may recall some of them more vividly than I do. Among the minor roles were Hubert Peabody on the Jack Carson–hosted "Camel Comedy Caravan"; the horn blower on "Nitwit Court"; and Floyd the Barber on "The Great Gildersleeve," a "Fibber McGee and Molly" spin-off and the first of its kind. Today, of course, developing new series around existing characters is common practice, but it wasn't back then. Speaking of "Fibber McGee," on that show I once acted the part of a fellow who'd been shocked by two thousand volts of electricity. Asked by McGee if he suffers from any aftereffects, he replies, "Well, it makes me speak with a little st-st-static."

In 1942 I played Uncle Petie and Rover the Dog on "The Tommy Riggs and Betty Lou Show," an NBC comedy that starred a dummy. No insult intended, just a statement of fact: Betty Lou was a ventriloquist's mannequin brought to life by Tommy Riggs, a musician from Pittsburgh. Such were radio's benefits that it didn't matter that he couldn't throw his voice à la Edgar Bergen. However, he did possess the ability to speak remarkably like a seven-year-old girl, a condition doctors at Cornell Medical Center described as "bivocalism." Riggs once told me that while a college football player, he used to scare the hell out of teammates emerging from the shower by piping up from behind the lockers in his innocent little-girl's voice.

On "Major Hoople," which first aired the same year, I shared the microphone with Arthur Q. Bryan. It was a familiar situation for both of us, only instead of Elmer Fudd, here he starred as Major Amos Hoople. The major was a dotty old windbag who endlessly told war stories, the details of which were dubious at best; it often seemed as if a Hoople ancestor had personally won every conflict waged since the beginning of time. He and his "everloving but not too trusting" wife, Martha, played by Patsy Moran, ran the Hoople Boarding House, which is where I came in, as longtime resident Tiffany Twiggs. Twiggs was the biggest doubting Thomas of them all, replying to Hoople's grandiose claims with scathing sarcasm.

Those were some of my lesser-known roles. Far more memorable was the Happy Postman, whom I portrayed for many years on "The George Burns and Gracie Allen Show." Despite his name, he was anything but cheerful, always verging on tears.

"Good-bye, Mrs. Burns," he'd lament, as if just notified of an impending income-tax audit. "And remember, keep smiling." His forlorn voice was derived from that of an old beachcomber I once encountered begging for spare change. While buying him coffee and a sandwich, I studied his peculiar speech pattern, later incorporating it into the Happy Postman.

George and Gracie were a delight to work with. Like many stars, they were so convincing in character that audiences truly believed Gracie was a scatterbrained brunette. Far from it. Off mike she was soft-spoken and so sharp-witted, some Hollywood wags called her "the smartest dumbbell in the history of show business." In fact, in 1939 she appeared on NBC's brainy quiz show "Information Please" and stunned the audience by more than keeping pace with her fellow panelists.

Likewise, George's straight-man role was carefully contrived. He and Gracie met in 1922, when Burns was twenty-six and already had as many years in show business under his belt as Gracie was old: seventeen. Some time before, he'd changed his name from Nathan Birnbaum to the less ethnic-

Gracie Allen and George Burns listen sympathetically to my Happy Postman character, whose name was a misnomer. "Good-bye, Mrs. Burns," he'd say forlornly, **"and remember, keep smiling."** *NBC Photo by Elmer W. Holloway*

sounding Burns. Grace Ethel Cecile Rosalie Allen, a petite gal from San Francisco, had dropped out of convent school to become a hoofer and actress with the Larry Reilly Company. But when she and Burns were introduced, stage work was so scarce that she was enrolled in secretarial school.

They first teamed up at the Hill StreetTheatre in Newark, New Jersey, for five dollars a day. Few folks know this, but in their original act Gracie played it straight and George reaped the laughs; what there were of them, that is. Then it was decided to reverse the dynamics. In his gruff voice George fed her questions and each time struck the jackpot:

"Gracie, did the nurse ever happen to drop you on your head when you were a baby?"

"Oh, no, we couldn't afford a nurse; my mother had to do it."

Demand for the pair soared, as did their monetary compensation. George liked the idea of being able to afford higher-quality cigars and from that day on happily tolerated Gracie's lighthearted quips insulting everything from his vocal talent to his virility. He even wrote many of the jokes for her. But then, Burns was always a savvy fellow. He once recalled for me how back in his days as a stand-up comic on the Orpheum vaudeville circuit, if he ever flopped in a particular town, rather than revamp the act, on his next pass through he simply adopted a new name.

Oddly enough, though both Burns and Allen were established stage actors, Gracie initially suffered from mike fright. To help calm her nerves, spectators were herded into the radio studio, so that the atmosphere was more like that of a vaudeville show. From then on, she was fine. She wasn't the only former vaudevillian to find the silence of the studio daunting. A decade earlier, when Ed Wynn starred in "The Perfect Fool" on New York's WJZ, he asked his announcer to round up everyone from electricians to cleaning ladies. In order to carry on, he *had* to hear people laugh at his jokes.

Gracie's comedic talent was her manner of delivering malapropisms, non sequiturs, and perfectly circuitous logic in a

The Burnses and me with Clark Gable (left). Gracie may have portrayed a dizzy dame publicly, but privately she was extremely sharp-witted. *Photo by Jack Albin*

girlish voice and with a sweet smile. She always kept audiences (and George) off balance, wondering, *Is she serious?*—especially when she talked about her oddball family. For instance, there was her brother Willy, who "wears a high collar to cover the appendicitis scar on his neck."

Burns: "Grace, your appendix is around your waist."

Allen: "I know, but Willy is so ticklish, they had to operate up there."

In 1950 the couple took their show to television. At the time I was too involved with other commitments, and so the

Happy Postman was retired, no doubt giving him something else to moan about.

Burns and Allen had been married for thirty-eight years when Gracie passed away from a heart attack in 1964. It was apparent to me that they had a good marriage and loved each other very deeply. A duo between whom there was no love lost, however, was Bud Abbott and Lou Costello. They got along well enough at first, but from 1945 on they barely spoke to each other. Yet both were such pros, the mutual animosity wasn't at all evident in their unforgettable comedies and if anything, might have given their professional rapport a sharpened edge.

Though Costello was constantly looking to replace his partner, I think that deep down inside he knew he'd never find a better straight man. It was true that Bud liked to drink, but he had impeccable timing and was highly disciplined, never stealing gags from Lou. Despite the acrimony and their recurrent separations, they remained in professional wedlock for over a quarter century—perhaps because each feared that without the other, oblivion beckoned.

Before merging in 1931 neither Abbott nor Costello had what you would call a glorious past. Bud dropped out of school when he was ten, worked as assistant cashier at Brooklyn's Casino Theatre, saved enough money to operate several burlesque houses with his brother, and became widely known as a first-rate straight man on the burlesque circuit. But somehow he wound up back behind the register at the Casino, which is where he met Lou.

Costello had been a luckless prizefighter and Hollywood stuntman, with the lumps and bruises to prove it. Eight years Abbot's junior, he was teamed with another comic. I don't know how factual this is, but the story goes that when Lou's partner took ill, Abbott offered to fill in for him and never relinquished the spot.

Abbott and Costello were the epitome of opposites attracting, even down to their physical size: Lou was paunchy

(Left to right) Abbott, rabbit, and Costello. By the mid-1940's Bud and Lou barely spoke to each other. But mutual animosity didn't diminish their comedy's brilliance.

and short, Bud was lean and nearly a foot taller. To top it off, their personalities were a combustible mixture. But their on-stage chemistry was another story. Both were gifted comedians, with Abbott playing the brainy one, and Costello, the infantile stooge who needed constant attention and frequent scoldings. Together they went from earning one hundred twenty-five dollars a week on the burlesque circuit to making twelve thousand dollars weekly appearing on radio and in nightclubs. This was even before the first of their many films, in 1941.

I can't say which man I liked better, although you couldn't help but feel sorry for Costello. So many tragedies befell him, people privately started referring to him as "Hard Luck Lou." In March 1943, with their radio program at its peak, he came down with rheumatic fever, forcing a premature end to the season. Confined to bed for months, no sooner did Costello finally recover than came a blow mightier than any he'd ever taken in the ring. I'll never forget that day.

We were in rehearsal at NBC's Hollywood studios for the 1943–1944 premiere, when around five o'clock Lou's manager was summoned to the telephone. It was Costello's sister on the line, bearing the tragic news that his eleven-month-old son, Butch, had drowned in the family swimming pool. Lou raced home, then phoned an hour before airtime to say he would be back in time for the broadcast. Evidently Butch had planned to listen to his father on the radio for the first time that evening, and heartbroken Lou was determined not to let the child down.

The premiere went on at seven o'clock as scheduled, Costello bantering with Abbott as if nothing were the matter. You can imagine the misty eyes among the cast, which included me, Sid Fields, Frank Nelson, Artie Auerbach, and guest starlet Lana Turner. As soon as we signed off, Lou broke down sobbing, and Bud had to quietly explain to the studio and radio audiences about the tragedy. Many of those close to him insist that from that day on, Costello was never the same, consumed by sorrow. And his wife, Anne, racked by guilt that she hadn't been home when the accident happened, took to drink.

Abbott, too, had a string of bad luck, being diagnosed as having epilepsy. Some say that his fear of suffering a seizure while performing contributed to his escalating intake of alcohol. By the time his and Costello's partnership dissolved for good, Bud had accrued so many tax debts that he was forced to sell his home and property, the Internal Revenue Service confiscating most of his income from the duo's salad days. But the tragedy of their private lives in no way diminishes the brilliance of their humor.

Many people remember Bud and Lou from their movies and TV show, which were chock full of slapstick and pratfalls. On radio, though, their comedy was quite cerebral, with word-plays their stock-in-trade. Some of the bits were merely extensions of those they had performed back in the 1930s, such as: "Hey, Abbott, where do all the little bugs go in the winter?"

"Search me."

"No thanks, I just wanted to find out."

In many of their classic routines Lou asks Bud a question, only to receive a long-winded, convoluted answer that leaves him more confused than before. The two become increasingly exasperated: Abbott can't fathom his partner's inability to grasp what to him is a basic concept, and though he always maintains his composure, his throaty voice sounds more pained with each successive explanation. Costello, meantime, is clutching his throat in frustration, as Bud's lengthy explanations lead Lou deeper and deeper into the morass.

Their most famous of this type is "Who's on first?" Since most readers have probably heard it so many times they can repeat it verbatim, let me cite an example in the same vein: "Flee fly flu."

Here Abbott lectures Costello, smitten with a cold, on how to steer clear of the flu:

Abbott: "The only way to avoid the flu is to flee."

Costello: "What's that?"

Abbott: "I mean that you've got to flee flu."

Costello: "Flee, flu? What kind of talk is that?"

Abbott: [*Impatiently*] "I'm trying to tell you that the only way to be free from flu is to flee when flu flies. When there's flu, everybody flees."

Costello: "Everybody flees?"

Abbott: "Certainly. I flee, you flee, he flees, she flees—"
Costello: "What have I got, a cold or a flea circus?"
Abbott: "You don't understand. To avoid the flu, you've gotta flee."

This signed photo to me from Abbott and Costello reads: "To Mel, the finest radio artist I know. Thanks a million for all you've done for the Abbott and Costello program. From your pals, Lou Costello, Bud Abbott."

Costello: "I've got a flea? Get him off of me, then. Get him off. I don't want him on me!"

This continues until finally Bud believes he's made a break-through: "I'm trying to tell you that to avoid the flu, you must flee. The only way to be free from flu is to flee when flu flies."

Costello: "Oh! You mean that to be free from flu, I've got to flee when flu flies! And the flea that flies has got nothing to do with the flu!"

Abbott: "Now you've got it!"

"Now I've got it?" Costello is ready to self-combust. *"I don't even know what I'm talking about!"*

Methodically Abbott keeps trying to enlighten his thoroughly befuddled partner about the spread of infection, asking, "Do you realize that germs travel at the speed of light? Now, one little sneeze—"

Costello selects that moment to unwittingly illustrate Bud's point, erupting with a volcanic wet one.

"'There you are!" Abbott exclaims. "There you are! The germs are off! They've already traveled from California to Maine. They are now crossing the Atlantic!"

"I didn't even say good-bye to them."

"At this very minute," Bud informs Lou, "someone in Europe is catching your cold." Before he completes the sentence, a telephone rings. Costello answers. It's me at the other end, as an enraged German screaming incomprehensibly into the receiver, climaxing the garbled tirade with a tremendous Teutonic *"A-choo!"*

Another of my characters on the show required a thick Scottish brogue. He was Botsford Twink, who lived in Bud and Lou's apartment building; unfortunately for him, on the ground floor. Whenever someone pressed the button for admittance to the entranceway, Twink yelled in annoyance, "Get yer finger off the buzzer! Yer usin' up the *electercity!*"

Appearing regularly on their show in a variety of roles provided me with an invaluable education. When I wasn't reading from my script, I'd watch them, marveling at their comedic timing and intuition. If Costello, the incorrigible one, started ad-libbing to an extreme, Abbott, the brainy one, subtly led him back on course by snapping, "Talk sense, Costello." And when Lou moaned his patented "I'm a *ba-a-a-d* boy" or shrieked, "Hey Abbott-t-t-t!" he had the listeners in the palm of his hand.

They were so attuned to each other, you'd never know they never socialized. Finally, three decades after they started together, the pair split up in 1957. Two years later Lou was dead of a heart attack, his wife going just months afterward, also of a heart attack. Bud died in 1974. I consider myself privileged to have witnessed them at top form.

Mexican accents were among the first I perfected as a youth, and I got plenty of mileage out of them on "The Judy Canova Show," which ran for ten years. Judy may not be as well remembered today as Burns-Allen and Abbott-Costello, but during the 1940s she was a bona fide star. Shortly after she bowed on CBS in 1943, thousands of faddish college girls took to wearing their hair in pigtails, in imitation of the "queen of the hillbillies," as Canova was called.

But Judy wasn't any more of a hillbilly than Gracie Allen was a dizzy dame. In real life she was Julia Etta, from Jacksonville, Florida. Her checkered career included Broadway appearances as the Singing Canovas, with her sister Anne and brother Zeke. She left the trio to work in films, but the down-home-gal image stuck, despite her attempts over the years to ditch it. Judy was actually a fine singer with a great range, but in character she vocalized with a nasal twang and a shrill yodel. And although she retained just a trace of a southern drawl, it was exaggerated for her comedy show. Together we played a couple of bucolic hillbillies, Maw and Paw, who . . . talked . . . real . . . slow . . . like, and raised preoccupation with minutiae to a conversational fine art.

I was also Roscoe E. Wortle, a pesky traveling salesman who always greeted Judy, "Hello, girlie, remember me?" in the same slobbering voice I would later use for the cartoon cat Sylvester. Another character of mine, Pedro the gardener, became such a listeners' favorite, he practically stole the show.

From his lethargic manner of speaking and his confounding illogic, you'd have thought the hours spent digging and weeding under the blazing sun had turned Pedro's gray matter to guacamole. "Thirty days hacienda," went one example of his south-of-the-border philosophy, "April, June, and sombrero. All the rest have thirty-one, except Gypsy Rose Lee. And everybody knows what she had, no?"

Pedro had an especially hard time mastering infant care and regularly plied Judy with ridiculous questions, such as this one regarding diaper-box instructions:

"They said to take the diaper off the infant and throw eet away," he tells her. "Lucky for me there was someone there to catch heem. . . ."

And the Mexican's ideas about infant nutrition would have horrified Dr. Benjamin Spock:

"I fed scrambled eggs with Tabasco sauce to the baby."

"Did you burp him?" Judy asks anxiously.

"No, he burped heemself. . . ."

Pedro's most famous phrase was "Pardon me for talking een your face, señorita!"—which he always blurted while Judy was in midsentence. Its origin is quite interesting, stemming back a few years to when Estelle and I were building our first house.

With Noel growing in leaps and bounds, it was only a matter of time before our apartment on Alta Vista Boulevard grew too cramped. So in 1940 we purchased a plot of land in Playa Del Rey, a moderately priced beachfront community just several miles south of Ocean Park, where Estelle and I had met. Charlie Chaplin lived nearby, but otherwise it was sparsely populated; Bel Air and Pacific Palisades were still the exclusive areas that attracted Hollywood stars.

My wife and I designed the home. Our method for mapping out dimensions would have drawn flak from any contractor worth his T square: We'd be visiting friends or relatives, and Estelle would comment, "You know, Mel, this living room would be the perfect size for our next home." So we'd excuse ourselves momentarily and, not having a tape measure handy, measure the distance from wall to wall in footsteps.

As haphazard as it seems, the house turned out just lovely, overlooking the Pacific Ocean and contoured to the land's steep incline. It was a modern structure with five floors, including a downstairs game room drenched gold with sunlight. And we landscaped it with ice plants and climbing geraniums. In all, a simply wonderful home.

What do blueprints and ice plants have to do with Pedro? This: One of the workers who laid the house's foundation was a talkative fellow named José, with whom I spent many hours going over plans and checking on his progress.

"Pardon me for talking een your face, señor Blanc," he said to me one sultry afternoon, "but thees ees a lot of work for one fellow to do in one day, *I theenk.*" I always loved listening to the peculiarities in people's speech, and José's presented a bumper crop. *Boy,* I thought, *his way of speaking can be turned into a great character.* Actually I was able to utilize José's fractured English for several characters: Speedy Gonzales, the Frito Bandito, the Little Mexican on "The Jack Benny Program," and Pan Pancho.

The latter was from one of radio's most listened-to Westerns, "The Cisco Kid," based loosely on the O. Henry character from "The Caballero's Way." Cisco was a Mexican outlaw, but the show's producers preferred promoting him as a prairie Robin Hood who robbed from the rich and gave to the poor. Pancho was his overnourished sidekick, so skilled with a bullwhip, he could probably paint a picture of a tumbleweed with it and not fudge a stroke.

There was something inherently unjust about their partnership: Cisco got all the pretty señoritas, while Chico, as he called Pancho, got only indigestion. He did, however, get to open each show with the shouted warning, "Ceesco! The sheriff, he ees getting closer!" With that, the two would spring atop their trusty horses Diablo and Loco, to roam the Western trail and unfailingly, to ride off into the sunset.

The show originally aired in 1942 with Jackson Beck and Louis Sorin in the lead roles, then was revived four years later

Judy Canova (left) and cast: (left to right) Joe Kearns, Sheldon Leonard, me, Ruby Dandridge, and versatile Verna Felton. *Photo Courtesy of Charles Stumpf*

with Jack Mather and a dear friend of mine, Harry Lang, as their successors. When Harry suffered a major heart attack, he asked me to be his substitute. I did so, but only after insisting that my wages be sent to him. I stayed with "The Cisco

Kid" for several years, and throughout my friend's convalescence, never took a penny. Harry remembered that till the day he died.

Jack Mather was splendid to work with; a great kidder. We used to joke around in character during rehearsals all the time, resulting in one of Pancho's biggest laugh-getters:

First there is the sound of gunshots, then Cisco inquiring worriedly, "Pancho, did they hit you? Are you shot?"

To which his sidekick replies, "I dunno. Gimme a glass of water, and I see eef I *leak.*"

Pancho didn't quite rival the popularity of Pedro on Judy Canova's show, the cast of which included many of my closest pals: Hans Conried as Mr. Hemingway, the terminally complaining houseguest; Sheldon Leonard as Joe Crunchmiller, Judy's Brooklyn boyfriend; and black comedienne Ruby Dandridge as Geranium the maid. The character Liz Pierce was portrayed by Verna Felton, one of the most versatile of all radio actresses. A matronly woman with a soft, kindly face, she and I appeared on many of the same programs, such as Jack Benny's, "Point Sublime," and "The Tommy Riggs and Betty Lou Show."

It was a terrific bunch, and Judy herself was delightful, the exact opposite of Al Jolson.

In fairness to the man called the World's Greatest Entertainer, when I joined his CBS show in 1938, Jolie's "The Lifebuoy Program" was on the verge of cancellation. And not without reason. It was an insipid variety-show hodgepodge. Hearing Jolson sing was still a treat, but the comedy segments (using a vaudeville colloquialism here) were *to die.* Just awful. Occasionally Al was joined by guest stars talented enough to rescue the sorry material, but most of the skits were dull, dull, dull.

Jolson knew this, and it irked him. You have to remember, here was a stage and screen star of great esteem who, for some reason, had never succeeded in radio. "Lifebuoy," in fact, was his fourth shot, following a trio of brief, failed stints on NBC.

Not only did this frustrate him, it had to shake his confidence, which was not helped by the fact that his ten-year marriage to former Ziegfeld girl Ruby Keeler was on the rocks. I personally never had any problems with Jolson but witnessed firsthand how unpleasant he could be.

With ratings dwindling, he attempted to monopolize creative control. Those who held differing opinions usually suffered swift humiliation. "Do you have a million dollars?" he would condescendingly bark. "Well, *I* do." Luckily for Al, he held on to his money longer than he did his radio show.

One thing, though, about Jolson's fierce convictions; he could be a loyal friend. One time I happened to overhear him on the telephone with someone from the show's sponsor. From what I gathered, they were discussing me; specifically, one of my characters, who sputtered when he talked. It was probably a Sylvester or Roscoe E. Wortle prototype. Just why, I don't know, but apparently the voice rubbed the sponsor the wrong way.

"Take him off?" I heard Jolson say indignantly. "No way." The conversation bounced back and forth until finally he issued an ultimatum: "If he goes, I go!" That was the end of that. Lifebuoy Soap knew damn well that their hotheaded star wasn't bluffing.

Still, cast morale was pretty low. To liven up the proceedings, I'd cut up with regular Martha Raye, who at the time was one of the busiest comediennes in Hollywood. How fitting that today she's a TV spokeswoman for denture cream, because we used to affectionately call her Mouth. My God, was it huge! I guess it helped her to sing, though, because she was a marvelous vocalist who was warbling professionally by the time she was just fifteen. That was before she took her stage name from a phone book, when she was still Margie Yvonne Reed from Montana.

Martha and I used to warm up the studio audience before the show, clowning around and dancing, groping each other. We were just kidding, of course, but the audience ate it up. Come to think of it, they seemed to enjoy the warm-up a good deal more than they did "The Lifebuoy Program" itself, which was canned during the 1939–1940 season.

Though I felt bad for Al, I wasn't worried about my own circumstances. In addition to my steady work at Warner Bros., I'd begun another lengthy association: with Jack Benny, whose Sunday-night program was as popular as Jolson's wasn't. Of all my radio memories the fondest come from my nearly thirty years with Jack, to this day the finest comedian ever to stand behind a microphone.

CHAPTER

7

Me 'n' Jack

Jack Benny was six years past his fabled thirty-nine when I joined the cast of his top-rated NBC radio show in 1939. The last time I'd seen him, from a seat in Portland's Orpheum Theatre, he was still going under the moniker Ben K. Benny, interspersing jokes with playing the violin. Now here I was working for him. It was hard to believe.

In the decade and a half since his Orpheum appearances, Benny had become a vaudeville sensation, at one point setting a house record by playing eight straight weeks at the Los Angeles Orpheum. Upon the advent of talking motion pictures, Benny transferred his talents from the stage to the screen, like so many of his vaudeville colleagues. But it was on radio that he would establish himself nationally.

America first heard Jack Benny on a 1932 Ed Sullivan broadcast. "Ladies and gentlemen," he said into the microphone, "this is Jack Benny talking. There will be a slight pause while you say, 'Who cares?' " Apparently both audience and sponsors did care, because two months later Jack was starring in his own show. It was an out-of-the-gate smash, consistently finishing near or at the top of the ratings.

Were it not for a family connection, I might never have gotten to audition for Benny. Estelle and I were dining with her parents one night when I remarked that of any radio show, the one I wanted to be on most was "The Jell-O Program," as it was then known. After broadcasting from New York for several years, the program now originated from Hollywood.

As Mrs. Rosenbaum set down her napkin, she said, "Mrs. Benny's mother happens to be a dear old friend of mine. Perhaps I can ask her to tell Mr. Benny that you do voices and would like a tryout." What good luck! But when Benny's mother-in-law, Mrs. Marks, asked him about giving me a test performance, he declined, explaining politely that he didn't do such things. I'm sure he figured this Mel Blanc fellow was just another talentless hopeful trying to break into showbiz.

I was very tenacious during those lean times; had to be. Boldly I contacted Benny's secretary, Burt Scott.

"I'm the guy Mrs. Marks told Jack about," I said earnestly, "and I'd really like to audition for him."

Scott was more sympathetic than most men in his position and promised he'd bring up my name again to his employer. "If we need another voice-man, maybe you'll get a shot." "But," he added, "I can't give you any assurances."

Sure enough, before the 1939 season, Scott called back to say that Mr. Benny would like to hear my stuff. "Be at the studio today at three o'clock."

While hustling over to Hollywood Radio City, I silently practiced my repertoire. I was ushered into a room where Burt Scott was waiting. A moment later the door opened, and Jack walked in. Unlike many Hollywood stars, who could be aloof and brusque, he shook my hand cordially. "Okay, Mel," he said, "let's see what you can do."

I voiced several dialects, ending with Porky Pig, my best-known character at the time. "How did I d— uh-d— uh-d—, uh, so how was I?" Jack howled with laughter, alternating between slapping his side and running a hand through his graying brown hair. As I would learn, he was not only a great comic but a comedy connoisseur; if something struck his funny bone, sometimes he laughed so hard that he'd collapse to the floor.

"That's great!" he enthused. "Listen, I need this voice . . ." He described what he had in mind: a ferocious polar bear, to guard his valuables. This was a fictitious scenario, of course. On the air Benny portrayed himself as a skinflint who stashed his money in an underground vault protected by a guard and more locks than a Manhattan apartment.

". . . So anyway, I thought it'd be funny to have a polar bear down there as well. Can you imitate one?"

Thinking to myself, *I've had some strange requests before, but . . .* , I nonetheless said, "Sure, Mr. Benny. He'd probably sound like this." I proceeded to emit a roar so savage, I nearly frightened myself.

Jack went into convulsions again before regaining his composure and declaring I was to be on the following week's show.

Benny further promoted his alleged cheapness by installing a combination lock on his refrigerator and a pay telephone in his living room, but in reality he was an extremely generous man who performed benefit shows at the drop of a hat and took a sincere interest in others' problems. Neither was he a Scrooge when it came to sharing the limelight, which ultimately was the key to his show's success. Most top bananas evoked laughs at the expense of their supporting players: the stooges, as they were known in the trade. Not Jack. More often than not the joke was on him, either through his own self-effacing quips or ribbing from a cast member. Then Benny would blurt, "Now cut that out!"

Jack deliberately embodied his on-the-air character with all human shortcomings—pettiness, vanity, stinginess—imbuing him with sympathetic charm. In addition, he granted his fellow actors the freedom to develop their own distinctive personas, working closely with his writers to ensure that the material suited each actor's identity and voice quality. He was a uniquely self-assured performer.

As a result, the Benny-show company became a virtual extended family, not only among ourselves, but in the minds of the audience as well.

One cast member *was* family: Jack's wife Mary Living-stone, the former Sadie Marks. They met when she was just fourteen years old, at a Jewish Passover seder in Vancouver, British Columbia. Benny attended with fellow vaudevillians the Marx Brothers, who happened to be distantly related to Sadie's family. It was only on arriving that he discovered "the party" to which Zeppo Marx had invited him was a religious observance. Don't you just wish video cameras had been invented then, so that someone could have recorded the evening for posterity? Imagine: a seder with Groucho, Harpo, Zeppo, Chico, and Jack Benny. It's supposed to be a fairly solemn ritual, with prayer, readings, and singing, but I can't imagine anyone remained straight-faced for too long, especially with the traditional imbibing of all that wine.

Benny, however, had a sweetheart back in Los Angeles and paid the young girl no mind; though he did fancy her older sister, Ethel. Four years later he and Sadie met again, at the May Company department store in downtown L.A., where she sold hosiery. Jack walked up to the counter to purchase a pair of stockings for his lady friend but realized he had no idea what size she wore.

"Gee, I don't know," he pondered aloud, while his eyes roved over the attractive, dark-haired salesgirl. "Actually, she's about your size."

Sadie lifted her skirt, giving Benny a magnificent view of her leg, and suddenly all thoughts of the girlfriend vanished. "Would you like to join me for lunch?" he asked impetuously. A courtship began, and within a year they were wed. Sadie not only became Jack's marriage partner, she eventually became his onstage partner as well and in 1934 joined the radio-program cast. She always claimed that performing made her jittery, and indeed, she did have a nervous habit of dropping each page of her script to the floor instead of shuffling it to the back. By show's end the studio was blanketed with white sheets.

But Mary Livingstone, as she was now known, was a natural comedienne. With her brassy voice and caustic delivery she proved a perfect foil for Jack. Interestingly, she didn't play his wife, although the couple's chance meeting at the department store was loosely recreated on her very first episode.

"Hey, you get a lot of strange customers in here, don't you," Benny observed.

Retorted Livingstone, "Aw, you're just self-conscious."

Before and after the show they were an adoring pair, pecking each other on the cheek and lovingly calling each other doll. But once positioned in front of a microphone, Mary's character taunted Jack about everything, from his miserliness to his miserable violin playing. Benny's favorite moment in the show's twenty-three-year history belongs to his wife. And all she did was to utter three words.

Announcer Don Wilson, a well-known classical-music buff, was engaged in a conversation about opera with guest Dorothy Kirsten.

"Well, Mr. Wilson," said the famous New York Metropolitan Opera soprano, "didn't you think in the aria 'Un Bel di Vedremo' that the strings played the *con molto* exceptionally fine, with great *sostenuto?*"

Jack didn't know a *sostenuto* from an antipasto but wanted to enter the discussion.

"Well, I thought—"

"*Oh, shut up.*" Mary cut him off with the finality of a Joe Louis sock to the jaw. The audience shrieked with laughter, and Jack could be found in his familiar pose, doubled over and gasping for breath.

About the only cast member to play fall guy to Benny was portly, silver-throated Don Wilson, a former sportscaster from Colorado. He joined Jack's show around the same time as Mary, but unlike many program announcers he was scripted into the plots.

Benny constantly chided Don about his girth, cheekily asserting that he'd made Wilson "the biggest announcer in radio." Actually Don stood six foot two and weighed a relatively modest two hundred thirty pounds. But he handled the digs with affable good humor and frequently targeted Jack with some stinging barbs of his own. Once asked to name his favorite radio personality, Wilson answered poker-faced, "Fred Allen," Benny's chief competitor. Then Don let out one of his ringing laughs.

He was a splendid announcer, reciting the six flavors of Jell-O gelatin with such relish, listeners suspected he snuck whole bowlfuls during breaks. However, he did have a tendency to flub lines, which inspired Bea Benaderet to organize a betting pool.

"Say, Mel, wanna get in on this?" she asked me before one show.

"What are you betting on?"

"Which line Don'll f**k up tonight."

His funniest miscue was the time he mispronounced journalist Drew Pearson's name as "Drear Pooson." Don continued reading sheepishly, the rest of us covering our faces with our scripts, cackling. And sound technician Eugene Twombly nearly knocked over whichever effect he was setting up. But Don hadn't heard the last on this, thanks to our quick-thinking writers.

Later in the program Jack was to ask actor Frank Nelson, "Excuse me, are you the doorman?" Nelson—famous for his unctuous "Yeeeeesssss?"—always played a huffy, insulting salesman or server of some kind. He was to reply sarcastically, "Who do you think I am in this red uniform, Nelson Eddy?" Instead, he responded indignantly, "Who do you think I am, *Drear Pooson?*"

Secondary cast members came and went over the years, but the nucleus of the Benny show remained virtually intact until its final 1953–1954 season; a testament to the mutual admiration, affection, and respect we shared. Phil Harris, who always addressed Benny as "Jackson," played the hard-drinking, fast-living glamor-boy bandleader and was a fine comedian in his own right. He and his wife, shapely blond singer/actress Alice Faye, had their own NBC comedy-variety program, which ran for eight seasons.

There was a succession of vocalists, but none stayed longer than Dennis Day, born Eugene Patrick McNulty, a baby-faced Irish tenor. It was always suspected that Mary Livingstone hired him more for his comic ability than his vocal talent. I remember him and the orchestra leader battling constantly because of missed cues, Day blaming the man with the baton, Mahlon Merrick, and vice versa. His character, however, was a meek little lamb with an overprotective mother, a role portrayed to perfection by Verna Felton. Braying like a lady marine drill sergeant, she constantly chided Benny about his alleged mistreatment of her allegedly gifted son. And whenever Jack attempted to apologize, she stridently cut him off with "Ehhhhh, *shuddap!*"

Two years before I came on board, the show enlisted a black vaudeville veteran named Eddie Anderson. Initially he was hired for a one-shot as a Pullman railroad porter, but Jack fell in love with Eddie's gravelly voice and wanted him added full-time to the cast. "You're a natural for radio," he told him, and the writers came up with the role of Rochester Van Jones, Benny's valet. Anderson attributed his peculiar vocal quality to throat strain suffered as a twelve-year-old newspaper hawker in Oakland. Off mike, it was deeper but just as raspy.

The Rochester character has absorbed much criticism over the years as a negative black stereotype and is usually spoken about in the same breath as the shiftless Andy and the shifty Kingfish from "Amos 'n' Andy," perhaps the most popular radio program of all time. How popular? In its early years as a fifteen-minute Monday-through-Friday NBC serial, the New York Telephone Company reported a sharp decrease in calls between seven o'clock and seven-fifteen. Amos and Andy were Harlem, New York, Negroes who ran the Fresh-Air Taxicab Company, so named because of its rickety, roofless jalopy.

Personally, I think most objections to "Amos 'n' Andy" stem from the fact that actors Freeman Gosden and Charles Correll were white. Having appeared on their show numerous times in an assortment of roles, I got to know both men well, and neither had a racist bone in his body. They'd been struggling entertainers for years until Chicago radio station WGN hired them to develop a series based on two black men, Sam and Henry, in 1926. The colorful characters, to be renamed Amos Jones and Andrew H. Brown, picked up such a devoted local listenership that three years later the show went national, on NBC Red.

Admittedly Andy and Kingfish were not exemplary role models. Neither were many radio characters representing other ethnic groups, but portrayals of Jews, Italians, and Irish that could be construed as defamatory were generally countered by more favorable characterizations. This wasn't true for blacks, in motion pictures as well as radio, and from that perspective I can certainly understand people's protests.

Eddie Anderson's Rochester was no Andy or Kingfish, however. He is often attacked for being subservient. Yet listen to "The Jack Benny Program" and you'll see that it's Jack, not his valet, who plays the fall guy. Like Mary Livingstone and the rest of the troupe, Rochester remarks sarcastically about Benny's execrable violin playing, his vanity, and of course his cheapskatedness.

A classic Rochester-Benny exchange pits the two of them on the golf links, where Benny insists on searching for a lost ball.

"We're never going to find it," Rochester says wearily. "Why don't you just give up?"

"Give up?" Benny is indignant. "Rochester, supposing Columbus gave up? He'd never have discovered America. Then what would have happened?"

"We'd be looking for that ball in Spain, boss."

As Eddie himself always pointed out, Rochester was no mere caricature or stereotype, he was a multidimensional, dignified, and very funny man. Radio history seems to omit the fact that forty and fifty years ago most blacks took great pride in seeing one of their own star on a national radio show. After broadcasts, Anderson and I frequently headed to a Sunset Boulevard bar for drinks, and I got to know him quite well. He was a warm, sensitive person, and the disparaging comments had to wound his feelings. It was as if his being a trailblazer had somehow made him a traitor.

Such claims hurt Jack as well, who was extremely sensitive avoiding racial humor of any kind. Other radio comedians frequently milked ethnic jokes for laughs, but Benny instructed his writers to forgo that route for fear of offending anyone. Racism was so foreign to Jack, he sometimes had a difficult time acknowledging its existence, so typical of his surprisingly guileless nature.

One time he and Eddie traveled together to a southern town; in Louisiana, I think it was. Checking into a hotel, they were confronted by the type of ugliness this country has been trying to eradicate ever since.

"I'm sorry, Mr. Benny," the desk clerk said, "but we don't have a room for him." Scowling, he pointed at Anderson.

Jack didn't understand the implication and asked, perplexed, "No room? But I made a reservation. Why no room?"

Because he's a Negro, he was informed.

Benny was incensed. "Because he's a Negro? You've got to be joking."

"I'm sorry, sir, but he can't stay here."

"Well, then I can't stay here either," Jack said through clenched teeth. "Come on, Eddie, let's go." The two of them stormed out the door. I think it was the first time Jack had encountered such blatant racism, and he was outraged. It was all he talked about for days and days.

Jack, Mary, Eddie, Don, Phil, and Dennis comprised the core of the cast. Then there were me, Artie Auerbach, Sam

Hearn, Sara Berner, Bea Benaderet, and Sheldon Leonard. Auerbach had been a New York *Daily Mirror* photographer and played Mr. Kitzle, the heavily accented Jewish frankfurter salesman who peddled hot dogs with a "peekle in the middle mit der mustard on top." Hearn, a veteran radio actor, was

Jack Benny and the "gang": (left to right) Eddie "Rochester" Anderson, Dennis Day, Phil Harris, Mary Livingstone, Benny, Don Wilson, and me.
Photo Courtesy of Charles Stumpf

an audience favorite for his portrayal of a lazy rube purported to reside in a Calabasas, California, vineyard.

Berner and Bea Benaderet drew laughs as NBC telephone operators Mabel Flapsaddle and Gertrude Gearshift, always gossiping derisively about Jack. And Leonard's character was identified only as "the tout," the kind of shady oddsmaker you'd find loitering at the Hollywood Park racetrack. Jack, however, constantly ran into him at the most unlikely places, such as a train station, where the tout whispered tips about which train to ride: "Psst! The El Capitan will beat the Chief into Kansas City by three lengths." Or: "Take my word for it, the Super Chief is a *sleeper.*" It was, too: a sleeping car.

Beginning in 1947 erudite film star Ronald Colman and his wife Benita Hume appeared frequently as the Bennys' next-door neighbors. Like Phil Harris, they were also awarded their own NBC program.

Fred Allen was not a cast member but might as well have been; even when he wasn't guesting on the show, his spirit was present. He and Benny engaged in an on-the-air exchange of insults that mushroomed into what the public was led to believe was a full-blown conflict.

Actually the two were fast friends, with strikingly similar backgrounds: both born the same year, both former vaudeville performers, both entered radio in 1932, and both worked their wives into their immensely popular programs. Allen was married to Portland Hoffa, whose screechy voice was once described by her husband as sounding like "two slate pencils mating." One of the few differences between Benny's and Allen's careers was that while Jack adapted relatively painlessly to television in the 1950s, Fred openly disdained the new medium, appearing only as a sometime emcee and "What's My Line?" panelist. He died in 1956.

The alleged feud began inadvertently on December 30, 1936, when Allen indirectly took a swipe at Benny's musical aptitude. Jack, in turn, needled Fred on his next broadcast, and the battle was on, much to their mutual delight. Both comedians were savvy enough to know that contrived enmity could be parlayed into a publicity bonanza. It was, reaching such a crescendo by the following spring that an announcement was made that the two would don gloves in a boxing match at New York's Pierre Hotel. Naturally the fight never came off, but ratings soared.

Though they shared much in common personally, their on-the-air personas were a study in contrasts. Benny's delivery was measured and deliberate; the Massachusetts-born Allen, on the other hand, practically broke speed limits in a voice nearly as harsh as his wife's. It was great fun whenever Fred came on Jack's program, or vice versa.

I remember one particularly riotous Benny cameo, from Allen's 1946–1947 season finale, in which Jack lost his pants, literally:

It begins innocently enough, with Benny and Allen discussing how some radio shows will not be renewed for the fall season. Fred piques Jack's interest by noting that in order to maintain an audience, several have resorted to giving away prizes.

"You mean, to stay on the air you have to give things away?" Jack asks, gulping.

"Yes."

"I'll *die* first," he declares.

Allen, however, claims that he's decided to host one of those giveaway shows: "King for a Day," a spoof of an actual Mutual Network program called "Queen for a Day." The idea of obtaining something for nothing appeals to Benny's legendary avarice, just as Allen knew it would.

"Well, Fred, as long as I'm here in the studio . . ."

One can imagine him casting a longing glance at a free icebox or washing machine. However, Allen halts him in midthought: "I'm sorry, Jack, professional people cannot participate. It's a rule."

Hmmm, Benny ponders, not easily dissuaded, *giving away things for nothing.*

In the next scene Benny returns as a contestant, adopting the pseudonym Myron Proudfoot. He winds up winning a bevy

of worthless prizes including a free pressing of his trousers
—which are forcibly removed from his person. I've never heard
a studio audience in greater hysterics as Jack stands there in
front of them clad in his underwear, yelling, "Come on now,
Allen, give me my pants!"

"Benny," responds his attacker, "for fifteen years I've been
waiting to catch you like this."

"Allen, you haven't seen *the end* of me!"

"It won't be long now!"

On another venture onto Allen turf, Fred began mercilessly taunting Benny, who replied defensively, "You wouldn't
have said that if my writers were here." It's true that without
the benefit of a script, Jack was no match for the man known
as the King of the Quick Quip, but his lack of ad-libbing ability
was really just another self-perpetuated Benny fallacy. Jack
was a consummate comedian and frequently broke up the
cast with his asides, such as the time he interrupted one of
my monologues to observe dryly, "Say, Mel, you did that pretty
good!"

Jack's most celebrated asset, of course, was his timing.
He believed in allowing a gag to build slowly and could wring
more laughs out of a moment of silence than most of his peers
could from a lengthy soliloquy. Sometimes all he had to say
was an exasperated ". . . Well!" Or "Hmmmm . . ." There is no
better example of Benny's humor than the "your money or
your life" routine, written in 1948 by the talented Milt Josefsberg and John Tackaberry:

Holdup man to Jack: "Your money or your life."

[*L-o-n-g pause.*]

Holdup man: "Look, bud, I said, Your money or your life!"

Jack: [*Testily*] *"I'm thinking it over!"*

Ed Wynn once complimented Benny by observing keenly
that he was the world's greatest at saying things funny, as
opposed to saying funny things.

He was also a tremendous editor who worked tirelessly

with his three- or four-man writing staff. On Monday mornings they began brainstorming the next show and by Tuesday
had hammered out a rough draft. Wednesday and Thursday
were spent polishing, adding, and deleting. Friday night we
rehearsed, often gathered around the piano in the living room
of the Bennys' handsome Beverly Hills home. Jack and the
writers then consulted on revisions, and the full cast returned
the next day. Benny always carefully assessed our reactions
to a bit; if no one was overly enthusiastic, out it went, to be
replaced by something else. It wasn't until the final rehearsal
several hours prior to broadcast that scripts were finalized.

Actually there were two Sunday-evening shows: one at
four o'clock for the East Coast, and one at seven for the West.
Between performances the cast was always invited to Mary's
parents' home for an elaborate buffet. Because Noel was still
an infant when I began working for Jack, I usually begged off
on dinner and dashed home to spend a few hours with my
son. Then it was back to Hollywood Radio City.

In the early 1940s, when my Sunday-evening schedule
included "The Great Gildersleeve," "Baby Snooks," and "Blondie," sometimes I'd simply stay put and study my scripts. If I
finished early, I'd wander over to the studio where Bob Hope
would be putting Jerry Colonna, Blanche Stewart, Barbara Jo
Allen, and the rest of his "Pepsodent Show" players through
rehearsals for their Tuesday-night broadcast.

Hope's rapid delivery was similar to Fred Allen's, but his
painstaking approach and collaboration with his writers was
more like Benny's. He'd rehearse and revise, rehearse and
revise, until he was fully satisfied with the material. What a
kick I used to get out of watching Hope and his famous profile
in action. I recall one especially funny routine he did with his
trumpeter and sidekick, Jerry Colonna:

[*The phone rings.*]
Hope: "Hello?"
Colonna: "Hope, hello, Colonna is this."
Hope: "Colonna, why are you talking backward?"
Colonna: "Put the nickel in upside down."

The Hope and Benny shows were always neck and neck for the radio-ratings lead, along with "Fibber McGee and Molly," "Amos 'n' Andy," "The Charlie McCarthy Show," and "The Fred Allen Show," among others.

I've told you about everyone's contributions to "The Jack Benny Program" except my own. For my first six months with Jack, all I did were the sounds of Carmichael the polar bear and the rackety Maxwell. A roar and a *p-tui*. Frankly, as much as I enjoyed being on the show, it seemed to me I was wasting away there.

So I approached my boss during one Friday rehearsal. "You know, Jack," I said nervously, "I can talk too."

Benny was sympathetic. "Tell you what," he said. "I'll have the writers put something in for you."

And they did. Most were one-shots, but several characters were written into the script regularly. Probably the best-remembered is the Union Depot train caller who announces out of the side of his mouth: "Train leaving on track five for Anaheim, Azusa, and Cuc-amonga!" It doesn't sound like much, but in typical Benny fashion, we used it to set up the audience like bowling pins and then knock them down. Countless gags were based on that line. Taking a cue from Jack, who was so expert at meter and rhythm, we began toying with it, lengthening the pause between "Cuc—" and "—amonga" until audiences practically leaned forward in their seats in anticipation.

The delay was stretched longer and longer, until on one show we inserted a completely different sketch between the first and second syllables. Jack and Mary usually shared a microphone, with everyone else except for Phil Harris congregated around another. I stepped back and waited patiently, watching the studio audience. The tension was so palpable, you could hear nervous giggles. Finally: "—amonga!"

The writers employed that cliff-hanger technique in other ways. For example, a series of public-address announcements are interspersed with dialogue among Jack, Don Wilson, Rochester, Harris, Sheldon Leonard's tout, and Frank Nelson.

First there's a standard "Train leaving on track five for Anaheim, Azusa, and Cuc-amonga." A minute later, with a touch
more urgency, "Train leaving on track five for Anaheim, Azusa,
and Cuc-amonga. Does anybody want to go to Anaheim, Azusa,
or Cuc-amonga?"

"Train leaving on track five for Anaheim, Azusa and Cuc-amonga!"
Gradually the pause between "Cuc—" and "—amonga" was stretched
longer and longer; one time we even inserted a different sketch between
the first and second syllables. *CBS Portrait by Gabor Rona*

Still later, voice quavering: "Train leaving on track five for Anaheim, Azusa, and Cuc-amonga. Aw, come on, *somebody* must wanna go to Anaheim, Azusa, or Cuc-amonga!"

And even *still* later, ready to concede defeat: "Train leaving on track five for Anaheim, Azusa, and Cuc-amonga. Look, we're not asking much. Two of ya, or even one of ya . . . just somebody to keep the engineer company!"

Meanwhile, Jack is being rudely informed by ticket-clerk Nelson that all trains to New York are booked. In a panic Benny shouts, "Well, think, man, think! There must be one train that has room for me!"

And at that moment, verging on hysteria: "Train leaving on track five for Anaheim, Azusa, and Cuc-amonga. Look, there must be five thousand people in this station. Isn't there somebody . . . *anybody?* Aren't there any volunteers? Please, please, please! I'll get fired if I don't get somebody on the train for Anaheim, Azusa, and Cuc-amonga!"

Frustration was a hallmark of many of my Benny-show characters, but none more so than poor beleaguered Professor LeBlanc, Jack's violin instructor. Now, truth be told, Benny was a highly capable violinist. He owned a rare Stradivarius worth many thousands of dollars, practiced two to three hours daily, and performed with dozens of the country's leading orchestras, even duetting with virtuoso Isaac Stern at a Carnegie Hall fund-raiser. But for the purposes of the program, he sawed away wretchedly, either at his "Love in Bloom" theme song or the eight-note musical exercise known as a Kruetzer étude.

To this, his French professor devised insulting rhyming couplets on the order of "Make the notes a little thinner/I don't want to lose my dinner" or "What a pain your fiddle brings on/How I wish it had no strings on"—sung with utter contempt. But Benny remained oblivious of his lack of talent, continuing to fiddle as LeBlanc slow-burned.

The long-suffering professor went to great lengths trying to convince Jack to give up the instrument. In one 1947 radio episode he is present when Rochester accidentally nicks Benny's throat while giving the boss a shave. As soon as Jack exits momentarily, LeBlanc whispers:

"Rochestair . . . the cut on Monsieur Ben-neé's throat; ees eet a bad one?"

"Naw, it's not deep at all. And it's all my fault."

"No, no, Rochestair," he says dejectedly, "eet was my fault. I didn't push your hand *hard* enough."

Each lesson was climaxed by the ringing of an alarm clock the professor carried with him, to spare himself from even one second of ear-damaging overtime. The moment the bell sounded, LeBlanc rejoiced like a condemned man who'd just been granted a stay of execution. "I'm free, free, *free!*" he'd scream before breaking into a jubilant rendition of the "Marseillaise."

Though my roles certainly improved once I accosted Jack in rehearsal that day, I still had to play nonhumans every now and then. One was Jack's parrot, which I was enlisted to voice when our real-life trained bird kept missing its cues. The feathered pet may have been the most vicious needler among the cast, cackling in a singsong, "Benny is a cheapskate, Benny is a cheapskate."

The authenticity of my parrot impression was proved on a ferry excursion Estelle and I took with another couple to Santa Catalina Island. Located off the coast of Long Beach, it's a sunny, lush spot inhabited by many colorful birds. The four of us were taking in the scenery and sunshine when I approached one and said in my parrot voice, "Pretty bird, pretty bird, pretty bird." Casting a sideways glance, it responded, "What are you, a wise guy?"

Eventually I played such a wide range of characters, the writers occasionally tried throwing me curves. I'd peruse the script and read, "Mel answers, using the voice of a Jewish fag." Not surprisingly, that one never made it past the censors. Or: "Jack talks to his goldfish, saying, 'Hello, itty-bitty fishy,' and Mel, as his goldfish, answers him." Never say no, is my motto, so I mouthed the largely inaudible sound of a fish blowing bubbles under water. Another time someone typed in, "Mel whinnies like an English racehorse," for a racetrack scene. This I did by whinnying, then placing an index finger over one nostril and emitting a stuffy British "a-haw." Benny and writers Josefsberg, Tackaberry, Sam Perrin, and George Balzer fell to the floor laughing.

All in a day's work.

The routine that cracked up Jack the most featured a character known both as the Little Mexican and Sy. Demonstrating that in comedy it's not always what you say but how you say it, this mournful man speaks only in monosyllables. For the benefit of the studio audience, I'd wear a serape and a sombrero while performing this minimalistic sketch.

Jack encounters the Little Mexican at the train station and asks, "Excuse me, sir, are you waiting for this train?"

"Sí."

"You're meeting someone on the train?"

"Sí."

"A relative?"

"Sí."

"What's your name?"

"Sy."

"Sy?"

"Sí."

"This relative you're waiting for—is it a woman?"

"Sí."

"Your sister?"

"Sí."

"What's her name?"

"Sue."

"Sue?"

"Sí."

"Does she work?"

"Sí."

"She has a regular job?"

"Sí."

"What does she do?"

"Sew."

"Sew?"

"Sí."

There were several variations on that basic theme, such as the following script. Here Sy graduates to using a full sentence or two and introduces his equally tight-lipped son, also played by me:

"Wanna shake hands?" Jack asks.

"Sí."

"Can I consider you my friend?"

"Sí."

"Will you always help me?"

"Sí. Before you leave, I'd like you to meet my six-year-old son, Thomas."

"Oh, hello, Thomas."

"He's learning to be a musician," Sy tells Benny. "He does a wonderful act on the stage with his sister."

"So, you're a musician, eh, Thomas?"

"Sí."

"Do you have an act?"

"Sí."

"With your sister?"

"Sí."

"What's her name?"

"Sue."

"Sue?"

"Sí."

"What do you do in the act?"

"Saw."

"Saw?"

"Sí."

"Who do you saw?"

"Sue."

"Sue?"

"Sí."

"Now, wait a minute!" Jack says, losing his patience. "Someone put you up to this. Who was it?"

"Me," Sy admits.

"You?"

"Sí."

No matter how much he tried to steel himself, Jack just could not keep from laughing. "I'm not going to break up tonight, Mel," he'd insist before the broadcast. But sure enough, he would. Of course I contributed to his hysterics by always maintaining a heavy-lidded, stoic expression throughout. One glance at my face and it was all over for Benny.

It reached a point where I was responsible for so many of his show's regular characters, Jack offered me a contract, for fear of losing me to another program. Until then, all agreements had been handshakes. At the end of each season he'd ask, "Say, you gonna be with me next year?"

"Sure, if you'll give me a raise and buy me a drink."

"Well, c'mon then, I'll . . . buy you a drink." He'd wink, and we'd both laugh.

Benny was one of the few Hollywood celebrities Estelle and I socialized with. The way I saw it, I spent enough time with my fellow actors in radio stations and animated-film studios and not enough time at home. Besides, whenever I did get talked into attending a party, everyone there discussed nothing but shop. Hell, I heard industry talk all day and night at work; I certainly didn't need to listen to it during my leisure time.

Jack and Mary, on the other hand, loved entertaining and putting in appearances at glittery functions. Though they willingly surrendered their privacy, it sometimes wore on Benny, who appreciated the comparatively quiet lifestyle my family led. He frequently escaped with us to our Big Bear Lake hideaway, located in the San Bernardino Mountains, about two and a half hours east of Los Angeles.

We discovered the vacation spot in 1938 and nine years

later built our own lakeside cabin there. Those readers old enough to remember the so-called Red Scare of the late 1940s will appreciate that its design included a hidden stairway. A lot of good that would have done us in the event of a Soviet "invasion."

Like television series today, radio programs went on hiatus for July and August, and so the Blancs spent many relaxing summers there. We loved the place so much that in 1949 I recorded a musical tribute, "Big Bear Lake," on Capitol Records, and in appreciation was made honorary mayor. The old-timers there have probably regretted it ever since. I don't know how much of a factor my song played in publicizing the area's charms, but Big Bear Lake's population swelled after that; much to some people's chagrin.

The first time Jack accompanied us, he brought along his adopted daughter Joan, fourteen at the time, and a girlfriend of hers named Hanna. We packed my black Cadillac convertible and took Route 18, to afford them the most scenic view. When Jack stepped out of the car, he pretended to wobble as if on legs of rubber. "I've never taken that many hairpin curves before!" he exclaimed, shaking his head. "It's worse than two weeks on the Queen Mary!"

"Would you like some Dramamine, Jack?" I joked. Benny was already in his early fifties, and the 6,700-foot elevation made it somewhat difficult for him to breathe at first. "And I was going to swim across the lake today," he quipped.

So that he, Joan, and Hanna could get acclimated to the thin air, we relaxed that first night, barbecuing some steaks. Around a crackling fire I related folklore such as the Indian legend about how the area had once been stalked by killer bears created by the Sun God to ward off evil spirits. After that, Jack and I took out our violins and proceeded to wreak havoc on a number of classics, Joan accompanying us on ukulele. I no longer practiced much and had a tough time keeping up with Benny, who could play any tune you named. The music filtered across the lake, and before we knew it the back porch was packed with neighbors, each wanting to hear a different song.

"Play 'Love in Bloom!' " someone shouted.

"Do 'I Tawt I Taw a Puddy Tat!' " came another request.

We fiddled until the crowd finally thinned and everyone was ready for bed.

"Tomorrow," I told Benny, "we're going water-skiing."

I was never too athletically inclined, but skiing came as naturally to me as walking. Of course, I couldn't have asked for a better teacher: national champion Elva Swaffor, who also happened to holiday at Big Bear Lake. To entertain Noel and the other children down by the dock, I'd sometimes ski around the seven-and-a-half-mile lake's circumference fully dressed and barely get wet. Or I'd hold the towline with one hand and light a cigarette with the other.

Jack's daughter and her friend were avid skiers, and Benny spent the better part of the afternoon watching us enviously. Suddenly he announced that he wanted to give it a try. "But I don't want to drown," he said worriedly. "What's the biggest life preserver you have?"

I tossed an enormous, twelve-pound Navy flotation collar at him, which Noel, Joan, and Hanna helped him into. "Even Don Wilson couldn't drown with that on," I observed, which seemed to calm his nerves a bit. Following some brief instruction, I handed Jack the baton, climbed into my speedboat, and looked back at Benny, bobbing in the water like a cork. Nearly three dozen people were lined up on the narrow dock, wanting to watch him ski.

They never got the chance. Just as the slackened towline began to tighten, Jack yelped rhetorically, "I don't think I should do this, do you?" With that he let go of the baton, which sped through the water in pursuit of the boat. Thus began and ended the water-skiing career of Jack Benny.

We decided to try fishing instead and drove downtown— all two blocks of it—to obtain a fishing license for Jack. That required a visit to a closet-size establishment called Fred's Sporting Goods. Since Benny was wearing sunglasses and a cap, no one recognized him, including Fred, whose last name was Bowen.

"If you'll just answer some questions," he said to Jack, taking out a form and preparing to fill it out. "Address?"

"One oh oh two North Roxbury Drive, Beverly Hills."

"Hair?"

"Brown," replied Benny.

"Eyes?"

"Robin's-egg blue."

Fred looked up at the stranger, wrinkled his brow, then shrugged and wrote it down.

"Age?"

"Thirty-nine." But of course.

"By the way," Jack asked wryly, "how much is this license going to cost?"

Big Bear Lake, 1949: The helping hand belongs to Benny's daughter, Joan. A few moments later Jack was scurrying out of the water, abruptly ending a skiing career that lasted all of about two minutes.

Four dollars, he was told.

"Hmmm . . . Do you think they'd take three?"

Fred, finally realizing the stranger's identity, did a triple take and stumbled over some fishing poles he kept behind the counter. "Jack Benny!" he shouted. Noel and I laughed heartily, and a sly smile flickered across Jack's face.

That afternoon the five of us ventured out in my fourteen-foot rowboat, which I'd outfitted with a small outboard motor. I know that vessels are traditionally given women's names, but mine? The *Bugs Bunny PTE #2,*"PTE" standing for "Pardon the Expression." We fished all day without a bite and around five o'clock were discouraged enough to pack it in. Suddenly Benny's pole was nearly bent in half. "I've got one!" he yelled. Then his exultation changed to apprehension. "Now what the hell do I do?"

With a little help from Noel, the girls, and I, Jack caught two bluegill that day. Not to mention hay fever.

Of all the performers I've worked with, none has had a greater impact on my life than Jack, whom I counted as my closest friend in all of Hollywood. He was an immensely talented performer, but more than that, he was a selfless person whose friends and admirers were legion. I think it's fair to say that Benny was probably the most beloved man in show business. One of the saddest days of my life was that Thursday, December 26, 1974, I learned of his passing from cancer of the pancreas, less than two months shy of what would have been his eightieth birthday.

He was buried at Hillside Memorial Park in Culver City, California, and entombed in the same mausoleum as Al Jolson and Eddie Cantor. More than two thousand spectators crowded around the glass-walled funeral chapel, where inside sat some three hundred celebrities. Groucho Marx was there, as were Milton Berle, George Jessel, Frank Sinatra, Danny Kaye, Johnny Carson, Henry Fonda—and of course, all of us from the old "gang," gathered together one final time. Fittingly, it was a Sunday.

Flanking me are two show-business giants, Jack Benny (left) and Al Jolson (right). I was a regular on Jolie's short-lived "The Lifebuoy Program" and Benny's long-running radio and TV series.

Wearing a Jewish prayer shawl about his shoulders, George Burns began the eulogy but broke down. He and Jack had been best friends for over half a century. Ironically, just before his fatal illness, Benny was to star in the film *The Sunshine Boys*. Upon his death the part went to Burns, who won an Academy Award for Best Supporting Actor. How appropriate that Jack should have a hand in revitalizing his old friend's career.

Obviously it was a sad afternoon, but one particularly moving line in the eulogy, completed by Bob Hope, brought a smile to my face.

"For a man who was the undisputed master of comedy timing," Hope read in a shaky voice, "you'd have to say that this was the only time when Jack Benny's timing was all wrong. He left us much too soon."

God bless you, Jack.

CHAPTER

8

Fighting the War, Hollywood Style

*I*t was just before eleven o'clock, Sunday morning, and the Benny-show cast was preparing as usual for its evening broadcasts. Suddenly there was a commotion outside: voices shouting and the sound of footsteps running up and down the corridors. A man burst into the studio.

"War! War's broken out!" he yelled, waving his hands. "The Japanese bombed one of our naval bases in Hawaii!"

Stunned, the dozen or so of us dropped our scripts and streamed out the door and into a reception area, where a radio blared scattered details of the surprise attack. ". . . At this time U.S. casualties cannot be confirmed. However, at least one battleship, the *Oklahoma*, has been reported afire, and many aircraft were destroyed on the ground.

"Repeating for those just tuning in: Less than an hour ago Japanese bombers launched an unprovoked attack on the U.S. Pacific Fleet stationed at Pearl Harbor, Oahu . . ."

"Oh my God," an NBC receptionist gasped, sinking into

a chair, "my brother is stationed there!" Tears trickled down her face, and a friend tried to console her.

As we were to learn throughout the afternoon and into the evening, the damage was much worse than initially reported: five battleships and several destroyers sunk, one hundred forty aircraft destroyed, over two thousand dead and more than one thousand wounded. I prayed silently that the young woman's brother was not among the dead.

"Those sneaky, slant-eyed sons of bitches," someone muttered. "On a Sunday morning! Do you believe it? I'll bet half those sailors were getting ready to go to church."

We continued listening to the radio newscaster, unable to speak.

". . . Other U.S. military bases, on Guam, Midway Island, and Wake Island, were also attacked by air. Details are presently sketchy . . ."

I don't recall much else from that day. Like everyone else, I was numb with shock. Although rumblings from Europe and Asia had been growing louder, few Americans were prepared for such a treacherous act of aggression. Especially since the U.S. and Japan had been in the midst of diplomatic negotiations to maintain peace. In fact, an hour *after* the bombing raids, the Japanese ambassador delivered to Secretary of State Cordell Hull a formal reply to a recent U.S. communiqué, as if the attacks had never occurred.

". . . There is some speculation that German planes assisted in the air strike, although this has yet to be confirmed." The information turned out to be unfounded, as did rampant rumors that swarms of Japanese warplanes were about to rake the California coastline. "I've got to get home right away!" one distraught man cried. I didn't believe Japan was bold enough to hit U.S. shores. Still, just to be safe, I phoned Estelle and told her to take Noel to her parents' house, inland. I was concerned because not only did our home sit right on the beach, but two potential enemy targets were just two miles away: the Douglas Aircraft plant and the Mines Field Army airfield. "Wait there until we hear something further," I said tersely.

The next evening we all sat in the Rosenbaums' parlor listening to President Roosevelt's radio address to the nation and to Congress: "Yesterday, December 7, 1941, a date that will live in infamy, the United States of America was suddenly and deliberately attacked by naval and air forces of the Empire of Japan . . ." He asked Congress to pass a declaration of war, and just like that nearly a quarter century of peacetime was shattered. Three hundred thousand Americans would lose their lives in World War II.

Estelle, Noel, and I returned to Playa Del Rey but to a radically different way of life. The first thing my wife did was to purchase yards of dark-brown material for covering the windows. Two months into the war it was reported that a Japanese submarine had shelled the Ellwood oil refinery north of Santa Barbara, and a Navy rear admiral's warnings that other attacks might follow made coast-dwellers nervous, as did U.S. Coast Guard signs posted along the beach:

Be Vigilant
No Landings Are Authorized on This Beach
Immediately Report *Any* Boat Actually Landing Persons on Shore
Here to the Nearest Military or Naval Post
and to the Sheriff and Police Forces

As unsettling as times were, it was heartening to see how citizens pulled together. In Playa Del Rey we set up a community watch, and I was appointed air-raid warden. Two, three times per week the warning siren sounded, meaning it was time for me to don a warden's cap and with flashlight in hand go from house to house calling, "Blackout! Please darken all windows!" Because of the nearby military targets, it was essential everyone comply with the blackout regulations.

My duties completed, I'd frequently head over to the bivouac and sit around telling jokes to the soldiers, some of whom were young enough to be my sons. Japan had caught America unprepared for war, and in the days following Pearl Harbor a mad scramble was on to assemble the military. The local Army base hadn't even set up a cafeteria yet. So, in the interim, Estelle's parents rustled up enough chili to feed . . . well, an army; several plastic tubs full. But how were we going to get it to the troops? was the question. Then inspiration struck.

Playing with my son in the backyard of our Playa Del Rey home, which, as you can see, sat right on the beach. This was a cause of concern during the war, when it was feared the Japanese might launch a coastal attack.

To my three-year-old son I said, "Daddy needs to borrow your wagon." In Noel's bright-red pride-and-joy, and in a bone-chilling downpour, we carted the steaming ground beef and red beans to the base. The boys cheered our arrival and were grateful for dinner, even if it was a bit watery.

Many of us in Hollywood aided the war effort by doing what we did best: entertaining the troops and boosting morale. The hub of activity for the armed forces was the Hollywood Canteen, a barnlike recreation center on Cuhuenga Avenue. On an average night 2,500 servicemen and servicewomen gathered under its wood-beam ceiling, from which were hung red-white-and-blue streamers and kerosene lanterns. Officers were not admitted—probably why some soldiers hitchhiked from bases as far away as fifty miles. At the Canteen they could count on a hot meal that must have tasted like haute cuisine compared to Army chow, plus music and comedy provided by some of the biggest names in show business.

Betty Grable would go dancing by, her partner a buzz-cut private with a blissful expression on his face. On stage her husband, trumpeter Harry James, would be putting his band through its paces. The busboy might be Walter Pidgeon, the coffee server, Hedy Lamarr, and the woman doling out sandwiches might be Rita Hayworth. Even Greta Garbo came out of seclusion to entertain the troops.

Celebrities are often stereotyped as superficial and self-absorbed, but the dedication shown by so many stars during World War II was stirring. Hell, I can remember washing dishes at the Canteen, asking the older gent next to me to pass the soap and realizing it was Buster Keaton, film comedy's Great Stoneface.

We struck up a conversation and a warm friendship that endured until his death in 1966. "I'm happy to be here," he told me, "because I know how lonely a soldier can be." Keaton, whose nickname was coined by magician Harry Houdini, had served in World War I. "Fortieth Infantry, France," he said proudly, a smile creasing his basset-hound face. Besides helping in the kitchen, Keaton would take to the stage, proceeding to demonstrate why many regard him as a comic genius second only to Charles Chaplin.

Military recreation was held in other places as well. I remember one in El Segundo that was a real sewer. Literally. It had been converted into a massive underground station, and there, in front of an enthusiastic platoon, actor Edward G. Robinson and I once swapped jokes. After that, whenever we saw each other, I'd kid, "Say, Edward, you wanna work the sewer again with me sometime?" and we'd laugh.

For those wondering, yes, Robinson talked every bit as tough as the gangsters he played in films such as *Little Caesar* and *The Racket*. But off camera his bulldog face softened, and he was one of the gentlest souls you'd ever met. He was a philanthropist, too, donating one hundred thousand dollars to the United Service Organization's (USO) campaign for military recreation facilities.

Robinson additionally contributed to the Allied struggle by broadcasting to European nations oppressed by the Nazis. He spoke seven languages, including that of his native Romania, from which he had migrated to the U.S. when he was ten. Incidentally, his middle initial *G* was adopted from his real surname, for he was born Emanuel Goldenberg.

Buoying up American soldiers' spirits was immensely gratifying, and I considered it my patriotic duty, but at times it was frustrating, too. Seeing our men in uniform always made me want to enlist. Once, after performing at a military-brass luncheon, I collared a high-ranking official and told him of my desire to serve.

He simply smiled.

"Mr. Blanc," he said, "I think you can probably serve your country better right here at home."

One way was through the Armed Forces Radio Service. I was a regular on several of its programs, including "Are You a Genius?", "Command Performance," "Mail Call," "Jubilee," and "G.I. Journal." The latter starred one of my most-requested characters, Private Sad Sack.

Since the Sack was a pathetic bumbler, I decided to grant

him Porky Pig's voice. Too, I wanted to use a characterization well-known to our fighting men and women overseas, as a reminder of home. The lowly private had dreams of grandeur, always introducing himself, with the de rigueur stutter, as "L-lieut—, uh, Corp—, uh, S-serg—, uh, Gener— . . . uh, Private Sad Sack." Undoubtedly his was the swiftest demotion in military history.

"G.I. Journal" was often broadcast live in front of a clamorous Hollywood Canteen crowd and featured many legendary entertainers: Bob Hope, Bing Crosby, Frank Sinatra, Dinah Shore, Alan Ladd, to name but a few. With such top-flight talent it was a huge hit with the troops, who sent fan mail from as far away as Australia; wherever they were stationed.

Two particular Sad Sack installments stand out in my mind: one with Groucho Marx and Lucille Ball, and one with Orson Welles. When you think of Welles, you usually reflect on cinematic achievements such as *Citizen Kane*, his keen intellect, his deep, stentorian voice. Always so profoundly *serious*. At least, those were my preconceptions. But Orson turned out to be quite jovial, calling everyone "loveboat," regardless of sex, and laughing easily.

Too easily, on the show we did together. Sad Sack's infernal stuttering eventually rubbed off on the guest star, who started tripping over his own words until he was helpless with laughter. It wasn't often that Welles lost his intense concentration like that.

Working with Marx and Ball was a real treat. Groucho was at the height of his career, while Lucille was still relatively untested as a comedienne. Recently wed to bandleader Desi Arnaz, she'd adorned a number of B-grade movies and was regarded by critics as more flashy than funny. Little did they know. Lucille *was* a knockout, though, with flaming red hair and a curvaceous figure, and Groucho was certainly intrigued by her. But then, Groucho was intrigued by anything in a skirt and didn't hesitate to tell them so. The writers took this into consideration, giving him lecherous lines such as:

Ball: "I insist that you carry on."

Marx: "Well, that's nice, because you're just the kind of girl I like to carry on with!"

Even though "G.I. Journal" was a radio broadcast, I'm sure that all the troops listening could imagine Groucho flicking his cigar and twitching his bushy eyebrows after each punch line.

The three of us performed a routine with Groucho as African explorer Livingston Marx and Lucille as his number one boy. They are combing the jungle for the Missing Linx. "Water, water," Marx calls, "I must have some water."

"Are you thirsty, chief?"

"No, but if I don't rinse my undies, who'll dance with me?"

Suddenly they spot something crawling out of the underbrush, but it's not the Missing Linx, it's:

"Private Sad Sack!" Groucho exclaims. "What are you doing in the heart of the Belgian Congo?"

"Belgian Congo?" The Sack is nonplussed. "I *knew* I shouldn't have turned left on Vine Street." And when Lucille Ball comes on to him—"Hello, Sackie darling"—he gets even more tongue-tied than usual.

Like many of the "G.I. Journal" shows, it was short on plot but long on gags, giving the guest stars ample opportunities to shine. And it typically ended with a salute to our boys in uniform:

"This is Groucho Marx saying, So long, men!"

Before he was on Armed Forces Radio, the Sad Sack had been a character in Allied training films produced by Warner Bros. Frank Tashlin directed the first one in 1942. The stuttering character also went under the moniker of Private Snafu, *snafu* being an acronym for "*s*ituation *n*ormal *a*ll *f***ked *u*p."

These three-to-four-minute, black-and-white animated shorts were included as part of *The Army-Navy Screen Magazine,* made exclusively for U.S. soldiers. The format was rigid: Snafu would be shown demonstrating everything from sexual hygiene to handling weaponry, but true to his name, he'd foul

During World War II I got to work alongside talents such as Lucille Ball and Alan Ladd on a variety of Armed Forces Radio Service programs.

it up. Then, with the guidance of a narrator, he would repeat the action again the correct way. Here's a sample plot, from a cartoon called *Going Home:*

Private Snafu is home on leave and blabs to his pals top-secret information, which somehow finds its way into the hands of Axis Power spies. Much to his horror he later learns that the entire ninety-ninth division he left behind was wiped out. The moral: Loose lips sink ships. All storyboards had to be Pentagon approved, yet the writers faced less censorship than they did for commercial cartoons. Humorous references to sex and bodily functions, for instance, were permitted. The series was cowritten by Ted Geisel, who would go on to gain fame as an author of children's books under the nom de plume Dr. Seuss.

These cartoons were very effective instructional aids. A military spokesperson once told me that a Sad Sack/Snafu training film on tailgunning had been shown to two Air Corps rookies with no in-the-air experience. After viewing it, they were immediately sent up in a B-17 bomber and came away with three "positives" (enemy aircraft hit and down) and three "probables" (planes hit but not confirmed down).

Pro-American themes pervaded commercially released theatrical shorts, too, with Bugs Bunny, Porky Pig, and the rest all drafted for the war effort. Despite President Roosevelt's assurances that wartime motion pictures were immune from censorship, a "Government Information Manual for the Motion Picture" urged the casual insertion of constructive "war messages" whenever possible. At every opportunity, it went on, American citizens should be shown "making small sacrifices for victory," voluntarily and cheerfully: bringing their own sugar when dining out; accepting dim-outs and restrictions on tires and gas; using public transportation instead of private automobiles. And so on.

According to the manual, each filmmaker was to ask himself, "Will this picture help win the war?"

Although these were purported to be "suggestions," the

film industry was ever-mindful that the government's War Production Board could place unprocessed film on a critical-supply list at any time, thus putting them out of business. So they complied to the letter. As it was, the plastics used in cel animation were limited drastically for private use, forcing the reduction of production. Warner Bros.'s output dropped from forty-one cartoons in 1942 to twenty-seven the following year. And in the war's final year, 1945, only eight were made.

Most of our animated films between 1942 and 1945 contained at least one reference to the ongoing fighting, such as Bugs Bunny's appeal for citizens to buy war bonds. Decked out in a red, white, and blue Uncle Sam hat, he sings:

> *The tall man with the high hat*
> *Will be comin' down your way.*
> *Get your savings out when you hear him shout*
> *"Any bonds today?*
> *Any bonds today?*
> *Bonds of freedom, that's what I'm sellin'.*
> *Any bonds today?"*
> *Scrape up the most you can.*
> *Here comes the freedom man.*
> *Askin' ya to buy a share of freedom today.*

Several cartoons were expressly war related. The first such offering from Warner Bros., *Wacky Blackouts*, was timed for release on July 4, 1942. Directed by Bob Clampett, it depicted the effect of blackouts and other wartime regulations on farm animals. Obviously, they symbolized the general population.

Other theatrical shorts, with self-explanatory titles such as *The Ducktators* (1942), *Tokyo Jokio* (1943), and *Bugs Bunny Nips the Nips* (1943), were blatant denunciations of the enemy. *The Ducktators* portrayed German, Italian, and Japanese leaders Hitler, Mussolini, and Hirohito as web-footed fowls, while in *Tokyo Jokio* a grotesque caricature of Japanese admiral Yamamoto Isoroku fantasized about one day occupying the White House.

In *Bugs Bunny Nips the Nips* the scrappy Yank rabbit inadvertently lands on a Japanese-occupied South Pacific atoll, where he's spied by two enemy soldiers. "Thassa Bugs a-Bunny," one says to the other, "we cap-cha heem." But instead, Bugs single-handedly takes them prisoner and cracks some insults that would have been considered defamatory had there not been a war raging. At one point he hawks the Japanese hand grenades disguised as "Good Rumor" ice-cream pops, barking, "Here y'are, slant eyes." And in another scene, he places an anvil in the hands of a bewildered enemy parachutist: "Here ya go, 'Moto, have some scrap iron for Japan."

Obviously, subtlety was not our intent. Comedy was. In spite of the war America maintained its sense of humor; even Jack L. Warner. With the mighty Lockheed Aircraft plant located close to his Burbank studio, the Warner's vice president had his set painters inscribe a twenty-foot arrow on a soundstage roof. And painted in giant block letters was "Lockheed: That-Away," for the benefit of any incoming Japanese pilots.

What with my radio and animated-film work for the Army, Navy, and Air Corps, I spent a great deal of time commuting back and forth from Playa Del Rey to Hollywood. To conserve gas I bought a scooter, which I stashed in the trunk of my car. I'd drive to Culver City, about halfway between home and work, then use the scooter to travel from job to job. At night I'd head home on Sepulveda Boulevard with my headlights off, flicking them on just long enough to make sure I was still on the road. Sometimes I'd go seven, eight miles in near-total darkness. Although the tide of the Pacific War began turning in the Allies' favor as early as mid-1942, we still lived with the omnipresent fear of a coastal assault.

Even with the scooter, getting adequate supplies of gas could be problematic. On account of my work for the government I was supposed to receive a "C" card, entitling me to tank refills. But I frequently ran into unexpected—and annoying—red tape. For instance, one time I pulled into a station and called to the attendant that I was low on fuel.

"I'm on my way to Walter Lantz's studio," I told him.

Warner's had given me permission to voice other houses' government-commissioned cartoons. One was a Navy medical film called *Enemy Bacteria*, which boasted a $100,000 budget. Milburn Stone, later to spend a history-making two decades as crusty old Doc Adams on TV's "Gunsmoke," played the doctor, and me, the animated germs. It was shown in medical schools for many years after the war.

"Where's your pay stub?" the attendant drawled. "I can't give you gas unless I see your pay stub."

"I don't have one. I'm doing it for free," I protested. But it was no use. I had to charge Lantz union scale and on the ride home present my pay stub to the attendant. Then I donated the money to charity.

When World War II ended, I returned to my old routine, which had gotten even busier, especially my radio work. Because of gas rationing and blackouts, Americans spent more time at home listening to the radio, comedy shows in particular.

In 1946 CBS and Colgate-Palmolive approached me about starring in my own series, and I jumped at the chance. Not that I had any complaints about playing a second banana a bunch (ahem!) of times. It certainly paid well, and it wasn't as if I felt slighted. Two years earlier I'd won a Distinguished Achievement Award for Best Male Supporting Player from the fan magazine *Radio Life*. But I owed it to myself to try being a leading man.

The setting for the program was Mel Blanc's Fix-It Shop, its motto, "You bend it, we mend it." The proprietor, whom I played using my own name and natural voice, could barely hammer a nail straight, making him the ideal person to own a repair shop. For comedy purposes, that is. Interestingly, "The Mel Blanc Show" was more autobiographical than most people ever knew.

The summer before we went on the air, I actually purchased a hardware store in Venice, a few minutes from home. Its name, naturally, was "The Fix-It Shop"; why not take advantage of the free publicity? Though originally an investment, it wound up a wonderful antidote to boredom for my father-in-law. He'd sold his thriving grocery and was losing his marbles trying to keep occupied. "Mel, this retirement business is for the birds," he kept grumbling. So, with some prodding from Estelle and her mother, we coaxed him into managing the store.

Owning the shop was a pleasant change of pace for me, and I stole as many hours as I could to run the fishing department. In addition, I did all of my own purchasing, paying my first visit to New York just to stock the place for its grand opening. However, much like my radio character, I didn't know a jigsaw from a hacksaw and returned with several tools that defied identification.

"Hopefully someone will buy them; then we'll know what they are," Mr. Rosenbaum suggested helpfully.

The Fix-It Shop wasn't much of a financial windfall but did inspire some suitable dialogue for the radio show. I'd relate everyday occurrences to the writers so they could incorporate them into the script. On the other hand, some of my repartee with customers was not appropriate for radio, such as the time a man came in and asked me if we had a small file called a bastard.

"No, we don't have a little bastard, sir," I replied, and held up a similar implement, "but we do have this big son of a bitch." If only we could have snuck it past the censors.

Numerous Hollywood personalities paraded in and out of the store: Jack Benny, for fishing tackle; Al Jolson, for a hunting knife; Roy Rogers, for toys for his children.

My Fix-It Shop remained in business for several years. Unfortunately the fictional store shut down after one season on the air. The half-hour program premiered on Tuesday, September 3, 1946, at seven-thirty, opposite NBC's "A Date With Judy." We had high hopes for it, as did the public and the critics, but it was plagued by several problems, most notably lackluster scripts. "A deplorable waste of Mr. Blanc's undisputed talents," wrote Jack Gould of the *New York Times*.

And in a letter to her local paper, a Mrs. V. S. Olsen from Vancouver, Washington, complained that while she remembered me fondly from my old "Cobwebs and Nuts" radio show, "this new one is just nuts."

"The Mel Blanc Show" did have its moments, though, and at least made one contribution to the lexicon of American popular expressions: "Ugga-uuga-boo, ugga-boo-boo-ugga." Come again? It was the password from the Loyal Order of Benevolent Zebras, a lodge my character belonged to, and it caught on like wildfire with the public—so much so that I wrote a tune with that title. Spike Jones and His City Slickers recorded it for RCA Records.

Few people know that I made my first record with Spike and his zany outfit back in 1942. The song was called "Clink! Clink! Another Drink!"—an ode to the joys of intoxication. It was a favorite jukebox item in taverns, from what I understand. I came to be paired with Jones through an old Portland acquaintance, Del Porter. As young men we'd played in an orchestra that toured the Pacific Northwest. He went on to become Jones's clarinetist and right-hand man.

In addition to that nonsensical saying, the show gave birth to a character named Zookie, who opened each episode by stammering, "Hello everyb— b-ba— b-ba— *hi!*" Porky Pig's voice again? Yes, I confess. It racked up a lot of mileage, as Porky, Zookie, Sad Sack, Private Snafu, and August Moon.

August, nicknamed "Moony," was featured on NBC's "Point Sublime," starring the delightful character actor Cliff Arquette. Readers will probably recall him as lovable country bumpkin Charlie Weaver on TV's "The Jack Paar Show" and on "Hollywood Squares" until his death in 1974. He had such a husky voice that even as a young man Cliff made a lucrative living playing old ones.

On "Point Sublime" he was Ben Willet, general-store owner in a quiet Pacific coast village. Moony was a railway clerk who doubled as Ben's assistant. For reasons the show's writers never clarified, he had a bizarre fetish for running his fingers through the rice bin.

Moony, helper in a general store; Zookie, helper in a fix-it shop. It did get confusing on occasion.

Other "The Mel Blanc Show" principals were Mary Jane Croft as Betty Colby, my good-natured girlfriend, and Joe Kearns as her father, a *harrumphing* old curmudgeon who found the fictitious Mel Blanc wanting as a prospective son-in-law. One of the show's better lines sums up our antagonistic relationship:

"Your father and I have a perfect understanding," I tell my sweetheart.

"You do?"

"Sure. There's nothing he wouldn't do for me, and there's

"The Mel Blanc Show" ran during the 1946–1947 radio season on CBS. Here Mary Jane Croft admires my lack of skill as a fix-it man.

nothing I wouldn't do for him. And that's the way it's been for five years: We haven't done a thing for each other."

Bea Benaderet played Mrs. Colby, and Jim Backus, Alan Reed, Hans Conried, and Earle Ross portrayed an assortment of colorful locals, such as old Mr. Brown, who says to me in passing, "I can't sleep, on account of milk."

"Well, if you can't sleep on account of milk, why do you drink it?"

"Oh, I don't drink it, I *deliver* it."

Although the program was not renewed for a second season, it enabled me to greatly expand my repertoire. For example, one episode has me attempt to fix Mr. Colby's radio but turn it into a heap of useless wires and tubes. To cover up for my blundering, I hide behind the set and imitate different programs as he rotates the dial: impersonations of Katharine Hepburn, Charles Boyer, a Russian—even a simulated soap-opera organ. Seven voices in all, I believe. Still, neither that nor an infusion of guest stars drew enough listeners.

And so it was back to being second banana. Tell you the truth, though I was disappointed the show didn't fulfill its potential, I was also a bit relieved. The experience gave me a newfound appreciation of the pressure stars such as Jack Benny faced, from the sponsors, the networks, the fans—and from themselves.

I learned that I prefer being part of an ensemble. Early in my career, back in Portland, I'd tried my hand at stand-up comedy and didn't like it one bit. Prohibition had just ended, and so the club's patrons paid far more attention to their drinks than to me. I remember feeling just awful, thinking, *Here I am giving it my all, and these lousy bastards could care.* My days—*day*—as a comic were finished.

One benefit of playing second fiddle was not having to live a star's fishbowl existence. Sure, my name appeared regularly in the radio columns, but I could still stroll anonymously to the local dime store most of the time. Benny couldn't do that. Or Bob Hope. Or Judy Canova, for that matter. Their ability to lead normal lives was impeded by fame, though they learned to accept it. Somehow, I don't think I ever could.

Neither Estelle nor I was a mingler. Having both come from closely knit households, family was extremely important to us. My father had died following a short illness in 1940, and my mother had moved down to Los Angeles to live with her sister. After many years of being separated by hundreds of miles, it was wonderful living near her again, and so we spent much time with her and with the Rosenbaums.

The only industry people we socialized with on a frequent basis were the Bennys and Warner Bros. colleagues such as Mr. and Mrs. Friz Freleng, Carl Stalling and his lovely wife, and Mr. and Mrs. Milt Franklyn. Radio and animated-film actors rarely traveled in the same social circles as movie stars, although of course I got acquainted with my share at various Hollywood functions. Two that come to mind were silver-screen goddesses Dorothy Lamour and Marilyn Monroe.

An amusing anecdote about Marilyn, whom I met for the first time at an awards dinner. It goes without saying that she was stunning; I don't think there was a pair of male eyes not glued to her as she moved through the banquet hall. The two of us were standing around chatting—she in breathy bursts, just like in her films—when a man interrupted us, steering her away by the elbow. "I want you to sit at my table and meet someone," he said to her. It seemed more like an order than a request.

"I can't," she squealed.

"Why the hell not?"

"Because," she said, glaring at him, "I can't sit down. I'm *sewn* into this dress."

Monroe was famous for the nude calendar she'd posed for. Dorothy Lamour, on the other hand, is famous for an article of clothing she didn't remove: a tropical-print silk sarong kept up with formidable muscle control. She is a lovely person, originally from New Orleans. We performed together a few times on Armed Forces Radio, with me as Private Sad

Sack. I don't remember if Dorothy was in character or just playing herself, but I can say for sure that she wore the sarong at least once. Some things embed themselves in the memory.

Not long after the war we ran into each other again. Dorothy mentioned that her young son, John, was a fan of the Warner Bros. cartoon stars. "Would it be possible for you to do a voice track of a couple of them?"

I told her I'd be delighted to oblige.

A week or two later she called me up to say, "You have no idea how much good you did with that tape you sent. He was absolutely thrilled."

"Well, then, when do I make the next one?" Whenever I had a chance, I'd duck into the studio and record more tapes for her youngster. She couldn't get over it.

Because of my ability to master dialects, I occasionally was asked by the Warner Bros. film studio to tutor some of its stars. Clark Gable needed a New *Yawk* inflection for an upcoming movie; Alan Ladd, a Texas twang; and singer Ezio Pinza required my coaching to minimize his Italian accent.

The Blancs may not have been Hollywood social butterflies, but our son, Noel, certainly couldn't complain of a humdrum youth. From the time he was four, he began accompanying me to work. Because no one under fourteen was permitted in the audience, he'd watch the proceedings from the sanctity of the soundproof client's booth and try listening to the dialogue over the incessant chatter of the cigar-chewing sponsor representatives.

Everyone made a fuss over him. Of course I'm hardly impartial, but he was a beautiful child, with my olive complexion and his mother's sparkling eyes. Sara Berner from "The Jack Benny Program," Judy Canova, Gracie Allen, Marilyn Monroe, and Rita Hayworth were just a few of the actresses who oohed and aahed over him—and spoiled him rotten on occasion. George Burns, "Great Gildersleeve" star Hal Peary, Jimmy Stewart, Clark Gable, Humphrey Bogart, Roy Rogers, Orson Welles—all would amble over, chuck him playfully un-

1945: Me in character as Private Sad Sack on "G.I. Journal." The lovely lady is Dorothy Lamour, sans sarong; much to my disappointment.

der the chin, muss his hair. And Jack Benny virtually became the kid's uncle. Were it not for its negative connotation, I suppose that you could say Jack was Noel's funny uncle.

Make that funni*est* uncle. Don Wilson, Phil Harris, Dennis Day, Sheldon Leonard, and the Benny-show writers adored Noel as well. All were in attendance at Santa Monica's Temple Beth Shalom for his Bar Mitzvah, which easily could have been mistaken for a Saturday rehearsal.

Because of the constant attention he received and because he was an only child, Estelle and I were careful not to over-indulge Noel. We knew all about the pitfalls of raising a youngster in affluent Hollywood, where children often grow up with swelled heads and an exaggerated sense of entitlement.

Nine-year-old Noel and me at NBC's Hollywood studios. From the time he was four, he often accompanied me to work, where Judy Canova, Marilyn Monroe, Rita Hayworth, and other actresses oohed and aahed over him.

Although we never hesitated disciplining him, we didn't believe in spankings—running contrary to popular wisdom.

The only time I ever took my hand to Noel was when he was about five years old. He and a friend from across the street were bouncing a ball in the bedroom, which had a crystal fixture hanging from the ceiling. "Please don't do that in here," I said to him. "You're liable to break something."

No sooner did he reply, "Nah, I won't," than the ball ricocheted straight up and smashed into the light, which shattered into hundreds of fragments. The other little boy, Butch, decided right about then that his mother must be calling him and raced home. I took Noel across my lap and started whacking his bottom.

My mother and my aunt were visiting, and from upstairs we heard Aunt Ray scream, "You're killing the child! You're killing the child!" Her hysteria was so out of proportion to the punishment, my son and I made eye contact, and we both started laughing and hugging each other. I never raised a hand to him again.

If Estelle and I were guilty of any overindulging, it was with attention. Noel's favorite time of day was breakfast, when I would read him comic books in my many voices. Sometimes I'd be sitting on the john, and he would come bounding into the bathroom, happily thrusting another comic book at me to read. He'd hop up onto my lap and stay there until I'd finished the last page.

Noel was a very inquisitive child and a quick learner, which posed some problems when he began kindergarten. For years he had pestered us from his high chair, "When can I go to school like the big boys?"

"When your feet get down to *there*," my wife would reply, pointing.

But the kindergarten at Nightingale Elementary School in Venice was comprised mostly of kids from backgrounds where education was not encouraged. To accommodate them, the pace was extremely slow, and every day Noel came home complaining about how much he hated school. At first Estelle and I simply attributed this to his being away from his mom and dad for the first time. But one day my wife received a call from Noel's teacher, a Miss Meyers. It was apparent to her, she said, that our son would not be happy in the local school.

"He just sits on the floor moping and says he can learn more at home. He's probably correct."

So we transferred him to another school, where he'd be properly challenged, and he took to it from the get-go. Normally he traveled by bus, but the first day of each term I drove him, singing, "In a little red schoolhouse with my book and slate. In a little red schoolhouse, I was always late." We'd pull up in front, and I'd point out the other children and their parents.

"Look, there's Cyd Charisse and Tony Martin, with their boy Nicky; Harry James and his sons Harry and Timothy. And say! There's J. C. Agajanian, the race-car driver, with his oldest, Cary, and J. C., Jr."

If I have one regret about how we brought up Noel, it was that Estelle and I unwittingly may have pressured him too much in one respect. My wife used a certain expression, "Johnny Boy," which was synonymous with being obedient. "Are you a Johnny Boy or a bad boy?" she'd say to Noel when he misbehaved.

"Oh, I'm a Johnny Boy, Mommy," he'd answer. In retrospect, it was the wrong approach, because he took it too much to heart. For a time he became timid, afraid that one miscue and he'd no longer be a "Johnny Boy." You have to remember that back then mothers and fathers didn't have the advantage of professional guidebooks on parenting as there are today. It was largely a hit or-miss proposition. For better or for worse, many of us adults from that era simply passed on the discipline we'd received from our own parents.

Overall, though, the Blanc household was a wonderfully happy one. If we were fated to have but one child, we couldn't have been blessed with a better son than Noel. He was, and still is, my pride and joy.

*   *   *

On May 30, 1948, I celebrated my birthday with—I admit it—some trepidation. It wasn't so much the fact that I was turning forty, making me older than even Jack Benny. For the first time in many years I harbored a lingering uncertainty over the future. My cartoon and radio careers were thriving, but looming on the horizon was a new medium that threatened to dwarf radio the same way talking motion pictures had brought down vaudeville twenty years earlier.

The entertainment industry is a volatile one, in which the phrase "job security" draws rueful snickers. Sometimes I couldn't help wondering if the end of the line was near. I'm sure many other radio actors shared the same concern about this thing called television.

CHAPTER

9

Television Enters the Picture

"**J**ust hold on to your horses, folks. This is gonna take a while."

The "Jack Benny Program" cast milled about the stage set restlessly while engineers and technicians repositioned TV cameras and adjusted lighting. It was October 28, 1950, our official entry into television. At the rate things were going, I wondered if we'd ever get the show on the air.

"Damn, these lights are *hot*," I remarked to Don Wilson, who was blotting perspiration from his face with a handkerchief.

"You're not kidding," he muttered. Just then a makeup artist looked at us, cocked her head, and declared she'd have to apply more powder. "The shine from your foreheads will blind the cameramen," she joked. Rolling our eyes, we followed her dutifully for another dusting.

The whole procedure smacked of film acting, which I'd flirted with through several bit parts. In *Neptune's Daughter*, a 1948 picture starring Red Skelton and lovely, water-winged

Esther Williams, I played a South American gaucho named Julio. And two decades later I would take on the role of Dr. Sheldrake in *Kiss Me, Stupid*, directed by Billy Wilder. Neither was much to write home about, nor did it whet my appetite for becoming a movie star.

No, I was content to remain behind the scenes in radio, which was so radically different from motion pictures—and now TV. Makeup wasn't required, you read from hand-held scripts instead of having to memorize lines, and action wasn't interrupted by the lighting crew alerting an actor he was out of range and obscured by shadows.

You want to know my initial impressions of TV? Frankly, I thought it *stunk*. And I was terrified.

I'd heard about television for some time but knew little about it. Primitive home-viewing sets had been on the market as far back as 1928, the same year that the first station, New York's W2XBS, took to the airwaves. Only a select hundred or so Americans owned a seventy-five-dollar set, but within twelve months twenty-six broadcasters were in operation. Los Angeles's first was W6XAO, an experimental channel that belonged to Cadillac dealer and KHJ-radio owner Don Lee.

Technology was expanding as rapidly as the number of outlets. Westinghouse developed an all-electronic television system consisting of a transmitting tube called an iconoscope and a cathode-ray-tube receiver, or kinescope. The original mechanical models had utilized rotating perforated scanning disks, through which reflected light was flashed to create a discernible, if somewhat murky, moving image. Electronic receivers were less bulky and formed sharper pictures.

But this 1929 breakthrough was ill-timed. Had it not been for the Great Depression, in all likelihood TV would have eclipsed radio within several years. But in a feeble economy a set was an unaffordable luxury. CBS's New York station, W2XAB, among others, suspended transmissions.

As the Depression lifted toward the end of the 1930s, production was gradually resumed. The first U.S.-made electronic television sets went on sale a day after their public unveiling at the 1939 New York World's Fair. The exposition's theme, appropriately, was "The World of Tomorrow." And tomorrow was precisely when most Americans planned to purchase a TV, still regarded as a mere novelty. Aside from the occasional sporting or news event, there was precious little programming to warrant such a lavish expenditure.

Once the Federal Communications Commission approved commercial broadcasting in 1941, scheduling broadened to include game shows. And commercials, lots of commercials. But once again the industry's progress was interrupted by fate: World War II. All stations closed their doors except for nine: three in New York City, two each in Los Angeles and Chicago, and one each in Philadelphia and Schenectady, New York. Programming was reduced from four days a week to just one. Factories that had once turned out television sets manufactured wartime goods instead. For the next four years, TV was all but dead.

When the shroud was raised at the war's end, there were three networks, CBS, NBC, and ABC, and a fourth, DuMont, on the way. And there was a surplus of sets. But by then radio had entrenched itself in America's consciousness. How could the budding medium hope to supplant Jack Benny, Bob Hope, Edgar Bergen, and "Fibber McGee and Molly"? It wasn't simply a question of replacing them with new faces, it required altering millions of people's nightly routine. Motion pictures and radio had caught on instantly with the public, but television's acceptance was going to take some time.

The first show I ever watched was the 1948 premiere of "Texaco Star Theatre," on a two-hundred-dollar, ten-inch Philco set that came complete with a plastic magnifying bubble lens. Conceived as a return to vaudeville's golden age, the program was hosted by Milton Berle, whose act I had witnessed several times many years before at the Orpheum.

Berle had attained only a modicum of success in radio and film, though he did forge quite a reputation among his peers for swiping material. Whenever someone plagiarized a joke, it was good-humoredly referred to as "a Berle." But once Milton began appearing weekly on "Texaco Star Theatre," he rocketed to national stardom. The show, later called "The Buick-Berle Show," then "The Milton Berle Show," consistently fared well in the ratings and remained on the tube for nineteen seasons. Berle was dubbed "Mr. Television," a title he surely deserves. His popularity spurred many radio stars to consider what impact TV could have on their careers.

Jack Benny, for one. He fielded several offers but viewed the medium guardedly. I think all of us on the show did, and not out of narrow-mindedness. Remember, after nearly twenty seasons, beloved characters such as Sam Hearn's rube and Sheldon Leonard's tout were implanted indelibly in the audience's minds. Each listener had his own perception of what Artie Auerbach's Mr. Kitzle looked like; or my Professor LeBlanc; or even the decor of Jack's home. Now we were faced with the daunting prospect of having to select just one image and present that to our viewers. What if they were disappointed?

Too, our writers, so adept at conveying mental pictures solely through words and sound, had to adapt to a visual medium. In radio it was necessary that they preface a character's actions with a descriptive statement; for example, "I think I'll go upstairs," which would be followed by the sound of footsteps ascending a staircase. But because television audiences could see the movement, such lines were redundant.

Other new aspects to contend with: blocking scenes, constructing props and scenery, and talent learning how to play to a camera. There was some question whether or not voice actors used to speaking into a microphone could adjust. It would take several episodes before writers, performers, and technicians were comfortable working in such a foreign milieu.

Cognizant of all this, Jack entered the television age cautiously, airing but four shows during the 1950–1951 season. Certainly our premiere did not make anyone forget the radio program, which continued broadcasting through June 1954.

A press photo of me around the time "The Jack Benny Program" made the transition to television. Most of the public had heard me but had never seen me before.

It featured regulars Don Wilson, Eddie Anderson, Artie Auerbach, the Sportsmen Quartet, and me. Mary Livingstone stated flatly she would not go before the cameras; radio was grueling enough. Though the Benny program became a television staple for a decade and a half, she remained true to her word, appearing only sporadically. We had two guests as well on that first telecast: singer Dinah Shore and comedian Ken Murray.

I was in a daze for much of it, feeling out of my element. We actors had to maneuver around an obstacle course of equipment that partially obstructed our view of the studio audience, and their view of us. And the constant motion of microphones, lights, and cameras was distracting. Most of all, I detested wearing makeup, which the kliegs melted so that it dripped down my neck. Because it was then believed flat photography produced the best picture, backgrounds were filmed brightly to minimize shadows and contrasts. If the heat generated didn't bother you, the glare did.

Some performers were so unaccustomed to the harsh lights, they donned sunglasses until showtime. Frankly, the brightness didn't disturb me half as much as the constant delays caused by the lighting technicians, most of whom were draftees from film studios and therefore were used to a more methodical, slower pace. They seemed to take forever to set up.

On that first program and those to follow, we discovered that some of our original apprehensions were well founded, and others, not.

As we feared, some viewers were disillusioned with the visual representations of several scenes and familiar characters. Certainly seeing Benny's ancient Maxwell wasn't as funny as simply hearing its wheezing engine on radio. And no matter what was tried, we never were able to construct a satisfactory underground vault for Jack's money. It was more effective to merely refer to it and let the public's imaginations take over; the same was true of the Union Depot train caller and of Carmichael the polar bear, whose roar I supplied off-camera.

But then there were those characters enhanced by TV exposure, such as Professor LeBlanc. We featured him in the opening skit of our fourth show, which aired on May 20, 1951. Having noted here the limitations television imposed, I should point out how it also increased comic possibilities through sight gags. In that first scene LeBlanc is giving Jack a violin lesson, and a camera focuses on two hanging pictures of eminent violinists Jascha Heifetz and Mischa Elman. As soon as Benny jerks his bow across the strings, both fall to the floor, as if unable to bear even one note. It received a hearty laugh.

Television proved to be the breeding ground for the definitive Benny-LeBlanc routine, which comprised a whole episode from our final season, 1964–1965:

Jack receives a phone call from a psychiatrist. A Professor Pierre LeBlanc is in his office, he tells Benny, ostensibly suffering from amnesia brought on by a nervous breakdown. Jack hurries over to the doctor's to find his instructor clad in a disheveled black tuxedo and beret, and staring catatonically into space. His lone movement is to fitfully pluck a tissue out of a box and absentmindedly stuff it into one of his pockets. A pitiful sight indeed.

The psychiatrist asks Benny to relate what he knows about the professor, touching off a series of flashbacks that begins with their very first lesson. For these trips back in time Jack and I had to pull on toupees of varying fullness, for our hairlines had begun their retreat long ago. As the years advance, Benny and LeBlanc are shown aging, and the professor's sanity is slowly unraveling, his clothes getting progressively shabbier. The only thing that defies Father Time is Jack's excruciatingly bad violin playing, which causes LeBlanc's composure to become as frayed as his garments.

Benny waves his bow menacingly, about to practice his Kruetzer exercises. "I'll start from scratch," he tells the professor, who snaps back, "*That* I am sure." You can see the agony on his face as Jack saws away. Finally, his patience eroded, LeBlanc starts screaming hysterically at his student to stop, but catches himself.

"I lost my tempair, Meester Be-neé," he says wearily. "I wish eet was my hearing."

After several more measures of grating notes:

"Meester Be-neé, could I have some water, please?"
"Water? Yes. There's some in the cooler down the hall."
"That ees not enough. I would like to drown myself."

Conducting Benny from the couch, the professor de-vises one of his rhyming couplets to complement—but not compliment—more études:
"Bend your wrist and slide your finger,
 Pull the switch, don't let me linger."
The show includes one of my favorite gags. "Professor," Benny asks earnestly, "how can I improve the tone quality of my playing?"
"Perhaps, Monsieur Be-neé, eef you wcre to hold zee vi-olin upside down . . ."
"Upside down? But Professor, if I hold the violin up-side down, the strings will be on the bottom. No music will come out!"
His teacher responds desperately, "We must try *any-theeng!*"
And then there's Jack's choice Benny-LeBlanc exchange:
"Professor LeBlanc, do you think you can ever make a good violinist out of me?"
"I do not know. How old are you?"
"Why?" Said defensively, of course.
"How much time have we left?!"

The scene returns to the present, in the doctor's office, where LeBlanc still sits silently, still squirreling away tissues.
There is but one way to reach the poor wretch, the psy-chiatrist hypothesizes: through music. Jack hurries home to fetch his violin. Back in the office he assumes his playing stance, wields the bow, and—
The room fills with sweet, lilting notes that awaken the professor from his stupor like the Prince's soft kiss upon Sleep-ing Beauty's lips. A crooked smile forms on LeBlanc's face. His eyes widen, and his narcose gaze traces the music to its source: *Jack Benny?* Impossible. He shakes his head and cleans

"Professor LeBlanc, do you think you can ever make a good violinist out of me?" asks Benny. "I do not know," says the beleaguered instructor. "How old are you?" "Why?" "*How much time have we left?!*"

out his eardrums with his fingers. But it *is* Jack Benny. Which means that he, Professor Pierre LeBlanc, is not a failure after all; even if it did take nearly twenty years. Completely recovered, he exits the office deliriously happy, but not before planting a kiss on his student.

Once Benny is sure the Frenchman is out of earshot, he appeals to the doctor, "I've made a lot of money and gotten a lot of laughs. Don't tell anyone I play that well."

After the show Jack hugged me and said warmly, "Mel, you're not only a great comedian, you're a great actor!" I took it, coming from such a giant, as a tremendous compliment. And it reminded me of my apprehension a decade and a half earlier, when I worried whether or not the coming of television might spell the going of Mel Blanc from the entertainment field.

My chief concern about performing before a camera had been, Will I be able to put across my characters visually? But just as when voicing Bugs Bunny, Porky Pig, Tweety, and other cartoon stars, my rubbery face automatically assumed the identity of whomever I played. Piece of cake.

And what about Jack, who'd harbored similar doubts? He took to the camera as naturally as he did to the stage, film, and radio. A born showman, he cultivated subtle but hilarious mannerisms to supplement his patented expressions: to accompany ". . . Well!"—a hand clapped to his cheek, a smirk, and an all-knowing glance at the camera. Or perhaps both arms folded protectively on his chest. Just as Benny brought forth laughter by pausing pregnantly before punch lines on radio, his understated gestures sent TV audiences howling. Far from inhibiting him, television enlarged his comedic scope.

Plus, for the first time viewers could see the famous effeminate Benny walk, which once prompted Phil Harris to quip, "You could put a dress on that guy and take him anywhere."

The bandleader was kidding, but some people in Hollywood actually believed his innocent remark contained an element of truth. Rumors are as rampant in Tinseltown as smog in the air, and even someone of Jack Benny's stature wasn't immune from them. At one stage, talk circulated that perhaps he was homosexual. In fact, I even know the person most responsible for perpetrating this outrageous falsehood: Benny himself. As usual, no one found Jack's mincing gait funnier than Jack.

The first three Jack Benny TV episodes received a cool reception from critics, and possibly deservedly so. But with the fourth one, the cast began recapturing the rhythm it was renowned for on radio. Six shows were produced during the 1951–1952 season, a far cry from the thirty-five to forty radio broadcasts during the same span. Yet "The Jack Benny Program" finished seventh in the A. C. Nielsen ratings that year. Out of its fifteen years on the tube, it would fail to rank in the Top Twenty just five times. CBS, and for one season, NBC, scheduled it on Sundays at seventy-thirty P.M. Between radio and TV, Sunday evenings in America were synonymous with Jack Benny for a total of thirty-three years.

Benny, Hope, Berle, Skelton, Burns and Allen, Abbott and Costello—virtually all of America's radio favorites triumphed on television. In a way these vaudeville veterans' careers had come full circle: from playing to an audience watching from a seat in the house, to playing to an audience watching from a seat in their own home. Little had changed except for the remarkable technology that made it possible. Ultimately, of the three mediums, radio turned out to be the curiosity, not TV.

Aside from "The Jack Benny Program," my only other regular on-camera appearances came by way of a short-lived and best-forgotten celebrity quiz show called "Musical Chairs" in 1955. However, TV provided me with nearly more work than I could handle, voicing cartoons produced specifically for it instead of movie theaters.

Persevere in the entertainment world long enough, and you learn it is governed by a sort of yin and yang: One opportunity goes under, but another emerges to take its place. At the same time it was contributing to the downfall of theatrical shorts, television was blooming into the near-exclusive province of animation. And beginning with the 1955 debut of "Mighty Mouse Playhouse" on CBS, Saturday mornings in particular became the domain of children.

Recognizing television's potential (and seeing storm clouds on the horizon, perhaps?), Warner Bros. sold nearly two hundred of its classic cartoons into syndication, to be shown repeatedly on 1950s kiddie programs such as St. Louis's "Cartoon Club," Philadelphia's "Willie and Carney," and Los Angeles's "Cartoon Carnival."

Two animated-film veterans who also envisioned the fruitful marriage of TV and animation were Bill Hanna and Joseph Barbera. Both had spent twenty years at Metro-Goldwyn-Mayer's studios, where they turned out winning theatrical shorts featuring Tom and Jerry. From 1943 to 1952 the most famous cat-and-mouse team of them all garnered a remarkable seven Academy Awards. Even such animated-film luminaries as Bugs Bunny and Mickey Mouse never came close to approaching that figure. How fortunate that Bill and Joe had scrapped their original concept: a fox-and-dog duo.

Based on their backgrounds and temperaments, there was little to suggest the two men would collaborate so prosperously. When Hanna joined the MGM cartoon department as animation director in 1937, he was a twenty-seven-year-old former engineer from New Mexico. His first apprenticeship in the field was served with Leon Schlessinger's Pacific Art and Title company. Dissatisfied with running for coffee and cleaning cels, in 1931 he joined Harmon-Ising Studios, which at the time was still producing theatrical shorts for Warner Bros.

Bill was private and mild-mannered, and a direct contrast to Joe Barbera, who was a gregarious twenty-six-year-old Brooklynite, the son of immigrant parents. He'd toiled behind a desk in an Irving Trust Company bank before landing at the

Van Beuren studio as a sketch artist and animator. Dark-haired, eyes set off by bushy black eyebrows, he looked much younger than his age, while his square-faced, prematurely graying partner appeared much older. The two hit it off grandly, though, and complemented each other artistically. Joe's talent was sketching storyboards, while Bill excelled at comic timing.

In 1957 MGM rewarded Hanna and Barbera for twenty years of racking up Oscars by ordering them to let their staff go. The company had discovered that rereleasing vintage cartoons netted it nearly as much in earnings as producing new ones, even though Bill and Joe had proposed switching to limited animation in the interest of cost-cutting. They responded by quitting and out of sheer desperation formed their own company.

Their first series, sold to NBC soon after they hung their shingle, was Ruff and Ready. Its stars were a dopey dog and a cagey cat. Budgets were shoestring, and animation was limited to approximately 1,500 drawings. At MGM the same five-minute short would have entailed 25,000. United Productions of America had pioneered this economical animation style, in which detailed backgrounds were eliminated; character movements were restricted to the basics, with few nuances; and reusable stock close-ups were employed as much as possible. Aesthetically, I prefer full animation. But simplifying the process had become a financial necessity.

After Ruff and Ready came series featuring characters such as Quick Draw McGraw, Yogi Bear and Huckleberry Hound, many of which were voiced by the talented, versatile Daws Butler. "Huckleberry Hound" was the first series to ever earn an Emmy Award for Outstanding Achievement in the Field of Children's Programming. That was in 1960, the same year Hanna-Barbera launched a novel concept: an animated series for adults called "The Flintstones."

I received a call from Joe Barbera about playing Barney Rubble, one of the four leads.

"What is he supposed to sound like?" I asked.

"A prehistoric Art Carney."

"Interesting," I said, "but I don't think so. I don't believe in impersonating others."

"Let me try to change your mind." Barbera supplied some more details about Barney: that he was an easygoing kind of Cro-Magnon and the ideal counterpoint to Fred Flintstone, who had a big mouth as well as a propensity for putting his unshod foot in it.

The pairing sounded full of comic potential. It also sounded an awful lot like Jackie Gleason's Ralph Kramden and Carney's Ed Norton from TV's "The Honeymooners."

"Listen, Mel, you don't have to copy Carney. Tell me: How do *you* think Barney Rubble would talk?"

"Well, I dink he'd talk like dis, Joe, with a silly hiccup of a laugh." And I broke into "A-hee-hee, a-hee-hee-hee."

"Love it. The part's yours if you want it," said Joe.

I wanted it.

It was strange at first, working with a director other than Friz Freleng, Chuck Jones, or Bob McKimson. Barbera was certainly talented, but he drove me nuts sometimes, not always being able to get across what he wanted. And he had this irritating habit of starting from the top every time an actor made a mistake. Recording sessions dragged on interminably, unlike at Warner's.

Frustrated, I suggested to him that we repeat only the misread line. "The engineer can edit out the flub and splice the tape back together." Sure enough, we cut down the time from seven hours to one and a half.

That beef aside, Hanna and Barbera were wonderful to work for: both creative professionals and marvelous guys. Plus, they surrounded themselves with some of the industry's brightest talents, including my former Warner Bros. colleagues Warren Foster and Michael Maltese, who had left the studio for greener pastures. The first time I sat in on a Hanna-Barbera story meeting, it seemed just like old times.

Yet it was even more exciting to be among new faces.

Back around 1950 I'd signed an exclusive Warner Bros. contract restricting me from accepting freelance assignments from other production companies. The money seemed attractive enough at the time, so I consented to it. In hindsight, it was one of the biggest mistakes of my career, if for no other reason than I had to give up voicing Woody Woodpecker.

If you recall, the redheaded bird's cackling laugh—"Hee-hee-hee eh-hoh!"—was the first I ever coined, in the hallways of Portland's Lincoln High School. I'd briefly tried it out on the incipient Bugs Bunny, but once the rabbit was redrawn, it no longer suited him. Finally, in 1940, I was able to place it with a proper owner.

Shortly after sketching Bugs Bunny, artist/director Ben Hardaway had quit Warner's to work for Walter Lantz, whose involvement in the field extends back to 1916, when the native New Yorker was a sixteen-year-old cameraman for the Hearst animation studio. Lantz first came to prominence in 1929, the year he unexpectedly inherited and began producing Walt Disney's Oswald the Lucky Rabbit series, for Universal. Several years later his agreement with the company was amended so that he was essentially independent, merely contracting distribution rights to Universal.

Lantz's first creation of note was lovable Andy Panda. But when he saw Warner's box-office success with vociferous Daffy Duck, he instructed Hardaway to come up with an equivalent. The result was Woody Woodpecker, who was to debut in a 1940 Andy Panda short called *Knock Knock*. "We should give him a distinctive laugh," Ben said to Walter, "and I know just who can do it: Mel Blanc."

He gave me a call, and I drove over to Lantz's studio to meet him.

"What do you think?" Ben asked me, holding up a prototype drawing.

"Ugliest damn thing I ever saw," I replied. And I was being polite. The original Woody was repulsive with a capital *R:* He had a peaked head topped with a sharply angled comb that looked like it had been styled in a wind tunnel. A narrow beak so long, its pointy tip was a zip code away. Short, swollen arms and legs. In all, a sorry spectacle. But it gets worse.

Hardaway must have been in a foul mood the day he designed the woodpecker, because there's no other explanation for its goofy grin: two pitiful little teeth set against an expanse of black, as if Woody had tried sinking his choppers into a petrified redwood. Mercifully, he soon underwent a transfiguration. His beak was pruned, his limbs thinned, and his red comb was drawn so that it fell forward like a feathery pompadour, making him much easier on the eyes.

Woody starred in his own short, *Woody Woodpecker (a.k.a. The Cracked Nut)*, the following summer and endured as a prolific screen presence for many years. I voiced roughly thirty

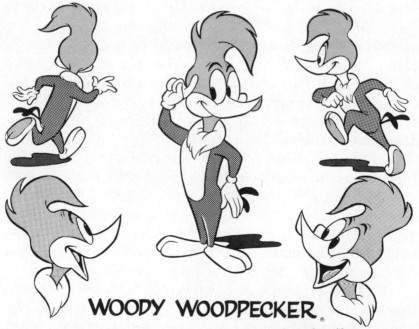

WOODY WOODPECKER ®

Woody Woodpecker's cackling laugh was the first voice I ever coined, when I was a teenager. However, it wasn't until seventeen years later that I matched it with Walter Lantz's red-headed troublemaker. *Woody Woodpecker © 1957 Walter Lantz Productions, Inc. All rights reserved. Courtesy of MCA Publishing Rights, a Division of MCA, Inc.*

cartoons, through 1949's oddly titled *Drooler's Delight*. Then I inked my name to that exclusive Warner Bros.'s contract prohibiting me from working for Lantz or for anybody else. Walter was forced to seek a replacement, which took him nearly two years. First Ben Hardaway tried filling in briefly but none too successfully. The part eventually went to the lovely and talented actress Grace Stafford, who later became Mrs. Lantz. I always kid Walter that he married her just to ensure Woody's voice wouldn't get away again.

Though my Warner's pact stipulated I could not portray the little redheaded troublemaker for cartoons, it did not apply to other media. I continued playing Woody on a Mutual Network radio show and also on disc. My first recording as the woodpecker, "The Woody Woodpecker Song," sold over one million copies in 1948 and reached number two on the singles charts.

Other Woody 45s and 78s combined music with children's stories and morals; for instance, 1952's "Woody Woodpecker and His Spaceship," in which Woody blasts off into outer space. His rocket comes to rest in "Double Land," the inhabitants of which possess two heads, speak in double-talk, and drink double-chocolate malts. However, not everything in Double Land is idyllic: They have to wash two faces. If only the sales royalties had been based on a similar mathematical principle.

Royalties and residuals are a touchy subject with most voice actors. The former is a percentage paid to an artist based on the number of units sold (such as recordings and videotapes), while the latter applies to the number of television-program and animated-film reruns. Generally speaking, cartoon studios took advantage of their performers for many years, me included. Let me give you an example that happens to involve Walter Lantz and Woody Woodpecker.

After I stopped playing his studio's most popular star, Lantz continued to use my prerecorded laugh in the Woody Woodpecker cartoons, yet I received not a single penny. Now,

I'd never been a terribly money-conscious person, but this struck me as enormously unfair. Why should everyone profit from my work but me? Besides, I originated the character's voice. I contacted Walter to air my gripe, and though he was sympathetic, his position was that he owned the rights to Woody—including his voice characterization.

I considered Lantz a friend; still do, in fact. But as a matter of principle I took him to court. We eventually settled, which I regret to some extent because the issue was never resolved. Warner Bros., too, claims the copyrights and trademarks on all its characters. So unless I obtain permission from the company, I cannot publicly say the expressions that made them famous. Can you imagine Bugs Bunny without "Eh, what's up, Doc?"? Or Tweety without "I tawt I taw a puddy tat"? I'm not legally permitted to identify the characters by name, either.

Ownership of a cartoon figure; it's a thorny problem, legally and ethically. Animators and directors have the same complaint and feel every bit as paternal toward the characters as I do. I guess you could say that we share joint custody of them.

Until the mid-1960s, when I negotiated a much fairer salary, I didn't earn more than twenty thousand a year from Warner Bros. The bulk of my earnings were derived from radio and, later, from television. Fortunately I invested wisely and was always able to provide well for my family.

One of my most lucrative investments also happens to be a favorite hobby of mine: collecting antique watches, a passion that started quite by accident. For my thirty-eighth birthday Estelle gave me an antique Patek Phillipe minute-repeater, made in Switzerland. Push a lever, and it chimed on the minute. Very unique.

And valuable, too, as I discovered several years later. Bud Abbott had long admired the timepiece, so I decided to get him one for his birthday. "Estelle," I said, "if you don't mind my asking, how much was that watch you bought me?"

Three hundred seventy-five dollars, she replied, at an antique store in Venice.

"Three hundred seventy-five bucks?" I couldn't believe my ears. "For a *used* watch?" Shows what I knew.

I called Tiffany's in Manhattan to see if they had one like it, and the salesman told me he did: for $2,040.

I became a watch collector that day.

Originally it was for financial purposes, but as I acquired other antiques, I grew fascinated by their intricate detail and craftsmanship. After a long day in the studio I found it very relaxing to examine them. Each one had its own history; not merely a timepiece, but a piece of time.

Today I own close to four hundred. Many are rarities, including what most collectors, or horologists, believe is the first watch ever made: a 1510 carrying timepiece measuring two and a half inches deep and two and a half across, hand-crafted by a German named Peter Henlein. Somehow it had come into the possession of a Frenchman employed by the Swiss Eturnamatic Watch Company. I met him in the 1950s, and badly in need of cash at the time, he sold it to me for just three hundred dollars. Neither of us realized its value. I wanted it simply because it was so unusual looking.

Fifteen years later Noel brought the watch to London for appraisal and was shocked when told it was worth over two hundred thousand dollars. I'd never sell it, though, for its historical value is priceless.

Another favorite of mine is an enameled pocket watch dating back to 1790. Made by Julian LeRoy for French King Louis XVI, its detail is exquisite. The face depicts a pastoral scene and three tiny gold figures: one strumming a mandolin; another, a lute; and another walking a tightrope. Their limbs actually move! Wind the watch with a key, and the musicians "play" a delicate tune. In addition, it strikes time on the hour and quarter hour.

Pieces don't have to be timeworn or expensive to be collectable, such as my 1904 Ingersol, which cost just one dollar. What charmed me was its inscribed manufacturer's guarantee, offering repair work for ten cents or a replacement watch for twenty-five. Other models are merely novelty items, like my Richard Nixon watch with eyes that move shiftily back and forth. I have a wall full of similar character-dial watches: There's Ronald Reagan, Little Lulu, Mickey Mouse, Bugs Bunny—even me.

The valuable part of the collection is stored in a bank vault, but I do keep some specimens at home. Those with melodious chimes, I wind, but not the more grating-sounding ones. One watch has a nine-foot mainspring that takes a half-hour to set.

Soon after joining the National Association of Watch and Clock Collectors, I tried involving Noel in my hobby, but at first it was nothing doing. Let's face it: Most kids just aren't interested in *anything* their parents enjoy. But today my son is a more ardent collector than I am, reading about antiques voraciously and traveling frequently to Europe, where he lectures to other hobbyists and procures new pieces. And to think that it all began when my wife "overpaid" for a "used watch."

Mid-1960, and I was nearing that time of life when most people receive a gold watch from their employer. I was fifty-two, thirty-one years of which had been spent in the entertainment industry. Retirement was out of the question, but I must admit I was anxious to expand into other areas of the field. The only question was, Which other areas?

That fall I was approached by former Warner Bros. executive producer Johnny Burton about going into business together.

"Sounds great," I enthused, adding almost as an afterthought, "What *kind* of business?"

For the next several weeks we brainstormed, finally deciding to start a commercial production company. What with my experience in voice characterization and Johnny's in production, it seemed an ideal venture. We were both well-known and boasted innumerable contacts between us.

And I might add, no business acumen whatsoever. Burton

and I rented a dingy, cramped seventh-floor office in the Taft Building, at the corner of Hollywood and Vine. To herald the formation of Mel Blanc Associates, we sent a cheesy brochure to every top advertising executive in the country. In Noel's opinion, it looked like a flyer from a used-car dealership. But at the time, what the hell did I know about running a company? As much as I knew about the hardware trade when I owned Mel Blanc's Fix-It Shop.

Seventeen hundred announcements were mailed on January 21, 1961. But by the time they were opened, newspapers everywhere were proclaiming that Mel Blanc was dead.

10

The Accident

"**S**well car, Mr. Blanc."
"Gee, Mr. Blanc, will you take
me for a ride in it someday?"

Several of Noel's friends were gathered around my newest
acquisition, a 1959 Aston Martin DB-2/4 Mark III. With sunlight reflecting off its brilliant emerald-green finish, the vehicle
seemed to glow incandescently. The neighborhood kids gaped
at it as if in the presence of royalty and touched its warm
metal with their hands.

Like many survivors of the Depression, I was frugal. Cars
were my lone self-indulgence. *Fast* cars. In the beginning I
bought them simply because they caught my fancy. But when
I discovered that certain models appreciated in value, what
started out as a hobby turned into a lucrative investment. It
was the exact opposite of how I came to collect watches.

The first auto I purchased was a green 1938 DeSoto that
belched choking black smoke each time it was started; then
a tan 1941 Packard, so heavily armored it was a wonder Cat-
erpillar traction and a flamethrower weren't options. That

same year I presented Estelle with a flashy lipstick-red 1941 Pontiac convertible but must confess that I probably spent more time behind its wheel than she did.

Cadillacs were my next fixation, followed by Rolls-Royces and Lincoln Continentals. However, my prize possession was a white 1957 Ford Thunderbird. What a machine. I loved racing it up and down the Pacific Coast Highway, listening to its hopped-up V-8 hum as I watched the waves lap against the coastline. One late afternoon while making my customary run, I thought contentedly, *Fastest baby in southern California.* Not by a long shot.

V-rooooom! Another vehicle streaked by me like an X-15 rocket-plane. "What the—?" By the time I whipped my head around to see what kind of car the driver was piloting, all I could make out were two red pinpoints of light way in the distance. Fortunately there was a traffic signal ahead, enabling me to finally catch up to him.

Over the rumbling of motors, I called out to the young driver, "Boy, that's a fast car. What is it?"

"An Aston Martin!" he shouted back. "Six cylinders! Engine's a two-point-five-litre!"

"Interested in selling it?"

To my amazement he replied that he was, for ten thousand dollars. The next day I was knocking on the door of his Bel Air mansion, check in hand.

"Good luck with it," he said as I prepared to drive away. "It's just too damn fast for me."

I hope you don't get the impression that Mel Blanc was some aging hot-rodder. Except for when on an empty freeway, if anything, I tended to be overly cautious. Especially when cruising along Sunset Boulevard toward Hollywood, which is where I was headed on the night of January 24, 1961.

After many years of self-management ("I handle myself," I used to joke), I'd finally relented and taken on an agent, a former radio sound-effects man named Jack Wormser. In 1959 he'd decided to change careers and asked me if he could claim publicly that he represented Mel Blanc. "It would really help me to attract clients, Mel, and I'd really appreciate it."

"Sure, why not," I said. "You can tell people anything you want." A short time later I really did hire him as my agent. Perhaps what convinced me was knowing he had this Mel Blanc fellow in his stable.

Wormser had booked me for a nine o'clock commercial taping session that Tuesday evening.

"It's only eight-thirty," I mused aloud, checking my watch. "I can take it nice and slow."

When the road sign for Bellagio Way swept past, I knew from experience to decelerate to just under thirty miles per hour. The upcoming curve was so treacherous, thirty-seven accidents had occurred there in the previous three years alone. It had well earned the designation "Deadman's Curve."

I eased my car into the right-hand lane and suddenly became aware of oncoming headlights. To avert the blinding glare I squinted and turned my head away, but the lights only loomed larger, brighter, closer. *I'm about to be hit.* The thought registered in my mind but for an instant. There was the screeching of rubber on asphalt, I screamed and—

That's it. That's all I remember. It wasn't until my wife explained the events to me later that I learned what had transpired.

An eighteen-year-old Menlo Junior College student was driving his father's Oldsmobile 98 west on Sunset. Apparently the power steering failed, causing him to lose control and careen across the white line into my lane, colliding head-on with my car. That he sustained only lacerations on his knee and forehead can be attributed to his American-made sedan's heavy steel construction.

Traffic officers P. C. Weir and L. J. Blunt arrived on the scene within seven minutes. They rushed over to the teenager, who was crouching by the side of the road, dazed and shivering. "He's all right," one said to the other. "Let's check on the second driver." Aiming their flashlights, they peered through the shattered driver's-side window of the Aston Martin, in which I lay unconscious, trapped by the steering wheel. The vehicle's lightweight aluminum body had crumpled like a wad of tinfoil upon impact.

"This is twenty-two J," one of them radioed. "We've got a two-car collision on Sunset at Groverton. Going to need a special unit with metal-cutting torches to get one of the drivers out. Better make it fast. Over." Half an hour would pass before I could be extricated from the wreck.

The officers heard the wail of sirens, and an ambulance lurched to a halt. One paramedic tended briefly to the boy's wounds before herding him into a police squad car and having him whisked to the UCLA Medical Center, just several blocks away. Meanwhile, the others paced around my car in frustration, unable to rescue me until the California Highway Patrol Special Unit got there. Knowing time was precious, they sighed in relief when it pulled up.

Within seconds torches were lighting up the sky, shearing through the soft metal as effortlessly as had the Oldsmobile. Four asbestos-gloved hands wrenched off the door, and while one paramedic maneuvered my body away from the collapsed steering wheel, the other reached inside my suit jacket pocket. Removing my black leather wallet, he flipped through credit cards and photos for identification.

"He's still alive," the first one said tersely, "but just barely."

"Holy cow!" exclaimed his partner. "It's Bugs Bunny! Look!"

He held up a color snapshot of me, dressed in a rabbit's costume and eating a carrot. It was signed, "Eh, what's up, Doc? Mel Blanc."

Jack Wormser was at the recording studio and glancing worriedly at the clock.

"Isn't Mr. Blanc here yet?" someone from the advertising agency asked him.

"No, he's not," Jack replied, "which is very unusual. Ordinarily Mel's the epitome of punctuality. Let me give his wife a call." He dialed the number of our home in Pacific Palisades, where we'd moved in 1954, and got Estelle on the line.

"Mel left over an hour ago," she told him. Sensing instinctively that something was wrong, the moment my wife hung up with Jack, she phoned the police to inquire if an accident involving Mel Blanc had been reported.

Informed that yes, there was such a dispatch, she nearly juggled the receiver. "He's in the intensive care unit at UCLA Medical Center," the desk officer said dispassionately.

In a matter of minutes Estelle had her black-and-white polka-dot coat on and was tracing the same eastward route I had taken. As her Jaguar neared UCLA, traffic slowed, and the night sky was illuminated an eerie magenta from the flickering flares set up by police.

She followed the caravan of cars slowly around the bend, torn between wanting to look and being deathly afraid to. A traffic cop was animatedly waving vehicles on, hoping to discourage rubbernecking, but without much success. It was a grisly sight. Bracing herself, Estelle glanced to her right, where the demolished Aston Martin sat facing in the wrong direction.

"Oh, Mel," she cried softly, just as the flow of traffic began picking up speed again.

She ran up the Medical Center's steps, where she was greeted by Noel, who had arrived scant seconds ahead of her. My twenty-two-year-old son had been dining in West Los Angeles with some married friends, Len and Selma Lewis, when Selma's mother came over to tell them about the TV news flash she'd just seen. Within seconds Noel was in his Porsche and racing up Westwood Boulevard toward the hospital.

Arm in arm, Estelle and Noel pushed open the glass doors and were met by press photographers and exploding flashbulbs. Already the story was all over the wire services. Momentarily disoriented, they were both pulled out of range by Jack Wormser.

"Jack, how is he?" my wife asked.

Critical, Jack told her, grimacing.

Noel's shoulders sagged, and his face went white. Estelle turned to him and said firmly, "Your father is a very strong man, Noel. If he survived that crash, he'll be all right." I think she said it as much for her own sake as for his.

Just then a doctor in surgical green walked up to the three of them and introduced himself as orthopedic surgeon Dr. Theodore Lynn. A team of eight physicians was working to save my life, he said, going on to explain, "Mel has numerous internal injuries, compound fractures of both legs, a fractured arm, and a severe concussion. But we're most concerned about pressure building around the brain. If it persists, we'll have to operate immediately. We should know in about six hours."

Finally, at four in the morning UCLA medical man Dr. Tracy Putnam and my personal physician, Dr. Ralph Dilly, approached Estelle, Jack, Noel, and his friend Richard Clorfene, an employee of the newly established Mel Blanc Associates. All were keeping vigil in the emergency waiting room and looked up expectantly. The doctors bore both good and bad news.

The swelling in the skull had abated, Putnam explained. Still, the overall prognosis was not good.

"It will be several days before we know whether or not he'll make it," he said. "I'm very sorry." With that, he excused himself and hurried out of the room.

"His recovery is in God's hands," Dr. Dilly said softly. "I suggest everyone pray for Mel."

I'd never been a particularly religious man, but I'm convinced those prayers—not only from my loved ones but from thousands of strangers as well—kept me clinging to life. Even though I was enveloped in blackness, people's kind thoughts somehow reached me.

The next morning, accounts of the accident were emblazoned across newspaper front pages. The *Los Angeles Times* understated, "Mel Blanc, Bugs Bunny Voice, Hurt," while the *Honolulu Herald* had me dead and gone. The Los Angeles *Herald-Examiner* was fairly accurate, its headline stating, "Mel Blanc Near Death in Car Crash; Comedian Fights for Life."

An ironic postscript: There was such public outcry over

my accident that while I lay in a coma, long-considered plans to eliminate Deadman's Curve were finally approved by the local council.

Already the UCLA Medical Center was besieged with phone calls from so many well-wishers that my family and friends were asked by hospital staffers to help man the switchboards. My private room overflowed with baskets of flowers, which Estelle and Noel requested the nurses distribute to other patients. I also received dozens of telegrams, from Mickey Rooney, Judy Canova, George Burns, Jerry Lewis, and many other associates past and present. "This is about the first time you have made so many people sad," wired Red and Valentina Skelton. Even a group of old friends in Oregon remembered me, sending a rose a day for two months, until I phoned one of them, Morris Rotenberg, and asked him to donate the money instead to a Portland youth facility.

Of all the get-well wishes, I was most touched by the fifteen thousand cards and letters sent from children around the country, many of which were addressed simply, "Bugs Bunny, Hollywood, U.S.A." To pass the time in the hospital, Estelle and Noel would open the envelopes and occasionally manage tired smiles. Inside were carrots wrapped in tinfoil, crayon drawings of the kids' favorite cartoon characters, and hand-scrawled cards.

Though I was still in a semicoma, my doctors were encouraged by the fact that my vital signs were strong. But they worried that prolonged unconsciousness might cause permanent brain damage. Every day my wife and son stood anxiously at my bedside, sometimes touching the plaster cast that covered every part of my body except for my left arm.

"Mel," Estelle would call gently. No response.

Noel, who had been scheduled to enter the Army Signal Corps on February 3, normally called me Dad. But out of respect, he felt moved to address me formally as "Father." No response.

Finally, on Valentine's Day, I spoke for the first time,

drawn out of my state by a resourceful surgeon, Dr. Louis Conway. Noticing the image of Bugs Bunny on the wall-mounted television, he thought to ask, "How are you feeling today, Bugs Bunny?"

My feeble reply, "Eh, just fine, Doc. How're you?" and another in Porky Pig's voice, sent him hastening to the nurse's station to telephone my wife with the heartening news.

Naturally I have no memory of that remarkable incident, and I remained skeptical about it for ages, despite Estelle's and Noel's assurances that it was indeed the truth. However, several years ago I was honored on the "This Is Your Life" TV program. And who do you think came out from the wings? Dr. Conway, whom I hadn't seen since leaving the UCLA Medical Center. He corroborated what my family had been telling me for nearly twenty-five years. "It seemed as though Bugs Bunny was trying to save his life," he told the audience. "And from then on, his health improved each day."

Once I regained full consciousness, my very first thought was to test my voice, for what if my vocal cords had been damaged? To say the least, it was a traumatic moment. I took a deep breath and trembling, uttered, "Hello?" in my natural voice. Then, louder, "Hello." Then, "What's up, Doc?" in Bugs Bunny Brooklynese. It was a miracle. Virtually every bone in my body had been broken, yet my larynx had been spared. I wanted to burst out of that cast and dance joyfully about the room.

Elation was a transient emotion, though, as I had to constantly ward off bouts of depression. Knowing that I faced another two, three months of immobility and hospitalization—well, it was easy to get downhearted at times. Luckily I had some of the world's top comedians to cheer me up. One of the first people I remember seeing after emerging from the coma was Jack Benny.

"J-Jack," I said groggily as his face gradually came into focus. "What are you doing here?"

"Oh, I just decided to come by and see how you were getting along," he replied offhandedly, as if I'd been admitted for minor elective surgery. Noel told me afterward that Benny had called the Medical Center every morning to ask if he could try rousing me. But until the sixteenth day, doctors weren't permitting anyone other than family in my room.

It was Jack who made me laugh for the first time, during his next visit. He strode into the room, kissed me on the forehead, and handed me two Ping-Pong balls, which he'd dipped in pink paint. On the accompanying card was written, "Noel told me that your voice was a bit higher in register and thought that these might be the reason. I found them near the scene of the accident."

During the next two months, whenever his schedule took him out of town, Jack sent me funny telegrams. One read:

"Dear Mel:

"I am just going to play nine holes of golf. Would you care to join me? I think eighteen holes would be too much for you without a caddy."

Another contained a mock display of Benny's legendary thriftiness: "How could you have done such an idiotic thing? You could have taken Wilshire, Olympic, or even Pico Boulevard. *Why Sunset?* You're fired, and I should remind you that this will not only cost you your salary, but also all of your hospital benefits."

As always, I chuckled, and it felt wonderful.

One of the most memorable days of my life is when I was brought home by ambulance to Pacific Palisades, where a year earlier I'd been elected honorary mayor. Despite a steady early-spring drizzle, more than one hundred friends and neighbors waited on Toyopa Drive to greet me. Clustered under umbrellas and waving flags, they spilled over onto next-door neighbor Walter Matthau's front lawn. To the accompaniment of kazoos, they sang a song they'd written, "Welcome Home Mel." And as my hospital bed was lifted out of the ambulance, I looked up to see a banner—"Hi Mel!"—that had been hung from our ranch-style home.

"I-I can't believe it," I stammered. I'd never been given to venting my emotions publicly, but let me tell you, I was moved to tears. I just broke down and cried. Besides feeling relieved to be out of the hospital finally, this outpouring of affection —I was speechless.

As soon as I was settled in my bedroom, the parade of visitors commenced again. What a delight it was to see my older brother, Henry, who had flown down from San Francisco with his wife. Not especially tight as youngsters largely because of the difference in our ages, we'd grown closer as we got older. Sadly, Henry battled alcoholism for most of his life, commencing to drink as a young man, then finding he couldn't stop. At the time it wasn't common knowledge that alcoholism was a disease, and there were few places inebriates could turn to for help. Henry would die an alcoholic in 1979. I never quite knew what to say to him about his drinking. But I never stopped loving him.

The most frequent visitor of all was who else but Jack Benny. Estelle recalls his coming to the door one afternoon and inquiring innocently, "Is Mel home?" Of *course* I was home. I was still confined to bed and would be for another seven months.

That didn't prevent me from working. Hell, there were theatrical shorts in production as well as an ABC-TV program, "The Bugs Bunny Show." Launched in September 1960, it aired Tuesdays during prime time and today is the longest-running animated series in television history. The show marked a first in that Friz Freleng and Chuck Jones collaborated on the cartoon direction, assembling vintage footage into a cohesive whole through the use of bridges and newly produced scenes.

Because it was one of the most widely watched programs of the season, Warner Bros. summoned some of cartoondom's most talented actors to substitute for me in my absence, but Freleng wasn't at all satisfied with their imitations. Sometime in March I received a phone call from him, requesting a favor.

"Do you think you're strong enough to record a scratch

track for us?" A scratch track is a casual reading of a cartoon script, which the animators refer to when sketching.

"You've got one hundred twenty-five people here waiting to go back to work," he kidded. "How about it?"

"Of course I'll do it," I said, looking straight at the three-foot card Warner's had sent: a full-color rendering of fourteen of my characters, all bedridden. "It's a baffling case, nurse," says their doctor, "they all seem to have temporarily lost their voices." *Tomorrow they'll regain them,* I thought to myself.

The next afternoon an engineer carted a heavy reel-to-reel tape recorder into my room. With assistance from Noel, who clutched the script and flipped the pages, and the engineer, who held the microphone to my mouth, I completed the reading without a flub. Listening to the playback, no one could have guessed that the actor responsible had been lying supine, encased in plaster, during the recording.

Warner Bros. called to thank me and to discuss financial compensation.

"I don't want a penny," I said. "I'm just glad to be able to put all those people back to work again."

Imagine my outrage, then, when Lloyd's of London refused to honor my long-standing disability policy. "Obviously Mr. Blanc is able to work," they contended. Able to work? I couldn't move! And I taped the one scratch track as a favor, at no charge. Yet the company remained steadfast. I'm sure Lloyd's of London wasn't too surprised when I canceled my policy immediately.

In three weeks, about the same time I was to be discharged from the UCLA Medical Center, Freleng would need me to record the final vocal track. At once my son and an engineer friend of his named George Travell got to work designing and building a home ministudio, so that I'd be able to voice cartoons while convalescing.

When I was wheeled into my bedroom, I couldn't believe the job the two of them had done. An adjacent room had been converted into a control room, with speakers, tape machines, microphones, and a console. Noel and Estelle knew that I'd mend more quickly, body and soul, if I could continue doing what I loved best. Not that I would have minded a week of rest at home.

Just four days after I returned to Pacific Palisades, two massive Warner Bros. eighteen-wheelers pulled up in front of the house. From the trucks were unloaded all sorts of magnetic-film recording gear.

An extension microphone stand, called a boom stand, was fixed over my bed so that the mike hung down directly over my mouth. By now I was able to grip the script with both hands but still couldn't be elevated at all. So the recording session was accomplished with me flat on my back again. "Beautiful job, Mel, beautiful," Freleng said, smiling, and several engineers broke into applause. The animated film was finished some months later, but because I was still homebound, I couldn't even go to see it!

The taping went so smoothly, I felt confident enough to take on yet more work. That came as welcome news to Hanna-Barbera, which was enjoying tremendous success with its Friday-night adult cartoon series "The Flintstones," on the ABC network. It would finish the 1960–1961 season as the country's eighteenth top-rated program, a feat unequaled by any other all-animation sitcom then or since.

The show's success was due in part to its sheer novelty: Rarely had cartoons been written for and about adults. "The Flintstones" was a playful satire of suburban life, albeit in a prehistoric setting. Fred and Wilma Flintstone's and Barney and Betty Rubble's Stone Age neighborhood was appropriately homogenous, though its uniform-looking houses were made of giant rock slabs and not aluminum siding. Fred didn't hunt for food like a true caveman; he brought home the bacon by working at the Rock Head and Quarry Cave Construction Co.

The Flintstones and the Rubbles reflected mid-twentieth-century viewers' experiences and problems back at them: having to contend with "modern-day" pressures while at the same

Fred Flintstone, voiced by Alan Reed, and my Barney Rubble character.
In its debut season, 1960–1961, "The Flintstones" was the eighteenth
top-rated TV program. *Illustration © 1988 Hanna-Barbera Productions, Inc.*

time enjoying "modern-day" conveniences. Of course, "modern-day" is relative, as are "civilized" and "uncivilized." America was going hi-fidelity crazy? So was Fred, only his stereo
consisted of a round slice of granite and a long-beaked bird
for a phonograph needle. The program's animators came up
with many other comical sight gags along this line: Barney's
lawnmower was a crab strapped to a sort of skateboard, clip-
ping the grass with his claws. Wilma's vacuum cleaner was a
baby elephant that inhaled dust through its trunk. And so on.
  Through humor "The Flintstones" pointed up how the

basic travails of mankind hadn't really changed all that much. In an increasingly tense world threatened by the so-called Cold War and the prospect of nuclear annihilation, it was good to be able to laugh at ourselves.

And at the characters, who were remarkably lifelike and believable. Credit that to a talented cast: Alan Reed as Fred, Jean Vander Pyl as Wilma, and my dear friend Bea Benaderet as Betty Rubble. In addition to voicing her husband, Barney, I was called on to play Dino, the Flintstones' incessantly yapping pet dinosaur; Bamm Bamm, the Rubbles' rambunctious son; and a dozen years later on "The Flintstones Comedy Hour," two supporting characters named Zonk and Stub.

The first time we taped the show at my home, it was quite a chaotic scene. Tangles of wires were scattered all over the floor, and chairs and microphone stands were arranged around my hospital bed. A speaker had been mounted on the wall so that Noel and producer Joe Barbera could communicate to the actors from the makeshift control room.

Sitting to my left were Benaderet and Vander Pyl. Jean was a pretty gal who commuted to taping sessions from her home in San Diego, two and a half hours away. Sitting to my right was Reed, gulping down spoonfuls of honey and lemon in preparation for his trademark exclamation, "Yabba dabba doo!" Director Alan Dineheart cued us from across the room, gesturing frantically as if he were Leonard Bernstein conducting the New York Philharmonic.

"Hope you're comfortable, Mel." Barbera's voice came crackling over the speaker. "We're in for a long evening." He wasn't kidding. We began sometime around seven and didn't finish until two in the morning. Every couple of hours Joe would ask if I was too tired to carry on, but I insisted on completing the show.

We recorded more than forty "Flintstones" episodes this way. Thankfully, by September my doctors allowed me to sit up a bit, elevated by way of a pulley-cable system to a semi-sitting position. It was no more than a few inches' difference,

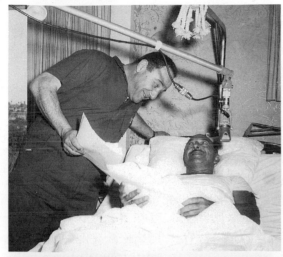

Producer Joe Barbera offers some last-minute suggestions before taping "The Flintstones" in my bedroom. I was still in a full body cast at the time.

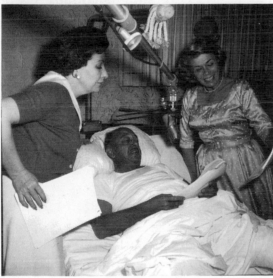

To record the prime-time cartoon show, a microphone was suspended above me, and the cast members gathered around my bed.

but as I laughingly told my colleagues, "How nice it is to be able to look at your faces instead of at the damn ceiling."

Following one session, Alan Reed asked if we could talk privately. I didn't know what was on his mind, but he seemed quite intense. Let me tell you about Reed briefly. Beginning in the early 1930s, when he still went by his given name of Teddy

Bergman, we crossed paths many times yet worked together only once. Alan played Mr. Potchnik the piano teacher on "The Mel Blanc Show." He and I were equally in demand in Hollywood but never got to know each other well.

Perhaps it was professional jealousy over my having my own program, but Reed confessed to me, "Mel, I used to think you were a conceited little jerk. Don't know why, I just did. But seeing your dedication and effort—Christ, doing a cartoon series from a hospital bed—changed my mind. I started thinking, 'Gee, what a brave little guy he is.' I just wanted you to know." From that day on we became better pals than even Fred and Barney, whom we portrayed on TV and in feature films for many more years.

Learning to work under such stressful conditions would prove valuable to me in the future. Twelve years after my accident, on the Fourth of July, I fell down while vacationing at our Big Bear Lake cabin. I broke the same leg that I had previously shattered in twenty-six places and which was still fitted with six silver screws to keep the bones in place. An ambulance whisked me to Santa Monica's St. John's Hospital, where I was tended to by the very same orthopedic surgeon, Dr. Lynn, as in 1961 at the UCLA Medical Center.

"Nice to see ya again, Doc," I quipped upon recognizing his face.

Once again I was back in traction, for two months. Rather than wait for me to return home, this time Noel set up the same ministudio in my hospital room. While nurses peered curiously through the door, their patient merrily voiced cartoons from his bed. "One of these days," I said poker-faced to my son, "I'm going to have to try this standing up again."

Following my first accident, it took ten months before I was able to walk, and then only on crutches. When I returned to "The Jack Benny Program" in late November to film the annual Christmas show, I had to act from a wheelchair. In the episode, Benny presents everyone on the program with gift boxes containing nothing but fresh air.

"Well," he says, "in Los Angeles, *that's* something."

But Jack was typically generous with praise, telling the *Los Angeles Mirror* he didn't know how he got along without me. Though I appreciated the kind words, if anything, the opposite was true. His caring and concern during those ten months unquestionably helped to speed my recovery. At a Friars Club dinner held in my honor almost exactly a year after the mishap, I tried my best to express my heartfelt appreciation, to him and to everyone else present. But first I had to endure a roasting from Benny and the other cast members.

"I don't think it was worth all you went through just for a dinner," Eddie "Rochester" Anderson said.

When it was his turn at the podium, Benny quipped, "That accident has got him more applause than he ever got on my show." Turning serious, he faced the dais, where I sat with Noel. "I can't love you more than everybody else in this room," he said, "but I certainly do as much."

Finally it was time for me to speak. I struggled out of my wheelchair, hobbled on crutches to the podium, and looked around the room at all the faces, many with tears in their eyes. Certainly I had to dab at mine with a handkerchief, I was so overwhelmed. I'd jotted down notes of what I wanted to say but never bothered to take the piece of paper out of my pocket. The words came pouring forth straight from the heart.

"You know, a year ago I was fighting for my life. I was in terrible pain. I didn't think I was going to live, and at times I didn't want to. I'm touched tonight, deeply. I'm blessed to have so many friends."

A year earlier I probably would have been too self-conscious to allow my feelings to surface; I would have most likely cracked a joke instead. But during my months of convalescence I reflected on my life and myself, and I mulled over ways of improving both. One personal trait I wanted to change was my deep-seated inability to express affection to others. My brush with death got me to thinking, *Imagine all the things that would have been left unsaid if I had indeed died.* I quickly began making up for lost time, possibly to the point of startling or even embarrassing others with my expressiveness. I found that saying "I love you" felt every bit as fulfilling as hearing it.

What else did I learn? That our deeds in life, good or bad, return to us: *karma*, according to Hindus and Buddhists. Whatever you want to call it, my trying experience left me certain of its existence. I'd always tried to help others as much as I could; now I was truly determined to perform more *mitzvahs*, the Yiddish word for good deeds, especially for incapacitated children. As soon as I was able to get around, I stepped up my number of appearances at Masonic and Shriners children's hospitals.

I had become a Mason in 1931, when I was still living in Portland, and a Shrine Mason in 1951. Because its 850,000 members wear black-tasseled red fezzes, or tarbooshes, and belong to the Ancient Arabic Order of the Nobles of the Mystic Shrine, all sorts of misconceptions persist about the Shrine.

It is not some Middle Eastern religious cult but an international fraternity founded in New York over a century ago. Four presidents have been prominent members, including Franklin Delano Roosevelt and Harry Truman. And what of the Masons' and Shriners' foreign-sounding salutation "es Selamu Aleikem"? It simply means, "Peace be with you." The Shrine is dedicated to philanthropy, operating a network of free orthopedic hospitals and burn institutes for kids under eighteen. When I was a teenager, I used to pass by the Portland Shriners hospital, located not far from my parents' home. Hearing about the work they did with crippled children was what initially piqued my interest in the fellowship and prompted me to seek admission.

I've visited many of their facilities and have spent countless hours with the youngsters. I don't know who appreciates whom more, me or them. "Do Bugs Bunny!" "Do Tweety!" they never fail to shout excitedly. Hopefully I'm able to bring them laughter and a respite from their pain. But it in no way equals the untold enrichment they bring to my life with each smile. There isn't a time that I walk out of their rooms without tears in my eyes. Honestly, sometimes I don't know how I manage to blink them back until I'm out the door. One thing I do know: Visiting these brave kids makes you count your blessings, and your own troubles seem very small by comparison.

I love entertaining children. Here I am with a youngster at a school for the blind. Visiting these courageous kids makes your own troubles seem insignificant by comparison. *Photo by Delmar Watson Photography*

Returning to the Los Angeles Shriners Hospital for the first time since my accident was very emotional for me. I'd always taken my talent for granted before, but as I sat talking in Sylvester's voice to a darling little girl, I thanked God for not revoking this undeserved gift.

I also thanked Him for however many years I had left and

vowed I would live them to their fullest. Maybe I was fifty-three and slowing down somewhat, and I'd led a most contented life. But having come to so many important realizations, I felt that the next ten, twenty, thirty years were going to be even better.

CHAPTER

11

That's Not All, Folks!

I was sitting up in bed, still in a leg cast, and finishing an interview with Hollywood gossip columnist Hedda Hopper.

"Last question, Mel," she said, adjusting one of her outlandish hats. "For other people who've suffered a debilitating injury, what does it take to overcome it?"

"Courage, patience, and a wonderful wife," I answered, although in retrospect I should have switched the order. My ordeal was as much a hardship for Estelle as for me. Yet if she ever felt dispirited by my lengthy recovery, she never let on, expressing only encouragement. Courage and patience? Mine came mostly from her.

I also owed a debt of gratitude to my son, who displayed a surprising maturity for his age during my convalescence. Nineteen sixty-one was a trying year for Noel. He had a lot on his plate at the time: graduating magna cum laude in theater arts from UCLA, then entering the U.S. Army Signal Corps and ascending to first lieutenant's rank. Initially he was stationed at Fort Monmouth, New Jersey, but he gradually journeyed back west, with stops at Fort Hood, Texas, Fort Ord, California, and Fort Lewis, Washington. Whenever possible, he flew home to assist me in recording Warner Bros. cartoons and "The Flintstones."

Just twenty-two, Noel also took over the reins of Mel Blanc Associates, which, to put it mildly, was in shambles. Our January launching having been thwarted by my accident, we'd tried again in March, informing advertising agencies that radio and television commercial production would commence from my home studio immediately upon my release from the hospital.

In the interim, responsibility for the company's day-to-day running had fallen to Johnny Burton. Now, my partner was a delightful fellow, but nervous and insecure; certainly not cut out for the business world. Whenever Noel visited our Taft Building office, poor frazzled Johnny could usually be found at his desk in one of three standard positions: shouting hoarsely into the telephone, with his hands covering his face, or staring wishfully out his seventh-floor window as if ready to jump. The company had become a captainless ship adrift at sea: saddled with a dearth of accounts and a surfeit of spiraling operating costs, as well as two salaried, incurably eccentric copy writers.

As best he could, Noel took over the helm, first as production manager. He'd long been interested in radio, television, theater, and film. As a UCLA film student he'd apprenticed with Sheldon Leonard, my onetime colleague from "The Jack Benny Program" and now an acclaimed director/producer. My son learned the fundamentals of directing from working with Leonard on the sets of two hit TV series, "The Danny Thomas Show" and "The Dick Van Dyke Show." Then, while in uniform, Noel had been assigned to head the U.S. Army Signal Corps' Motion Picture Unit at Fort Ord, producing and directing training films. That, too, was beneficial for an aspiring director, despite mundane subject matter such as "How to Write Checks" and "How to Clean Your Weapon."

I'd never actively encouraged my son to enter the business, for fear of pressuring him. One hears too many woeful tales about entertainers' children who were overburdened by the expectations of their parents, the press, or the public. I told Noel at a young age, "Be whatever you want, except a bank robber." But if he decided to take a chance on my profession, I was certainly going to be supportive, just as my own parents had been.

For a time he claimed he wanted to be a doctor, so my wife and I bought Noel his own little doctor's kit. But he was always very musical and theatrical. When he was no more than five, he began playing piano and within a year was giving recitals. I think that the sound of applause had the same intoxicating effect on him as it did on me twenty-five years earlier. From that day on, the little ham's mind was made up.

Once I was finally able to take an active role in the business again, in 1962, Johnny Burton asked to leave.

"What's the matter, Johnny, don't you like it here?"

"I love it, Mel," he said, "but it's just too much work for me."

So, when Noel exited the Army for good in December, he officially joined the company as general manager. And to make it a full family affair, Estelle started supervising the secretarial and legal work. She was also the creative department's sounding board, obliged to endure all of our comic ideas, both good and bad. You should have gathered by now that my wife has a lively sense of humor. Therefore, those times she didn't get a gag, staring at us blankly, we knew it wasn't much of a gag.

The father-and-son team created, if not a storm of interest, at least a squall in the advertising industry. Just four months after Noel came on board, our billings had risen twenty-five percent over the previous year, when Mel Blanc Associates produced one hundred consumer-product and general-industry spots. We felt optimistic that perhaps our trade-mark—humor—was catching on.

Today comical commercials are commonplace. Hell, many of them are better written, acted, and directed than the TV programs themselves. But back when Johnny Burton and I first conceived Mel Blanc Associates, the majority of advertisements were dull and unimaginative. My experience in early radio—when product endorsements were routinely incorporated into the scripts—had taught me that applying humor *judiciously* was a tremendously effective selling tool. Throughout the years I'd often proposed to sponsors how to improve their commercials, and on more than one occasion they'd said to me, "Why are you giving away your suggestions for free? You should make your own commercials."

Swell idea.

Notice the emphasis placed on the *judicious* application of humor. I always stress that our commercials are entertaining, not funny; a crucial difference. Too many contemporary radio and TV ads seem more intent on peddling a director's or writer's talents to Hollywood than on selling the product. They're cleverly scripted, boast big-name actors—and obscure their original intent. Ask a viewer to name the product, and he might reply, "I don't remember . . . *but the commercial was great!*" That's not what the art of advertising is about. To some extent I suppose that Mel Blanc Associates was responsible for creating a monster.

As sorry as business had been the first year, Noel and I had at least glimpsed what could be. Our first noteworthy radio ad campaign was for the then small Midwestern Clark Oil and Refining Corporation. For it we and Tatham-Laird Advertising devised two characters, Fisby and The Chief, who became highly familiar to listeners. Using radio as its sole advertising medium, Clark grew into the largest independent oil company in the country. My son and I knew we were on to something.

Another of our earliest commercials was a ten-second spot for Pepsodent toothpaste. With no musical background (called a "bed" in the trade), an announcer stated matter-of-factly: "The makers of Pepsodent, in an effort to promote dental hygiene, will now demonstrate the right way and the wrong way to brush your teeth." First listeners heard the everyday sound of teeth being brushed. "That is the wrong way." Then the sound of more brushing. "And that is the right way." Its very absurdity grabbed radio audiences. And while they were involved, being entertained, we slipped the product's name into their memory banks. And there you have the key to advertising.

At first many advertisers and agencies resisted humorous commercials, but they were here to stay; a favorable set of circumstances for Mel Blanc Associates. Seemingly overnight we became an industry force with which to be reckoned, and I began speaking frequently at advertising seminars around the country. In 1964 I delivered the keynote address at the American Association of Advertising convention, held that year in Omaha. When we celebrated five years in the business, our client roster included Volkswagen, Ford, Pontiac, and Avis Rent-a-Car, and billings were well over a half-million dollars a year.

Noel was now vice president, and for the first time since 1961 I was finally able to walk without the aid of a cane. To build up the muscle tissue in my legs, I'd had to undergo two years of rigorous physical therapy, including weight lifting and underwater exercises. Essentially I had to learn to walk again, first with a walker, then crutches, then the cane. I can't even begin to describe the exhilaration I felt the first time I took a stroll without any support.

Mel Blanc Associates branched into other areas as well, producing programs for radio syndication. "Inside Show Business With Mel Blanc" was a revealing, lighthearted, behind-the-scenes look at the entertainment industry. It was so well received, we immediately went to work on another, "Super Fun." This was a series of records containing comedic one-liners and brief vignettes for disc jockeys to air between songs. Such budding talents as Albert Brooks, his brother Bob Einstein, and future "M*A*S*H" producer John Rappaport, plus seasoned pros such as "The Jack Benny Program" 's George Balzer were among our twenty-three-man writing staff.

We recorded about four thousand of these bits using a

1967: Noel at work in the Mel Blanc Associates office ministudio, under the watchful eye of his dad. Always a creative kid, today he is an award-winning commercial producer. *Photo by Mark Gottlieb*

stable of actors that included me, Don Knotts, Hans Conreid, Lenny Weinrib, Joan Gerber, Joe Sirola, Henry Corden, Bob Crane, June Foray, Sid Melton, Ed Prentiss, John Stephenson, Lee Zimmer, Lou Horn, Byron Kane, Daws Butler, Howard Morris, Jesse White, Dave Ketchum, Hazel Shermut, Pat Carroll, Naomi Lewis, Leo Delyon, Rudy Hoffman, and two relative unknowns who would soon become national TV sensations on "Rowan and Martin's Laugh-In": Arte Johnson and KMPC Los Angeles disk jockey Gary Owens.

I'd fulfilled many of my life's ambitions, but one that still remained was to establish a commercial-actors' training school. Frankly, I never thought I'd see it happen, but in 1972 the Mel Blanc School of Commercials opened, housed temporarily in the Westwood United Methodist Church. We offered six courses and an impressive faculty: Veteran radio, TV, and film actress Lurene Tuttle taught a beginner's course in radio and TV voice-overs. Stanley Ralph Ross, the Emmy-Award-winning producer/director, gave instruction on camera techniques. Advertising whiz Dan Vinokur taught commercial-acting principles. And with assistance from the incredible diction and dialect coach Larry Moss, I personally conducted a class called Cartoon Dialects and Character Voices.

Its curriculum was unorthodox, to say the least. If you were to have walked in during a lesson, I might have been exhorting a pupil, "No! Open your mouth wider and let your tongue roll down your cheek!" What was the instruction in? How to speak like a giant hippopotamus. But of course.

The Mel Blanc School of Commercials wasn't an acting school, it was an *un*acting school, because the essence of a good commercial actor is to appear natural before a camera. This is not at all as simple as it sounds; it takes a long time and much hard work before most actors are able to overcome self-consciousness.

In addition to the regular teaching staff there were frequent guest speakers: Sheldon Leonard, Gary Owens, Walter Lantz, TV game-show host Monty Hall, to name a few. Professionals also played a vital role in the school's most unique feature: a talent-review board. To the best of my knowledge, no other institution, before or since, has offered anything of equal caliber. Between Noel's and my connections we were able to prevail upon ninety-five professionals from all phases of the industry to serve on it: advertising- and talent-agency executives, directors, producers, casting officials, studio talent scouts, and well-known performers such as Kirk Douglas, Jack Palance, and Vincent Price.

For each pupil's final exam, he or she was audiotaped or videotaped, depending on the nature of the class. These cassettes were distributed to the board, which reviewed and graded the students' work. Undergrads not only received constructive criticism from those in the field, their taped performances sometimes impressed the board enough to result in job offers. I'm happy to say that many found instant employment upon graduating from the six-week course.

Unfortunately, the venture was prohibitively costly, and we had no recourse but to shut its doors after two years. I was disappointed, naturally, but on the brighter side, Mel Blanc Automedia, as we were now known, was expanding yet again.

On the company's thirteenth anniversary it became a full-service ad agency, Blanc Communications Corporation. We conceived ad campaigns and produced them from start to finish. More spacious quarters were necessary: a suite of offices on Wilshire Boulevard. When I noticed a sign above our new address that read, "Glendale Federal Savings—Assets Twenty-Five Billion Dollars," I observed to my son, "We can now tell everyone that Blanc Communications Corporation's ass sits on twenty-five billion dollars."

Noel, incidentally, was company president, and me, chairman of the board. From father and son to son and father. I was glad about that, to tell you the truth. I know that it often bothered Noel when others suggested that he worked for his dad. Hell, it was more the other way around. Noel was the expert in commercial production, as should be proved amply by his more than two hundred forty national and international broadcast honors, including several Best Commercial awards from the American Advertising Federation.

It's not easy being the child of a well-known personality. First, there's all that pressure to match the parent's achievements. And if the child does succeed, it's automatically assumed that nepotism had something to do with it. Many offspring of the famous change their last names, so as to avoid the comparisons or unwarranted resentment from others. But everything Noel has accomplished he's done entirely on his own. Is it any wonder I'm so proud of him?

While my son was producing commercials, I continued making them. The work was financially rewarding, such as the time I received fifty thousand dollars from Paper Mate pens for saying but four words: "With the piggyback refill," in Porky Pig's voice.

But when I taped a TV spot for the American Express card in 1975, I got much more out of it than a paycheck. For those too young to have seen "The Jack Benny Program" and "Musical Chairs," it was the first time they'd actually *seen* Mel Blanc. Mel who? You know, Bugs Bunny. The commercial, filmed in a restaurant, played off of my peculiar combination of anonymity and celebrity:

"Do you know me? Would you believe I'm Bugs Bunny? I'm also the voice of many other cartoon characters. But in here, they don't care if I'm Daffy Duck. Desth*pic*able." It ended predictably: "Why, without this, the only way I'd get any attention is by saying, 'Th—uh-th—that's all, folks!' "

Well, let me tell you, once it aired, I couldn't walk down the street without passersby shouting, "Hey, Mel, got your American Express card?" I received more public exposure from a thirty-second TV spot than I did in nearly fifty years of radio and cartoons! And I have to admit, I enjoyed the recognition and being asked for my autograph. Certainly I'm not as inundated with requests as some other actors, but I've always made it a point never to refuse a single person. If someone wants me to sign something for them, hell, I'm delighted to do it.

It upsets me when I hear about celebrities acting rudely to their fans, although courtesy should be mutual; I've witnessed occasions where fans reacted insolently if their demands weren't met at once. *Everyone* is entitled to respect, a point I once had to make clear to a Warner Bros. executive at a VIP cocktail party being thrown for Bugs Bunny Birthday Call. This was a promotion whereby for five dollars children could receive prerecorded birthday greetings by name from their favorite rabbit.

One young suit-and-tied man scanned the guest list and grumbled, "What the hell is this? There's not one really important person on the list!"

Such arrogance. Slamming my fist on the table, I looked him in the eye and said, "Son, you'll never go anywhere until you realize that every person is important." I meant every word.

Just entering my seventies, I was signing more autographs than ever before, on college campuses. From 1978 to 1983 I spoke at nearly two hundred institutions and must have heard the following at least once per engagement:

"I grew up with you," a young man or woman would say to me.

"So did your old man," I'd reply.

Many old-timers were in the audiences, made up of an eclectic mix of age groups: long-haired college kids sitting next to conservatively attired adults sitting next to excited children, all sharing a common love for cartoons. Without trying to sound boastful, my appearances broke attendance records nearly everywhere I went.

I always used the same warm-up:

"Eh, what's up, Doc?"

"Duh, my name is Barney Rubble, and I live next door to Fred Flintstone."

"Ooh, I tawt I taw a puddy tat!"

"Thssufferin' thsuccotash, you did see a puddy tat."

Once the laughter died down, I'd say, "Now that you know who the hell I am, how're you doing?"

For forty-five minutes I'd relate anecdotes about the origins of each cartoon character, interspersed with clips from favorite animated films such as *Birds Anonymous* and *Knighty Knight Bugs*. Then the floor was opened to questions and shouted requests for other characterizations and routines. "Do Sí-Sy-Sue!" "Do Pepe Le Pew!" Many of the questions I'd answered literally thousands of times before during my career, but I was happy to do so again. Seeing the impression the old cartoons and radio shows made on fresh-faced kids made me feel several years younger myself. How gratifying to know that the impact of something you've had a hand in creating spans generations. If you had told me fifty years ago that 1980s youngsters would laugh just as hard at the antics of Porky Pig or Bugs Bunny or Daffy Duck, I'd have thought you were looney tunes.

Because the characters and I have stuck around for so long, we've received many honors. I have my own star at 6385 Hollywood Boulevard, on Hollywood's Walk of Fame. So does Bugs Bunny. The honor that means the most to me, though, is my inclusion in the Smithsonian Institution's National Museum of American History, which maintains a collection of U.S. entertainment history. There's the villainous J. R. Ewing's cowboy hat, a set from the "M*A*S*H" television show, comedian Rodney Dangerfield's shirt and red tie, and "All in the Family" patriarch Archie Bunker's favorite chair. In 1984 I donated videotapes, vintage photographs and movie posters, and talking puppet recreations of some of my most popular characters.

While in Washington for the Smithsonian ceremony, I was contacted by the White House about visiting an old friend: Ronald Reagan. Besides being former Pacific Palisades neighbors, the fortieth president and the first lady were onetime acting colleagues of mine. Forty years ago or so, Reagan called me to ask if I would entertain children at the Boys and Girls Club of Brentwood with him. We had a marvelous afternoon. He was a Democrat back then and a much better actor than people give him credit for.

Before Estelle and I were ushered into the Oval Office to catch up on old times with the President, I was introduced at the regular noontime news briefing. Not as Mel Blanc, however. With April Fools' Day coming up, we decided to play a prank on the press.

Struggling to keep a straight face, deputy press secretary Larry Speakes announced, "Mr. Pierre Lapin, visiting from France." I was, he claimed, "a renowned scholar in the field of cybernetic cellulose performance, a subject the President himself has increasingly had great interest in."

In my heaviest Gallic accent I addressed the gathering by apologizing for my poor English. "In this country," I said, "I talk like a rabbit." And I did: like Bugs Bunny. Only then did the men and women of the fourth estate realize who I was and begin to tear up their notes, sheepishly. Speakes's facetious introduction, by the way, contained several arcane truths. *Lapin* is French for "rabbit." And cybernetic cellulose performance? The art of speaking on film. The President, who's had his, shall we say, differences of opinions with the press corps over the years, laughed quite heartily when Estelle and I filled him in on our little joke.

Vocally tricking people has always been a pastime of mine. A favorite is to discreetly study someone's tone and inflection, then repeat it back to them. The looks I receive in return are hilarious. Because they're not used to hearing themselves, they act startled at first, as if wondering, *Gee, that voice sure sounds familiar* . . . It usually takes several minutes before they realize that it's familiar, all right.

The best practical joke I ever pulled was on a good friend who owned two restaurants in San Francisco's Chinatown district. It was such a cruel trick, I must preface telling it by noting that this friend of mine was also a jokester and had victimized me on more than one occasion.

I waited for revenge. And waited. Until Chinese New Year's Eve, when both of his establishments were sure to be wall-to-wall with revelers. I telephoned him and in a woman's voice, pretended to represent the city's water department. "This is to alert you that due to a broken water main, all water will be shut off in approximately one hour," I said authoritatively. "Thank you."

Because Chinese cuisine is prepared with enormous amounts of water, this news was about as welcome as "Mozzarella Declared Illegal Substance" at a pizzeria. After placing the call I drove to the corner of Grant and Clay streets and observed the chaos I'd generated: White-aproned employees of both restaurants were dashing about, frantically trying to find barrels, buckets, pots, pans, dishes, bottles—anything that could be filled with water. And there was my friend, shouting out orders and tearing at his hair.

Mel, show some compassion, I admonished myself, and ducked inside a nearby phone booth. In the same female voice I called back to say, "I'm sorry to have inconvenienced you, but I've made a terrible mistake. The water will not be shut off until *tomorrow* night."

It wasn't until two years later that I could bring myself to confess the deed to my friend, who, thankfully, was not given to violence. You'd think I'd have learned my lesson from my school years, when my proclivity for mimicking voices landed me in more hot water than a boiled egg. "Bugs Bunny made me do it," I told my friend, winking.

On the subject of the gray-eared rabbit, he and the other Warner Bros. characters have continued to air on television. Since the 1960s, Bugs, Daffy, Sylvester, Tweety, Porky, and Roadrunner and Wile E. Coyote have all starred in their own series at one time or another. But in addition to reprising the old gang, I launched many new voices as well, mostly for Hanna-Barbera. Test your memory by seeing how many of these animated programs you recall watching:

"The Alvin Show" (1960–1961, CBS-TV); character: Salty the parrot, whose squawking delivery was borrowed from Jack Benny's smart-aleck bird.

"The Atom Ant/Secret Squirrel Show" (1965–1967, NBC-TV); character: Secret Squirrel.

"Captain Caveman and the Teen Angels" (1977–1979, 1986–1988, ABC-TV); character: Captain Caveman, billed as the world's first superhero. I don't know what Superman

**In 1984 I donated numerous mementos from my career to the
Smithsonian Institution's collection of U.S. entertainment history.**

thought of that claim. This cartoon show was a spin-off of a segment from "Scooby's All-Star Laff-a-Lympics" (1977–1979, ABC-TV).

"Curiosity Shop" (1971–1972, ABC-TV); characters: various. This charming thirty-minute educational program reunited me with former Warner Bros. director Chuck Jones, who hosted.

"Heathcliff" (1986–1988, syndication); characters: Heathcliff and the fishmarket owner.

"The Jetsons" (1962–1963, ABC-TV; 1985–1988, syndication); character: Cosmo G. Spacely. The youngest network's first in-color program, "The Jetsons"'s premise was akin to that of "The Flintstones," only set in the future. Mr. Spacely was the ill-tempered boss of George Jetson, whose wife, Jane, was played by Penny Singleton, for years the voice of radio's and film's Blondie Bumstead.

"Lippy the Lion" (1962, syndicated); character: Hardy Har Har.

"The Magilla Gorilla Show" (1963–1967, syndicated); character: Droop-a-Long. Magilla, as per his namesake, was a devilish simian squatter who refused to vacate Mr. Peebles's Pet Shop. One of the show's segments starred sheriff Ricochet Rabbit, tormented by a trio of bumbling deputies, including Droop-a-Long.

"The Perils of Penelope Pitstop" (1969–1970, CBS-TV); characters: Chugaboom, Yak Yak, the Bully Brothers. Penelope was a female race-car driver preyed upon by the nefarious Sylvester Sneekly, voiced by the late Paul Lynde.

"The Peter Potamus Show" (1963–1967, syndicated); character: Sneezly the seal.

"Speed Buggy" (1973–1974, CBS-TV); character: Speed Buggy. For the role of a remote-control auto owned by three adventurous teenagers, I essentially resurrected Jack Benny's Maxwell, except that Speed Buggy not only sputtered, it talked.

"The Wacky Races" (1968–1969, CBS-TV); characters: various.

"Tom and Jerry" (1965–1972, CBS-TV; 1975–1979, ABC-

TV); characters: Tom and Jerry, but briefly. MGM, if you recall, had let go award-winning directors Bill Hanna and Joe Barbera in 1957, only to watch enviously as the two enjoyed considerable success with TV cartoons. So the company brought the famous cat and mouse out of mothballs for a series of theatrical shorts that were then sold to television.

Tom and Jerry had been mute since their 1940 debut, *Puss Gets the Boot,* but as an experiment I was asked to devise voices for them. We recorded just two cartoons before it was decided not to tinker with a formula that had netted seven Oscars.

"Where's Huddles?" (1970, CBS-TV); character: Bubba McCoy, gridiron center. Three-fourths of "The Flintstones" cast were brought back together for this cartoon about the misadventures of the wretched Rhinos football team. Alan Reed played the coach, and Jean Vander Pyl, the wife of quarterback Ed Huddles.

Bubba McCoy, Hardy Har Har, and Yak Yak. No, not exactly Bugs Bunny, Daffy Duck, and Tweety. But to compare Hanna-Barbera's made-for-TV cartoons to Warner Bros.'s theatrical shorts is unfair. Not only were their budgets substantially smaller, production time was virtually cut in half. Whereas Warner turned out an average of twenty-five cartoons annually during its heyday, Hanna-Barbera and other TV-cartoon studios produced about twice that number.

It would be dishonest of me to claim that the abovementioned animated films were on a par aesthetically with Warner Bros.'s. Hell, I realized as much at the time. But I have always taken great pride in *all* of my work. Despite what some might term the "frivolous" nature of my job, I consider myself an artist, and cartoons, art.

Because of my deep affection for animated films, I have to say that I am saddened by the execrable quality of most of today's cartoons. I'm not referring so much to the limited animation as I am to the limited imagination exhibited by their directors, writers, and actors. The majority of contemporary voices are uniformly characterless. Either that, or they're thinly veiled approximations of well-known characters'. I've heard some of my own pilfered and altered slightly, and it burns me up.

Did you know that no legal protection exists for voice actors? That others can blatantly plagiarize Bugs Bunny or Woody Woodpecker, and there's nothing I can do about it? Unfortunately there are so many thieves in this business, it's laughable. What's not so laughable is having to *listen* to some of these god-awful Mel Blanc imitators, who can be heard on commercials, radio-station IDs and children's records. Several years ago I came across an English LP called *Bugs Bunny Comes to London,* on which the impostor rabbit speaks with the pear-shaped tones of a British barrister! Not a hint of Brooklynese; not even a single "Eh, what's up, Doc?"!

Another complaint I have with modern cartoons is that they merely mirror children's realities instead of transporting them—back in time, for instance. Historical references were common in Warner Bros. animated films, something you rarely see today. Perhaps that's more of an indictment of the educational system and the fact that kids read less than it is of cartoon makers. But to me it's both shameful and cynical when the leading Saturday-morning heroes are little more than animated versions of popular toys; contrived, naturally, to sell more toys.

Then there's the issue of brutality in children's fare. Warner Bros. was accused of depicting too much violence in its cartoons, but I have to disagree. To me, there's a huge difference between the realism portrayed in today's cartoons and the slapstick we plied for laughs. The Warner animated films showed obvious *un*reality. Yosemite Sam gets flattened by a falling drawbridge, only to return in the next scene unscathed.

At Warner Bros. we always felt a responsibility to the youngsters. Friz Freleng was particularly astute at determining what was and wasn't appropriate, and he was affectionately called "the Censor." Yet the Warner cartoons never proselytized morality—the surest way to alienate kids.

I don't try couching my disdain for today's cartoons. Therefore, you can imagine how delighted I was when Warner Bros. opted to produce its first theatrical short in nearly twenty years. *The Duxorcist*, released to selected movie theaters in late 1987, was the first in what we hope is a return to the big screen for the beloved Warner characters.

It came about because of the originals' ongoing popularity. The cartoons are regularly shown in revival houses and on college campuses, and the "24-Karat Collection" home-video series released in 1985 and 1986 (including *A Salute to Mel Blanc*) has been fabulously well received. Of the eleven available videos, *Bugs Bunny's Wacky Adventures*, *Daffy Duck—The Nuttiness Continues*, and *Porky Pig's Screwball Comedies* went gold, selling over 75,000 copies each. Contemporary parents want to expose their youngsters to the cartoons that meant so much to them when they were kids—and I suspect, want to relive some of those childhood memories, too.

The studio gave the go-ahead for a seven-and-a-half-minute, $200,000 animated film, shot in the old square-screen format of 1.33:1.

Since his last outing, 1968's pedestrian *See Ya Later, Gladiator*, Daffy Duck had gone into hiding, presumably out of embarrassment. He surfaced but once, for the feature-length movie *Daffy Duck's Movie: Fantastic Island* in 1983. Not only was it a thrill to play the obstreperous little black duck again, but it was additionally pleasurable to work with a multigenerational production team. The two background artists, Dick Thomas and Alan Bodner, were forty years apart in age: seventy-two and thirty-two respectively. Thomas, in fact, had worked on the first Bugs Bunny cartoon, *A Wild Hare*, in 1940. And one of the three animators, Norman McCabe, had been a Warner's artist/director in the late 1930s and early 1940s.

The Duxorcist was a parody of the 1973 film *The Exorcist*, and it turned out wonderfully. Younger fellows such as writer/director Greg Ford and cowriter/director Terry Lennon maintained a respect for Daffy that would normally be reserved for

Devilish Daffy Duck returned to theatrical shorts for the first time since 1968 in *The Duxorcist* (1987), shot in the old square-screen format. *Photo copyright © 1987 Warner Bros. Inc.*

a star the magnitude of Sir Laurence Olivier. If I said to them, "I'm sorry, but Daffy wouldn't say something like this," it was changed without debate.

So the film undeniably remains true to Daffy Duck's heritage, as well as to other elements of the original Warner Bros. cartoons: from the familiar bull's-eye logo to the music, culled from the best of the late Carl Stalling and Milt Franklyn. And unlike much of today's animation, which is delegated to cheaper studios overseas, *The Duxorcist* was made entirely in Burbank, a fact duly noted in its opening credits. About the only difference between the 1987 Daffy and the 1947 Daffy, as a *Wall Street Journal* writer noted wryly, was that today the cartoon might be the most profound thing on the screen.

Already a second Daffy short, *Night of the Living Duck,* is finished. If it is as well received as *The Duxorcist,* perhaps Warner Bros. will revive production full-time—though not back in Termite Terrace, I hope.

With that possibility in mind, I've already taken steps to ensure that the voices of Daffy, Bugs Bunny, Foghorn Leghorn, and the rest are around long after I'm gone. The notion first occurred to me following my 1961 accident. I'd never thought about what would happen to my characters if something happened to me, but after Bugs Bunny and Porky Pig

Noel, Estelle, and I celebrate a birthday. My wife has been extremely supportive throughout my career, even during the early, lean times.

helped to save my life, I felt a responsibility to try to preserve theirs.

Having heard nothing but horrendous impersonations over the years, however, I wasn't very optimistic about finding someone who could perform them accurately. Racking my brain one night, I thought, *I've got to get somebody with the same kind of throat musculature as mine.* Then it hit me: Noel! Why didn't I think of him before! Like most kids, he'd been imitating his old man since he was about twelve. No, let me take that back. Noel first impersonated me when he was just three years old.

I was fixing a broken leg on Estelle's favorite mahogany end table. My son had accompanied me to the garage of our Playa Del Rey home and was watching intently as I hammered my thumb instead of the nail.

"Son of a bitch!" I roared, hopping around the garage with one hand clasped around the red, throbbing finger.

"Sum bitch!" Noel repeated blithely. "Sum bitch! Sum bitch!"

I was so appalled that my mind left my pain momentarily. "Don't *ever* say that word!" I cried, then hurried into the kitchen for some ice.

Several weeks later Estelle, Noel, and I were at an elegant Christmas luncheon thrown by Mrs. Cecil B. DeMille, wife of the legendary film producer. The affair was a Hollywood society columnist's dream, held at the DeMilles' sumptuous DeMille Drive mansion. Unable to locate a baby-sitter, we brought along our son, who was generally extremely well behaved.

To occupy Noel while she chatted with some of the other guests, my wife gave him her key ring to play with. Suddenly the buzz of polite conversation was interrupted by a tiny voice yelping, "Sum bitch! Sum bitch!" Our son had caught his finger in the metal ring. Believe me, I stuttered more than Porky Pig trying to explain (unconvincingly, I'm sure) to the astonished hostess how a three-year-old had picked up such salty language.

* * *

When I first broached the subject of his carrying on the Warner Bros. characters, Noel was reluctant. He had successfully strived to establish his own identity, and here I was asking him to essentially follow in my footsteps. After much persuasion I finally convinced him, and we began practicing together. It didn't require much, though. My son picked them up as if he'd been doing them all his life. Occasionally I'd offer suggestions. For example, his Sylvester was off; he was spraying too much with his tongue and not enough with his lips. The only character he has yet to master is the same one that's always given me the most difficulty: Yosemite Sam.

Initially Noel felt uncomfortable emulating me—"I'd rather just listen to you, Dad," he told me—but today we often read scripts together: Bugs and Elmer Fudd; Sylvester and Tweety; Foghorn Leghorn and Henery Hawk. It's funny to watch the expressions on people's faces when we conduct conversations in character. Their eyes dart back and forth as if watching a tennis match. Then they usually blurt, "Amazing! He sounds exactly like you!"

It's true. Noel performs my characters so well, I could sue him.

In May of 1988 I celebrated my eightieth birthday with a huge party thrown by Warner Bros. on its Burbank lot. And again I was asked the same question I've heard on every damn birthday since I turned sixty-five: "Mel, when are you going to retire?"

I'll tell you when:

The day I drop.

Why would I want to stop doing something that I love so much? There is no greater joy than to be able to make people laugh, especially children. I may have but one son by birth, but I sometimes feel as if every boy and girl who ever chuckled at Daffy Duck or Speedy Gonzales is a relation. That includes grown-up boys and girls who still find humor in an animated rabbit being chased by an animated hunter. I feel blessed,

"So, Mel, when are you going to retire?" When I drop, that's when. I still record several times a week. Who would want to quit making people laugh?

which is why I continue to record three or four days a week in my sixteen-track home studio.

When you reach my age, you're expected to dispense sage-like wisdom like a guru atop a mountain. "What's it all about, Mel?"

"What's *what* all about?"

"You know."

Oh. The big *L* word. Life.

I wish I had something more profound to offer, but it's really very simple:

Enjoy yourself. Try pursuing a career you enjoy; one that gives you personal satisfaction and not merely financial com-

In the future my characters' voices will live on through Noel, who has learned them all so well, I could sue him.

pensation. Believe in yourself and never allow others to discourage you. Like my returning to Warner Bros.'s Termite Terrace, enduring rejection after rejection, keep at it, and you will succeed. I firmly believe that.

Whether I'm speaking at a college, being interviewed by a reporter, or appearing on radio or television, it's become something of a tradition for me to conclude using Porky Pig's famous farewell. So here goes:

"Th— uh-th— uh-th—"

Aw, you know the rest.

Philip Bashe is the author or coauthor of several books, including *How to Keep the Children You Love Off Drugs, Dee Snider's Teenage Survival Guide, Heavy Metal Thunder, Rolling Stone Rock Almanac*, and a forthcoming biography of Rick Nelson. A former magazine editor and radio/TV announcer, he lives with his wife and three cats in Baldwin, New York.